# THE HEALING OF AMERICA

# The Healing of America

## Welfare Reform in the Cyber Economy

James L. Morrison, Ed.D.
*Department of Consumer Studies*
*College of Human Resources, Education,*
*and Public Policy*
*University of Delaware*

With Michael Lieberman, P.C. &
Pamela P. Morrison, Ph.D.

## Ashgate

Aldershot • Brookfield USA • Singapore • Sydney

© James L. Morrison 1997

Published by
Ashgate Publishing Limited
Gower House
Croft Road
Aldershot
Hants GU11 3HR
England

Ashgate Publishing Company
Old Post Road
Brookfield
Vermont 05036
USA

Reprint 1998

**British Library Cataloguing in Publication Data**
Morrison, James L.
    The healing of America : welfare reform in the cyber
    economy
    1.Public welfare - United States 2.United States - Social
    conditions - 1980-
    I.Title
    361.6'8'0973

**Library of Congress Catalog Card Number:** 97-61059


ISBN 1 85972 666 6


Printed and Bound by Biddles Limited
Guildford and King's Lynn.

# Contents

# Figures and tables

# Acknowledgments

A book of this nature is not possible without contributions made by individuals who have shared their thoughts and creativity throughout this project. Special thanks must be given to three individuals who approached welfare reform with rather varying views. Michael Lieberman, an attorney-at-law, provided the incentive for designing a model for welfare reform quite different from that appearing in the literature. Pamela P. Morrison provided a sounding board for ideas and also was instrumental in seeking out and obtaining important resources which have been dispersed throughout this writing. Special thanks are also in order to Ayana Chisholm, Jennifer Denaro, and John Brunhammer, majors in consumption economics, whose research and input played an important role in the development of the concepts used in this test. It takes a team to build a model, and the result has been an accomplishment of an extraordinary challenge in scholarly research.

# Preface: Accepting the challenge

This country is about opportunity, that is equal opportunity for all Americans. What makes this nation so great is its willingness to give individuals a second chance, an opportunity that may change one's life forever. The challenge is to assist those families who find themselves, for one reason or another, not being able to succeed within a democracy. An important aspect of our democratic form of government is the importance attached to preserving individual freedom. In this instance, freedom is associated with the 'right' of individuals to make choices as to what is in their own best interest. Making personal choices without interference from government at the city, county, state, or national level is part of the American way of life and part of both economic and political freedom that binds citizens of this country into a powerful force capable of overcoming obstacles to fairness and equality.

Accompanying the respect for individual freedom is the empathy Americans have for one another, especially in time of need. Americans have traditionally come forth to help others either by personally donating money to those who have been subjected to a tragedy or by requesting their government to assist. Such financial assistance often comes directly from the Federal government in the form of low-interest rate loans, direct grants, food stamps, rental subsidies, and child welfare benefits. Other assistance comes from personal donations from one group of citizens to another through private local community agencies and programs such as the United Way, Meals-on-Wheels, and Neighbor-to-Neighbor.

The current controversy involves whether poverty is the result of laziness on the part of heads of households or whether it is the result of imperfections in the marketplace that prevent families from determining their own destinies. The extent to which heads of households of families in poverty should be required to work (especially those where there are single-parents) remains the primary point of contention among welfare reformers. Dealing with the harshness that is associated with welfare reform measures is quite emotional in that the lives of many children are affected by new public policies that drastically change the way public perceives assisting those in need.

What is suggested here is welfare reform that reflects a changing U.S. economy where lifestyles are becoming more dependent upon electronic communication and new methods of interaction. The emergence of the electronic society that promotes open communication, the rights of all individuals, and the focus upon civility requires a rethinking of welfare reform. What makes this proposal different from others being suggested is its distancing from the current trend of thought whereby the focus is primarily upon limiting welfare benefits and corresponding job training to two or three-year commitments with the expectation of finding employment. Welfare reform proposed here expands upon the current dialogue by offering a mechanism which builds upon individual pride, the achieving of the American dream to own one's home, and the instituting of family support systems to enable career advancement. What is required to 'heal America' is a new wave community whereby parental involvement becomes the centerpiece of a new form of civility. Long-term solutions to raising the standard of living of families in general will only come about if commitments are made by both the private and public sector to assure those willing to work can find employment that provides a 'living wage.'

An innovative use of a readily available resource will be suggested as a basis for a model of a new kind of community. In this regard, a new form of government involvement that could significantly impact upon families where poverty is most evident is suggested, resulting in a new kind of residential and working environment for those in need of a second chance in life. A need for a different kind of philosophy based upon the principles (primarily economic) that are so basic to accomplishing the American dream--a good job, home ownership, and community identity--forms the basis of a proposed model which illustrates the formation of a community with 'a new attitude.'

As you make your way through this book, there will be selected terms *highlighted*. Each term represents an important element related to the proposed model for welfare reform described in this treatise. The challenge is to use *as many of these terms as possible* when formulating your ideas as to what you believe represents your model for welfare reform. You may take aspects of the model proposed here or propose your own. The challenge is for you to take a position as to how your vision differs or is similar to the model described here. Please send your responses to Dr. James Morrison by email to jlm@strauss.udel.edu. We invite your comments. What you are about to read is our dream of welfare reform. It is hoped that you will be inspired to enter into the dialogue as we move in the direction of welfare reform that reflects the best interests of both families in poverty and those of our nation.

# Overview: Framework of analysis

The framework for this book is derived from theory fundamental to the disciplines of family economics, microeconomics, and consumption economics. The inclusion of these three disciplines reflects the complexities of family structure and the economic system within which families generally function. In this regard, families generally cope within the constraint of limited resources, and their actions within a free enterprise system generally reflect considerable ingenuity as they analyze competing alternatives for enhancing personal as well as family welfare.

Family economics studies financial activities along two dimensions--personal and managerial. The personal strand examines the impact of values, beliefs, and attitudes upon family decision making related to short-term and long-term financial goals. The managerial dimension focuses upon how families apply specific skills and knowledge for controlling financial resources. Included here is the implication of time, money, and energy as families attempt to devise strategies for improving their standard of living. In addition, family economists are also intrigued as to how personal and managerial perspectives interact. Therefore, the discipline of family economics creates a framework that combines the study of three crucial factors: the level of economic resources, the degree of knowledge and skills possessed by heads of households, and the influence of values, beliefs and attitudes upon desired outcomes.

Microeconomics theory provides the dimension to the study of families based upon the premise that localized solutions have benefits to solving problems. The examination of the free enterprise system within the context of microeconomics brings into play the significance of establishing one's own destiny by capitalizing upon the rewards attributed to hard work and the corresponding strengths of freedom of choice. It is the interacting of the motivational aspects of the free enterprise system about which competition evolves that generates acceptance of change for the benefit of the many rather than the few. For example, the reliance upon the supply and demand theory in microeconomics enables individuals to make decisions without reliance upon outside interference. It also provides an intriguing direction for the model in welfare reform that is to be proposed. The outcome of these decisions influences a family's current and future economic situation but also a family's ability to remain intact by creating a bond that enables individuals to endure through difficult times as well as enjoy those successful periods of accomplishment.

Finally, the discipline of consumption economics enables us to focus upon the particulars of consumer money management practices. Consumption economics enables us to analyze family spending strategies for designing new and perhaps more appropriate alternatives for enhancing family welfare. It introduces the significance of saving, investing, and budgeting one's funds through a systematic plan that enables families to be goal-oriented. The discipline also emphasizes the significance of having control and an awareness that one can modify an existing environment by changing money management strategies.

A large number of individuals continue to clamor for welfare reform. In spite of the rhetoric that citizens must work for their own good by obtaining employment within a 5-year window, there remains concern over the future of many of these families who have had in the past the security of a safety net for providing their basic needs. Over the past several decades, many suggestions have come forth on how to provide a transition from a world of dependency to that of a world of self-initiatives for families in poverty. As early as 1965, researchers began sounding the alarm that there was a breaking down of family values and structure, especially in the poorer neighborhoods of the U.S. There has been a continuing attack on public welfare policies with the expectation that solutions must include incentives that enable heads of households of families in poverty to assume responsibility for their own future. Some notable publications which have guided our thinking over the past decade are:

- *Beyond Entitlement: The Social Obligations of Citizenship* (1986)
- *The New Consensus on Family and Welfare: A Community of Self-Reliance* (1987)
- *Poverty and Social Justice* (1987)
- *The Tragedy of American Compassion* (1992)
- *The End of Equality* (1992)
- *Reviving the American Dream: The Economy, the States, and the Federal Government* (1992)
- *Tyranny of Kindness: Dismantling the Welfare System to End Poverty in America* (1993)
- *Welfare Realities: From Rhetoric to Reform* (1994)
- *Poverty and the Underclass* (1994)
- *Rosa Lee: A Mother and Her Family in Urban America* (1996)

Each of these writings documents a rise of a dependent underclass in America that has resulted in families having little, if any, opportunity to benefit from the economic freedom which citizens enjoy in a democracy that is the envy of the world.

The general direction of welfare reform appears to be quite clear. The welfare system in the U.S. is no longer going to provide subsidies to families who qualify based upon arbitrary income limits. It is clear that welfare reform must have as its objective the reduction of dependency on federal programs on the part of families in poverty. Welfare reform includes reducing and possibly eliminating federal cash assistance programs such as Aid to Families with Dependent Children (AFDC), food stamp subsidies, and grants to immigrants, among many other programs. In their place will be the institution of state block grants for enabling states to establish and run their own welfare programs through greater accountability. For example, teenage mothers are likely to be required to stay in school, get retrained, or live with their own parents in order to get assistance from either state or federal programs.

However, in terms of assisting those in need of long-term assistance, the assumption here is that there must be a better way to help those who are less fortunate without having to resort to a continuous stream of 'public handouts.' Proposed here is an aggressive strategy that suggests that consumer welfare may be more appropriately enhanced by a different kind of assistance, one that reflects individual pride and accomplishment. What most individuals desire is the ability to experience success to the degree that they can rely upon their own abilities and talents to produce a decent living wage, not only for one's own personal satisfaction, but for others in a family.

Preserving the family and the community within which that family resides is an essential component of a healthy society. The future of our society relies upon the way its citizens transmit to the next generation those values which reflect the 'rich' traditions of our heritage. The stronger our children hold to these values, the stronger they will be in terms of eventually assuming those positions of leadership required to advance American ideals.

The welfare reform model to be proposed here uses generally accepted principles and practices associated with the three disciplines of family economics, microeconomics, and consumption economics. What is suggested here is simply a reorganization of existing structures that enable families in need of a second chance the opportunity *to achieve the American dream.* Achieving this dream has been a reality for many immigrants who have also had a second chance to start a new life. Such dreams are readily apparent in the corporate area whereby ideas among everyday citizens resulted in huge success stories as demonstrated with the creation of Ford, Microsoft, and Intel. The basis for this model is similar in that it is the 'average' everyday person who through personal imagination and drive can have a great impact upon society through inventions that reflect ingenuity, freedom, and individual ability.

# Part One

## WELFARE  REFORM

## WITH PASSION

# 1 Welfare reform: a model with conviction

The model for welfare reform being proposed describes a flexible plan for attempting to instill a 'winning spirit' into the lives of those individuals who have not been able to reap the benefits of the free enterprise system. The plan consists of several key components, each carrying significant weight in terms of enabling individuals to set their own destiny but within expectations of the neighborhoods. What is suggested here is the need for a 'new attitude' on the part of our political leadership and those organizations which make up the 'backbone' of a neighborhood. Such a plan is required in view of a 'new economy' in which knowledge, cooperation, and sharing are important attributes.

Today, many heads of households presently receiving aid through Aid to Families with Dependent Children (AFDC) who seek employment are concerned with the low-paying wages that are associated with many of the jobs in the service sector. While no simple solution has been found for transforming the lives of those in poverty, a fundamental change in the way government assistance is provided is direly needed. The need to employ or re-employ large numbers of persons for reducing welfare subsidies comes at a critical time as another transformation of the American marketplace occurs. The moment of truth is now at hand, and how we cope with welfare reform while coping with significant changes in the expectations of future workers will determine if we truly mean business. With the U.S. economy changing right before our very eyes as witnessed by the downsizing of many companies, having true welfare reform becomes even more of a challenge.

As governors seek waivers from the federal government to initiate innovative strategies to help the less fortunate turn their lives around, many other more affluent Americans in the middle class are at the same time pondering their future. In this regard, the middle class in particular is leery about possibly having to sacrifice some of their success in order to enhance the lives of others. Whatever signals we send to AFDC heads of households in terms of placing them in jobs, those in the middle class also need to be reassured that such jobs will not be taken away from them. Job creation is a fine objective, but if it is perceived as a trade off by playing one group against another, chaos will no doubt result.

This doubt on the part of many in the middle class poses a serious threat to any attempt to end public welfare. According to many economists, Generation X, a label often used to identify our next generation of leaders, may be the first generation in American history whose standard of living is to decrease when compared to that of their parents. This anticipation may be 'hard to swallow' for our youth because they have typically enjoyed a secure feeling of living in a country with the world's highest standard of living. However, this feeling of security is starting to waiver from comfort to bewilderment. Economic security is very much on the minds of today's American family, including those families on welfare who are now being targeted with reduced public support. However, there is much doubt among Americans as to how we can assist AFDC families to become more independent without committing additional resources for solving this problem. Can we implement true welfare reform without reducing or eliminating important services presently being provided to those of the middle and upper socioeconomic classes of the American society?

**Welfare reform and the free trade movement**

One way that the U.S. is trying to create a sufficient number of new jobs is by attempting to lead a 'free trade movement' among countries around the world. Historically, an example of this interest is agreeing to be a participant in the General Agreement on Trade and Tariffs (GATT) initiated in the 1940s. The GATT agreement enabled U.S. exporters to ship goods more cheaply and allow service companies to enter foreign markets. In similar ways, we allowed foreign competitors to sell their goods and services in the U.S. In reality, GATT was considered by many to be the world's biggest tax-cut, with 117 nations lowering or eliminating tariffs.

This attitude among our political leaders at that time was that GATT would result in an expansion of exports which will result in the creation of thousands of new jobs. According to the U.S. Department of Commerce Bureau of Economic Analysis (1996), the U.S. had consistently exported more than it imported from 1965 to about 1973. It was during this period that the citizens of this country generated much new wealth which came about through plentiful jobs paying higher wages. It was during this time that the American work ethic was considered the role model for the world. It was during this time that manufacturing sectors throughout the country produced products that were in demand worldwide.

However, the pendulum swung quickly in the opposite direction beginning in the mid 1970s. As shown in Figure 1.1, it was during this

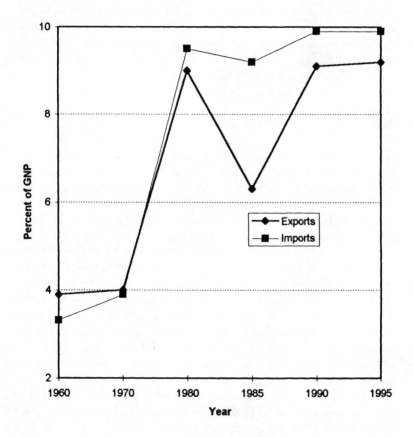

**Figure 1.1    Exports & imports as percentage of GNP**
Source:        Brookings Institution, 1996

5

time period that imports began to exceed exports. With this new allegiance between American consumers and products and services made in other countries came the realization that wealth is leaving the U.S. This realization showed up quickly in yearly large trade deficits frequently in the $150 to $250 billion range. In 1996, the yearly trade deficit continues to be over $150 billion. In spite of yearly trade deficits, exports in the U.S. continued to grow. Between 1990 and 1995, it has been estimated that U.S. exports accounted for half of total U.S. economic growth, supporting more than nine million jobs. *It is estimated that for each $1 billion increase in exports, 10,000 new jobs are created.* Therefore, increasing exports is extremely vital if we are going to create additional jobs in sufficient numbers to employ those individuals who have been outside of the workforce over the past years. This is an excellent time to initiate a new comprehensive welfare policy and the model community that is to be proposed enables those presently on welfare to become part of this strategy for generating new wealth.

*There is a whole new opportunity out there*

The World Trade Organization is beginning to supersede GATT. If there is a continual trend towards free trade among countries throughout the world, millions of new jobs are expected to become available to American families, including those on welfare. A likely outcome of free trade agreements between the 1996-2006 era will be American households possibly experiencing an average increase in income of up to $1700 per year. The continuation of the GATT agreement by the World Trade Organization (WTO) could be considered just the tip of the iceberg. Other regional agreements may also spur free trade among countries that find themselves with common interests. For example, the North American Free Trade Agreement (NAFTA) aims at reducing and ultimately eliminating most of the remaining barriers to trade and investment among Canada, Mexico, and the U.S. Under NAFTA, the United States joins with its first- and third-largest trading partners as part of the world's largest common economic market.

According to statistics reported in *North American Free Trade,* the combined Gross Domestic Product (GDP) of the three countries was about $63 trillion in 1990, with a population of 363 million. The U.S. economy accounts for 87 percent of the GDP of these three countries and 69 percent of the population. By comparing trade balances between the U.S. and Mexico, the potential strength of the U.S. economy is evident. Between 1986 and 1991 U.S. exports to Mexico grew at an annual rate of 22 percent and imports only by 13 percent. According the Los Angeles

Times, record growth in U.S. exports to Mexico is expected to continue as a result of the NAFTA agreement.

The easing of tariffs that began when NAFTA took effect on January 1, 1994, has already helped boost U.S. exports to Mexico to $11.8 billion in the three months ending March 31, 1994, which is 16 percent higher than the first quarter of 1993. It was the highest quarterly level of *exports* to Mexico ever recorded. First quarter *imports* of Mexican goods and services grew to $11.3 billion, up 22 percent from the same period in 1993. What is good for American is also good for Mexico. Canada similarly experiences growth in their exports to the U.S. as well as reaping the benefits of importing quality products and services from their southern neighbor. Therefore, regional trade pacts are likely to assist the workers of the three countries by increasing the opportunities for additional employment as well as expanding the choices for goods and services available in the marketplace.

As illustrated in Table 1.1 below, while the per capita income among residents of Canada and the U.S. are relatively the same, that of households in Mexico is much lower. However, regional trade agreements may be one alternative for bringing the three countries closer

**Table 1.1**
**Relative size of the Canadian, Mexico and U.S. economics, 1990**

| Item | Canada | Mexico | U.S. |
|------|--------|--------|------|
| GNP ($ billions) | $ 572 | $ 214 | $ 5,514 |
| Per capita GDP | $ 21,527 | $ 2,490 | $22,055 |
| Average wage per day | $ 67.98 | $ 8.11 | $ 69.14 |
| Population (millions) | 26.6 | 86.1 | 250.0 |

Source: Brookings Institution, 1996

together in terms of economic gains for its citizens. In a similar regard, welfare reform in the United States may have a positive effect upon the general welfare of the citizens of these three countries.

Entering into global trade agreements symbolizes the beginning of a new era for the American economy. By voluntarily entering into trading agreements with other countries and adhering to an international legal body for resolving complaints, the U.S. government has set the stage for enhancing the standard of living of all citizens. Those citizens who can band together in innovative schemes can reap the benefits of world trade.

This proposal for welfare reform calls for the reinstitution of 'social capital theory' that requires a new attitude towards work and community. The free trade movement is about rekindling a new spirit, a new direction, and a new camaraderie. With some ingenuity, welfare reform can be integrated into the free trade movement through a renewed spirit of adventure.

**Taking advantage of other new opportunities when they arise**

One of the demands upon the political leadership in the United States is to assure its citizens a smooth transition from a military dominated market place to one based upon a 'peace time' economy. As America goes through this important transformation, new opportunities arise. These opportunities can result in significant gains. However, timing is not the only significant factor to consider. A political leadership must be willing seize an opportunity by targeting newly available resources.

The downsizing of the military complex in the United States provides one of those timely opportunities for solving one of America's most pressing problems; that being, getting residents off public welfare programs and into the workplace. The military has played a major role in the American marketplace ever since this country was founded. The Revolutionary War, Civil War, World War I and II, the Korean War, the Vietnam Incident, and the Gulf War are just some of the conflicts that are part of American history. Each and every one of these wars has had a profound impact on the kinds of new products that have made their way into the marketplace. Such products as the television, personal computer, radar, automobile technology, and many household appliances have resulted from military research. Many of our advances in space technology has resulted in 'leading edge' advances such as solar energy, laser technology, and genetic engineering. Not only has war boosted our economy, but it also established a sense of dominance that has enabled our country to remain as a superpower for so many years.

However, the days of a military complex driving the American economy are now over. Future advances in product design and availability to the public will more likely have to come from a peace-time economy driven by the ingenuity of the everyday citizen. Similarly, the need for a military complex to manage huge numbers of individuals in the army, navy, air force, and marines also appear to be over. In their place are high-tech weapons capable of considerable destruction with pinpoint accuracy. Lethal, specialized assault equipment has taken the place of the unknown soldier. Anyone who witnessed the Gulf War in the early 1990s remembers the numerous aerial assaults on Iraqi military targets using electronic sensing ballistic missiles.

In view of the entrance into a high-tech mobile military force, the U.S. Government now finds it unnecessary to maintain the number of military bases that have existed for decades. The surge to close unneeded military bases came to a head in 1988 when Congress enacted legislation to set up a commission to identify those military bases that could be closed as a money-saving move. A 12-member panel, called the Commission on Base Realignment and Closure (BRAC), was created. The panel initially identified 16 bases indicated in Table 1.2 that could be closed. The estimated savings that would be accrued annually because of these closings were estimated to be in the millions of dollars, (Base Realignment and Closure Report, 1988).

### Table 1.2
### 1988 BRAC commission report on military base closings

| | |
|---|---|
| Chanute AFB, IL | Mather AFB, CA |
| Pease AFB, NH | George AFB, CA |
| Norton AFB, CA | Naval Station Brooklyn, NY |
| Phila.Naval Base, PA | Naval Station Galveston, TX |
| Naval:Lk.Charls., LA | Presidio of San Fran, CA |
| Fort Sheridan, IL | Jefferson Proving Ground, IN |
| Lextng.Army, KY | Army Mat. Tech Lab, MA |
| Fort Douglas, UT | Cameron Station, VA |

Source: BRAC = Commission on Base Realignment and Closures, 1988

But the federal government did not stop with the 1988 commission. Two more commissions were established. A second commission was established in 1991, and this committee identified 26 more bases listed in Table 1.3 on the next page that they felt could be closed. Many of these military bases are located near large cities in which there is a considerable population of AFDC families. For example, the Philadelphia Navy Yard is located in a large metropolitan areas which as easy access to roads, entertainment, and educational facilities.    A military base in San Diego

## Table 1.3
### 1991 BRAC commission report on military base closings

| | |
|---|---|
| Naval Long Beach, CA | England AFB LA |
| Moffett NAS, CA | Eaker AFB, AR |
| Tustin MCAS, Ca | Carswell AFB, TX |
| Chase Field NAS, CA | Bergstrom AFB, TX |
| Brissom AFB, IN | ENGR CTR, San Diego, CA |
| Fort Ord, CA | Naval Station Puget, WA |
| Fort Devens, MA | Phila Naval Shipyard, PA |
| Fort Harrison, IN | Naval Station Phila, PA |
| Loring AFB, ME | Sacramento Army Depot, CA |
| Wurtsmith AFB, MI | Myrtle Beach AFB, SC |
| Castle AFB, CA | Richards-Gebaur ARS, MO |
| Lowry AFB, CO | Williams AFB, AZ |
| | Rickenbacker AGB, OH |

Source: BRAC = Commission on Base Realignment & Closures, 1991

has also been  targeted  for closing in an area where a large Hispanic AFDC population resides.  Also a number of military bases located in the state of Texas targeted for closing are also located in areas easily accessible to AFDC families

A third commission was established in 1993, and they identified an additional 28 bases for closure (depicted in Table 1.4 on the next page). Based upon statistics supplied by the United States Senate, these military bases are located throughout the country, with a considerable number targeted in California, Texas, and Pennsylvania, (United States Senate,

1988). By the third commission report, approximately 70 military bases were identified as having potential for being closed. However, it should also be noted that there are approximately 500 military bases as part of the military complex, and at the time of this writing, only 14 percent have

**Table 1.4**
**1993 BRAC commission report on military base closings**

| | |
|---|---|
| NESEC, St. Inigoes, MD | Naval Station Charleston, SC |
| Vint Hill Farms, VA | Naval Station Mobile, AL |
| MACA El Toro, CA | Naval Air Station Alameda, CA |
| Naval Air, Cecil Field, FL | Naval Air Station Agana, Guam |
| Plattsburgh AF Base, NY | Homestead Air Force Base, FL |
| Naval Air Alameda, CA | Naval Station Mobile, AL |
| Naval Station Staten Island, NY | Defense Personnel Sppt. Center, PA |
| Naval Air Station Barbers | Naval Station Treasure |
| Point, HI | Island, CA |
| O'Hare IAP ARS, IL | Naval Depot, Pensacola, FL |
| Mare Island Naval Shipyard, | Naval Air Station Dallas, TX |
| Vallejo, CA | |
| Naval Air, Glenview, IL | Gentile Air Force Station, OH |
| Charleston Naval Shipyard, SC | Naval Aviation Depot |
| | Alameda, CA |
| Naval Aviation Depot | Naval Training Center |
| Norfolk, VA | Orlando, FL |
| Newark Air Force Base, | Naval Training Center San |
| OH | Diego, CA |
| | K.I. Sawyer Air force Base, MI |

Source: BRAC = Commission on Base Realignment and Closures, 1993

been suggested for closing. Currently, some of these bases have already been either sold or contracted out for other purposes. However, there are considerably more bases available to become part of an innovative scheme for creating communities with a new spirit for enhancing the lives of AFCD families currently desperate in search of a future

In terms of these initial commissions which targeted military bases for elimination, Table 1.5 on the next page indicates that 495 still remained as part of our national security. It should be noted that at the time of this writing, discussions on eliminating an additional 50 to 100 military bases were also being held.  No matter what the outcome, a new resource has now become available, one that reflects the new opportunity for solving the welfare problem in this country.

## Table 1.5
## Major domestic closures

| BASES | BRAC88 | BRAC91 | BRAC93 | LEFT | REDUC. |
|---|---|---|---|---|---|
| Army | 109 | -7 | -4 | -1 | 97 | 11% |
| Navy/ | | | | | | |
| USMC | 168 | -4 | -9 | -20 | 135 | 20% |
| Air | | | | | | |
| Force | 206 | -5 | -13 | -5 | 183 | 11% |
| Defense | | | | | | |
| Agencies | 12 | 0 | 0 | -2 | 10 | 17% |
| Totals | 495 | -16 | -26 | -28 | 425 | 15% |

BRAC = Base Realignment and Closure Reports

*A diamond in the rough*

How can the U.S. benefit from closing all of these military bases?  Earlier it was stated that a new attitude was needed.  No longer should big business receive all of the benefits of change.  These military bases can be described as a 'diamond in the rough.'  This analogy depicts an available resource that could be molded into 'sparkling new communities.'  Many of the military bases have everything that a community needs; and with them   soon to be vacated,   why not turn them into self-contained communities?  Jobs could be created and lives could be restored.  Some 158,000 jobs have been created at military facilities closed between 1961 and 1990, more than replacing the 93,400 lost defense jobs, (Wall Street Journal, August 1993).

The subsequent series of maps illustrates the numbers and locations of military installations, state by state.  Former bases housed schools for 160,000 individuals, support 75 industrial and office parks, and provide 42 airports, (U.S. Dept. of Interior, 1992).  New Jersey's Raritan Arsenal, now an industrial park, employs 13,100 people, compared with 2,610 as a military facility.  The first of the three maps shown depicts the number of military bases across the U.S. Figure 1.2 reports data from the United States Department of Interior Geological Survey. It illustrates that military bases are located throughout the United States, providing an opportunity to have a national impact in terms of creating new kinds of neighborhoods in which residents can participate in seeking the American dream. As noted in Figure 1.2, the five states with the largest number of installations are California with 102, Virginia with 56, Florida with 41, Texas with 36, and Pennsylvania/Maryland tied with 23.

On the other hand, the those regions where there are the fewest number of installations include New England, the Midwest, and the far west, excluding California. It may be concluded that there is a resource presently available for changing the lives of many Americans in poverty, and with a little ingenuity, a significant impact could be made upon turning around the lives of millions of individuals presently in poverty. Creating a city from scratch is nothing new to America. With the creative talent of the building industry readily available, the challenge of succeeding at such an attempt represents the American spirit which has traditionally come through when tasks appear to be insurmountable.

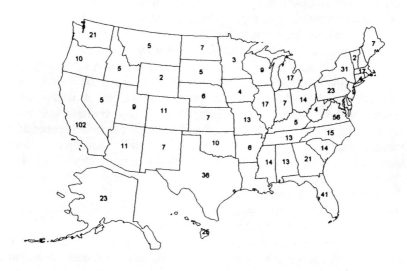

**Figure 1.2    Military installations by state, 1995**
Source:          U.S. Dept. of Interior, Geological Survey, 1995

However, with the profit motive and the current needs of business to expand their markets as well as to find appropriate workers in a tight labor market, the incentives are basically in place. What the political leadership must do is put the finishing touches on such a plan to recreate peace-time communities on military bases which are in reality mini-communities providing many services to residents.

The second map shows the major bases which are closed or are soon to be closing. In Figure 1.3, the data indicates that 32 major bases have been closed or realigned at the time of this writing. As shown on the detailed map, a vast majority of the military bases already targeted for closure are east of the Mississippi River. A considerable number are located either on the Eastern seaboard between the states of Virginia and Massachusetts. Similarly, six major bases have been scheduled to be closed in the state of California.

A major base closing is one in which at least 300 military and civilian jobs will be lost. The state of Florida has also been targeted in that five major base closures have been consummated. These bases have customarily been part of contractual agreements with states or local governmental units for specific uses other than military. Some have already been transferred to businesses while others have been adopted for social causes. However, even though 32 have already been targeted, there are substantial numbers of military bases in existence and their future in many cases has not been determined.

The key concern in closing military bases is the economic fallout such an action would have in the communities which surround the facility. In terms of estimated job losses, California and Texas would be impacted the most heavily. Therefore, there has been some urgency in finding new owners for the military bases in order reemploy those civilians who have depended upon these sites for their jobs. Therefore, our model proposals a viable alternative for these military bases. Instead of leasing or selling these bases to the commercial sector with the aim of expanding only employment, it may be to America's advantage to redesign the sites for the purpose of establishing whole new communities. The number of jobs created would no doubt be significantly more than those associated with a few companies that set up business operations.

The boom to the local economies would be significant. Such a policy would meet the needs of huge numbers of Americans who desire a second chance at life. Pockets of poverty exist throughout the United States. The military bases scheduled to be closed are conveniently distributed throughout the countryside. Some are located near small towns, others within easy commuting distance to large cities. The intriguing aspect of adapting the military bases to residential use is that they can be designed to reflect the unique characteristics of the different regions in the United States. Therefore, there has to be no one model community for welfare reform. Depending upon the ingenuity of community planners, welfare reform can be instituted from many different perspective. Although the model communities should reflect the diversity of cultures in the nation, they can attract citizens with selected interests in terms of job skills. Such communities can be designed on a foundation of science, the theater and the arts, tourism, or financial services.

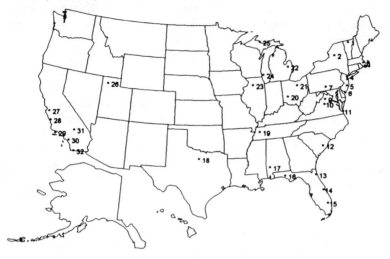

**Figure 1.3   Major base closures and realignments, 1993**
Source:       U.S. Dept. of Interior, Geological Survey, 1993

Legend:
1. Plattsburgh AFB, NY
2. Griffis ARB, NY
3. Naval TC, RI
4. Naval Staten Island, NY
5. Naval AWC, NJ
6. Defense Clothing Fact., PA
7. Nat. Capital Region, DC
8. White Oak, MD
9. Vint Hillls, VA
10. Fort Belvoir, VA
11. Norfolk, VA
12. Charleston, SC
13. Cecil Field, FL
14. Orlando,FL
15. Homestead AFB, FL
16. Pensacola, FL
17. Mobile, AL
18. NAS Dallas, TX
19. NAS Memphis, TN
20. AFS, OH
21. Newark AFB, OH
22. NAF, Detroit, MI
23. Chicago, IL
24. NAS, IL
25. Sawyer AFB, MI
26. Toole Depot, UT
27. SF, CA
28. Monterey,CA
29. P. Hueneme, CA
30. Tustin, CA
31. March AFB, CA
32. San Diego, CA

In Figure 1.4, a third map identifies five military bases which may become pilot communities as we learn how to establish new neighborhoods that are all inclusive. These five military bases were selected because they are different characteristics from each other. Some of the bases are larger than others, some provide more services than others, and some are located in different regions from others. These five possible pilot communities illustrate the flexibility of the model being proposed. Not all communities must have the same design, purpose, or size. The newly designed communities can be generated according to the specific characteristics and needs of a region. The employment component of a particular community can reflect the past successes of a region. Therefore, the model being proposed does not adopt one particular set of parameters but allows for flexibility according to the style of the anchor business or businesses that form the commercial center of the neighborhood.

**Figure 1.4   Pilot communities for welfare experiments, 1997**

16

A more thorough description of each possible pilot community depicting five bases that could be converted into self-managed communities is provided here.

*Alameda Naval Air Station.* One pilot community found on the map is in California. The Alameda Naval Air Station is a division of the Navy and is closing. It is a very large air station, covering almost 2,842 acres. It is on the east side of the San Francisco Bay and conveniently located close to a number of cities and suburban communities. It has ample housing, a retail store, a barber shop, a dry cleaners, a food shop, a florist, banking, a service station, a bakery, a convenience store, an auto hobby shop, child care facilities, an elementary school, a library, a medical clinic, and a dental clinic. This base also has a bowling alley, a movie theater, a pool, a gym, a recreation center, tennis courts, racquetball courts, a ticket office, clubs, a baseball diamond, a football field, and even a pitch and putt golf course. All this community needs is a few families, and we have ourselves a legitimate neighborhood.

*Plattsburgh Air Force Base.* A second pilot community could be located in New York. It is called the Plattsburgh Air Force Base, and it is expected to close by the time of this writing.. It houses around 11,000 people and consists of about 1,600 acres. The services that Plattsburgh offers a potential community are many. They include: a commissary, a retail store, a barber shop, a dry cleaners, a food shop, a florist , banking, a service station, a day care center, a home day care program, a kindergarten, a preschool, an elementary school, a library, a hospital, a medical clinic, a dental clinic, a bowling alley, a movie theater, a pool, a gym, a recreation center, a golf course, a tennis court, a racquetball court, a skating rink, a fitness center, a softball field, a football field, an auto shop.

*Glenview Naval Air Station.* The third pilot community that could be considered is the Glenview Naval Air Station, located in Glenview, Illinois. It consists of 1,200 acres. It is 20 miles north of Chicago and about 10 minutes from the O'Hare International Airport. It has housed about 3,800 people consisting of military personnel, family members, and civilians. The services that Glenview offers are ample housing, a commissary, a retail store, a day care center, a medical clinic, veterinary services, a medical clinic, a bowling alley, a movie theater, a pool, a gym, golf, tennis, racquetball, a fitness center, an auto shop, a camping site, a youth center, and even skeet shooting. Because of the location of this based, it could become a welcome alternative for those on welfare in the Chicago area.

*Dallas Naval Air Station.* The fourth new kind of community could be situated in Dallas, Texas. The Dallas Naval Air Station is located on 840 acres and is located 13 miles west of Dallas in Grand Prairie. The services that currently exist on this station are a commissary and exchange, a retail store, a barber shop, a dry cleaners, a florist, banking, a service station, a convenience store, personal services shop, an optical shop, a beauty shop, a fast food restaurant, a day care center for up to 50 students, a library, a medical clinic, a dental clinic, a bowling alley, a pool, a gym, tennis, racquetball, a fitness center, a softball field, a football field, an auto shop, even a marina and picnic area.

*Central Florida Research Park.* The fifth possible pilot community could be in Orlando Florida. It is located on 40 acres in Central Florida Research Park. It is 15 miles from downtown Orlando and about 17 miles northeast of the Orlando International Airport. This military base is quite small in size as it customarily has housed about 1,250 residents. Although smaller than the most of the other military bases destined for closure, there are considerable services available such as a base library, a naval hospital, a bowling alley, a movie theater, golf, tennis, a softball field, an auto shop, and clubs.


**Reinventing power neighborhoods**

What is proposed is a new form of government assistance. Our model allows for the creation of new kinds neighborhoods consisting of welfare recipients who desire a second chance. Using military base closures, short-term moneys would be required to redesign, upgrade, and expand existing communities which are now available. The idea is to move families on a voluntary basis from the inner cities where crime and despair are prevalent to a revived self-contained community. Over the long-term, the residents of the community will eventually take on the responsibility of funding their own public services as job training is completed and employment is obtained. It is argued that a pilot community could be established in any one of the five locations previously identified. Change is happening all around us, and an opportunity to assist thousands of families in need of public assistance is now at hand.

What is typical of many communities today? They consist of people who live in *separate* homes, have *separate* decks/porches, have their *own* cars, work out at their specific fitness clubs, have their *own* personal computers... and the list goes on. What did you notice about this description of today's community? Terms like *own and separate* are words that *divide*. Where there is division within a group of people, there can be no *community*, no *communion*, and no *togetherness*. In the 1992 Webster's Dictionary and Thesaurus, the word community is defined as 'a group of people living in the *same* area and under the *same* government; a class or group having *common* interests and likes'. What did you notice about this definition of a community? This definition uses words like *same and common*--words that bring individuals *together*.

Establishing communities in which families can bond through home ownership is critical to the success of any plan to reform welfare. What is proposed here is adapting military bases scheduled for closure into a self-contained *power community* in which government in partnership with business take on the responsibility of helping others enhance their quality of life. Therefore, by creating power communities--away from inner cities and rural communities--families can experience the American dream while learning to become part of a society where law, education, and work are readily attainable.

In such a community of renewal, families will be given the opportunity not only to receive training for employment, but also have the 'right' to own their own homes and participate in their own communities. A comprehensive community consisting of health care facility, a school, training centers for displaced workers, a commercial area of stores, and companies which 'anchor the community' provide a new perspective to welfare reform. Of course, criteria for admission to these 'renewal' communities would be developed, but such a criteria would attempt to incorporate as many different kinds of families as possible, including two parent, single-parent, divorced, and single. The idea here is to develop a multicultural neighborhood where differences among residents are respected rather than challenged.

The funds to remodel existing military bases would come through tax incentives to business and other investors who would join in new venture teams for creating a community where individuals can shape their own future. The power community is based upon commitments that would result from contractual agreements among the participants. Eventually, families could have the option of remaining in that community where jobs could be attained, begin to make payments on their residences, or leave the community to seek employment elsewhere after agreed upon time limits..

Attaining the American dream of home ownership is the basis of a contract. On the one hand, the individual on welfare is provided a support system of health care and day care as long as he/she remains in a training program which guarantees a job at its conclusion. Once the individual gains full employment in that community, he/she would begin paying taxes to support that community. Therefore, the community eventually becomes self-supporting, relying less and less on public funds from the federal and state levels over the long-term.

At such a time when independence is achieved, the new employee can select an option which includes the purchase of a personal residence for a family, a very important incentive to participate. The power community can be laid out in a similar fashion to that of a wheel in which all activities revolve around the hub and the spokes reflect the solidarity of a neighborhood. It takes all parts of the wheel to make it work perfectly, and the same is true for the renewal community. The term *renewal or power* is critical in that the families who voluntarily join together are attempting to gain control over their lives. To assure that families do not get 'lost in the redesigned neighborhoods' or lose interest as the aura of the new community wears off, a strong social bonding becomes the driving force for generating a feeling of security.

**Elements to the renewal community**

At the central core or hub of the community is a *Town Fellowship Hall*. It is considered the pivotal point from which all activities originate. It symbolizes the significance of the renewal community in that fellowship, sharing, and collaborating provide the basis for social empowerment. Revolving about the community hub is a public school, a residential sector, commercial center, a shopping district, and a community service unit (government). Residents are urged to seek employment in their community (in government or in the private sector) and use day care facilities to meet family needs. It is important to remember that renewal communities will likely vary in style according to regional priorities and in particular the job market in that area of the country. There is no one renewal community. Although the general layout of each community may be similar to one another, the employment sector may vary according to the needs of the companies that become part of a self-contained community.

The cost of remodeling military bases would be shared by companies, the government, and the eventual residents of the community. Welfare subsidies would likely continue until the initial group of citizens completed their training and were then classified as tax-paying residents. The communities would consist of between 5,000 and 15,000 residents, depending upon size of the military bases being transformed. Citizens who violate their contract would, after reasonable number of warnings, be required to leave the community. What is promised in the community is safety, education, jobs, and entertainment. What is not promised is a permissiveness towards crime, cheating on contractual agreements, and lack of commitment to meet community standards. Criteria for community expectations would be established by community councils similar to those now in place in many states. Such councils would provide the basis for law and order, similar to the way commissions operate in some states throughout the country.

Sounds impossible! Well, let's describe what a typical renewal community may look like once it is in place. We will initially identify particular segments of the community including the health care and physical fitness hub, education, housing, community service, a shopping district and commercial center. It is the concept that is significant and not the particulars as to size, diversity, and the kinds of businesses to be included.

*Health care and physical fitness hub*

At the center of the renewal community will be a health care and physical fitness complex (or a wellness strategy), which is the 'heart beat' of the Town Fellowship Hall. All community activities will emanate from the Fellowship Hall. Health care is not just medical care. Health care includes physical fitness, mental fitness, and enjoyment. In order to mobilize community resources, one large facility serving as a town center will be required. This is the focal point where neighbors come together to bond as they participate in activities which will lead to a healthy lifestyle. This facility could become a multipurpose facility which will include HMO facilities and equipment, day care facilities, athletic facilities, seminar rooms, and rehabilitation and post-surgery facilities. The main goal of the town center is to provide the families with a chance to stay within a 3-wide radius for fulfilling their needs.

The costs of operating such a facility will be shared by those companies which set up operations in the renewal community. Therefore, day care and health care will be provided to all residents who sign contracts to have their children enter public schools or to complete job training themselves. Partial funding will also come from state Medicaid funds to help support the community HMO. Once these individuals are fully trained and have obtained full-time jobs, they will be required to participate in a co-pay arrangement for these services on reduced fee schedules as long as their children attend school regularly.

Central to the town center is the Health Maintenance Organization (HMO). This area of the center will be called *the Salutary*, which focuses upon preventive care measures. *The Salutary* will also have a 24-hour hot line in case of emergencies. If, for example, a child falls out of bed and suffers from a mild concussion or broken bone, or if an individual overdoses on medicine or some other serious drug, all one will have to do is call the 24-hour *Salutary* hot-line and someone will be able to assist them.

Family doctors and a pharmacy will also be provided. Family doctors will give regular yearly checkups and provide his or her patients with the proper prescriptions. These prescriptions will be taken to the pharmacy and filled by a registered nurse. All patients will be entered into the database along with the drug, ailment, doctor, date of last checkup, and date of current issuance. Patients must have their prescriptions filled within two weeks of issuance or they will have to pay for their own prescription. The doctor and the pharmacy nurse will work from two interconnected databases so that the information is received as soon as it is input into the system.

*Day care with a new attitude*

Children between the ages of one and five may be cared for in the day care center. Therefore, within the town hub, a day care center or *Children's Room* will be provided and will remain available as long as the businesses are open. *The Children's Room* will also provide breakfast, lunch, dinner, and snacks depending on the time of day each child is present. The special facility will have cots in the nap area for the younger children or for the children who have to stay longer than five or six hours. There will also be an indoor and an outdoor playground in order to keep the children active and constructive throughout the year.

Children between the ages of one and five learn a lot about their surroundings. During the early stages of childhood, children can be taught their alphabet, full names, parents' full names, their addresses and other pertinent details of life. Day care will be the first contact many of these children have within the community; therefore, activities must be entertaining but also intellectually challenging. Taking care of toys and maintaining a safe-free environment are the basis of early childhood experiences, setting the stage for reinforcing community pride during later years of schooling.

Once the parents of these children are trained in the business field of their interest and begin working, they will enter 'attractive' co-pay arrangements with their employer for the family's day care services. A small fee is a symbol of commitment to the community and the business in which they are employed. Refunds may be an option in which residents may be able to collect part of their fees at the end of the fiscal year if the family remains healthy and does not have an excessive use of the community center. Such fees will also help prevent abuse of the system in that residents know if they use good judgment, they can get their portion of the co-pay back either from their employer in the form of a fringe benefit or from the HMO.

*Athletics and physical fitness becomes a passion*

As stated earlier, health care is also physical fitness and enjoyment. The next feature in the renewal community center is the athletic facility or *Physical Fitness Room*. This feature includes various recreational activities in which individuals can participate. Some of the activities can be merged with the activities of the high school such as the multi-sport gymnasium which can be used for volleyball, basketball, indoor track and tennis. A community field will be multifunctional in this new

22

neighborhood because it will serve as a place where cookouts, picnics or various outdoor games can be played. This field will give many residents the chance to get to know one another and work together as a team.

For fun and entertainment, there will be a separate hall. This hall will still be inside of the community center, but in another section. This facility will fulfill the role as a recreational center, especially for sponsoring concerts, plays, and other staged events. It will also served as a *Community Affairs Room* in which parents and children can enter into group activities from gamesmanship to discussion groups. The *Community Affairs Room* can also house children's talent shows, school plays and local celebrations.

*Rehabilitating services with compassion*

The health care and physical fitness hub (the core of the Town Fellowship Hall) will have a confidentiality room or *Support Room* for private counseling. In this room, individuals will be able to talk out their problems with others who are in a similar situation. Seminars will be conducted to show individuals that there *is* a way out besides violence or suicide. The counseling rooms will educate individuals on different ways to handle certain problems such as rebellious children, living with a person who abuses drugs, or living with an abusive person. The counseling rooms are open at all times and schedules will be posted weekly indicating who will be speaking and what rooms will be available for use. Individuals who are recovering from any kind of addiction or physical or mental abuse will also need rehabilitation.

Some individuals of the community may need surgery and may be required to go through a post-surgery rehabilitation program in order to get well. For this purpose the *Wellness Center* is useful. In the Wellness Center, there will be various types of equipment for limb or bone strengthening. There will be whirlpools and ultrasound equipment so that injuries can be doctored back to good health. There will also be weights, bikes, treadmills, benches, tables, ice machines and other types of equipment needed to restore individuals of the community back to good health.

The *Wellness Center* also works in conjunction with the *Support Room* in rehabilitating mentally and physically abused persons. The rehabilitation for victims of mental abuse helps the victim to build or rebuild self-esteem and confidence. Most mentally abused victims have low self-esteem because their counterpart has torn them down almost to the point where they think they are nothing. These individuals can become suicidal without help.

Physically abused individuals are either abused by others or abused by themselves. Individuals who abuse themselves have low self-esteem. For example, individuals who are bulimic think they are vastly overweight, so starve themselves because of this perception. Often, these individuals will have excessive weight loss resulting in a body weight of no more than 100 pounds. They need similar help as do individuals who are anorexic and starve themselves because they feel they are overweight. Overweight individuals also need help with self-esteem. However, being overweight is dangerous to one's health and most overweight individuals are teased, pointed at, and ridiculed making them feel inferior or giving them the feeling that they do not belong. There are programs for people like these individuals and others who have health problems. The Wellness Center can and will help!

### A techno-school with spirit

Quality of life is what most individuals want for themselves and their children, but what is the ideal quality of life? Quality of life is gaining the most from life based upon the resources at the command of the individual. Similarly, a quality school is one that provides those attending as many opportunities as possible to learn how to appreciate all aspects of life. This school will instill a respect for oneself, academics, job skills, as well as caring for others. The neighborhood school has four themes which will be integrated into a comprehensive package: *life experiences, spirit of social responsibility, technology, and employment preparation.*

The techno-school is a new, innovative, nontraditional school. The goal of the school is to get the parents of the community more involved in their children's studies and their schools' environment. The community school will have few administrators. It is to be operated under the principles of *Total Quality Management (TQM),* which will be adopted and implemented by the parents of the students who attend the school. This should decrease the amount of disruptive behavior since some children are less apt to 'act up' if they know that their parents could easily be reached. All parents will have weekly meetings to be kept up to date with how their child or children are doing in the area of getting along with teachers and other children.

Public education will include grades K-14 with the final two grades primarily focusing upon gaining those technical skills to complement the general education skills learned previously in grades K-12. The neighborhood school will have a guidance office, a nurse's office, cafeteria and a gymnasium as all schools do. Also, the school will be more project-oriented as opposed to paper-oriented, unlike other schools where written exams are about 90 percent of the students' grade. Moreover, the techno-school will emphasize hands-on projects emphasizing the development of logic skills, interpersonal communication, and collaborative problem-solving strategies. The grading policy for the techno-school will be based on the students attendance, problem-based learning, and impact their learning has upon the community in which they reside. The neighborhood school will be located near the center of the community; therefore, no buses will be needed to transport children or parents from home to school or vice versa.

*Life experiences emphasized*

*Life experiences* will be integrated into all aspects of the techno-school's curricula. In the school's counseling center, trained professionals will be able to meet with children and parents in order to increase the growth of the parent-child relationship. The counselors are also here to participate in the self-esteem and drug awareness programs. These programs are predominantly for the children, but parents are permitted to sit in at the child's request.

Also included in the curriculum is a *culture awareness* program. This is a mandatory program given to all who attend the neighborhood school. Everyone needs to learn the different cultures of the world in order to get along. This program will teach individuals not to fear or put down others because they simply look different or have different forms of celebrations.

An important segment of the curriculum is *social and family pressures*. Many times individuals are pressured into doing things because a friend or family member is doing the same thing. This program will teach each individual that he or she is unique and can have his or her own style as long as this style is not damaging or disrespectful to others. Other pressures to be studied are sexual harassment, family abuse, divorce, sibling rivalry, and parental pressures upon academics.

*Social responsibility and spiritual growth*

A *spirit of social responsibility* will become an integral part of  the learning style of the youth in the renewal neighborhood. What is meant by social responsibility is what individuals owe to themselves, their community and others around them. All youth in the community will take on some responsibility to help keep the community clean and safe. The creation of a *community maintenance team,* mostly run by students, will create an interest in protecting the environment by reducing litter, by beautifying public areas, and by assisting residents with special needs such as lawn care, painting, and carpentry.

Along these same lines, *volunteerism* on the part of all students is an expectation in the community. Volunteering means to willingly offer, extend, or present oneself or services for a good or worthy cause. It will be considered patriotic for students to practice in their neighborhood those ideas and projects which have been generated in the community techno-school. For example, the act of charity has been a very important aspect of the American way of life. In this regard, most individuals who attempt to be charitable often sacrifice their time, energy, and sometimes money as they go about their commitment. However, giving students at all age levels the opportunity to volunteer to help others also gives them pride in themselves. This helps them to feel good in that they are needed by others as well as those in need feeling good that the youth in their neighborhoods care about them. By including the element of volunteerism as an integral part of school life, the objective here is to broaden an awareness that assisting others is a way of life and is the 'heart and soul' of a community.

Problem-based learning will also become an integral part of the instructional process of children k-12. The curricula in the techno-school reinforce the importance of sharing both knowledge and self as community problems and issues are analyzed in the techno-school. This form of 'reality learning' coincides with the spirit surrounding volunteerism that permeates all aspects of the renewal community. For example, while participating in a problem-based learning exercise, each student in a group will be responsible for completion of a certain part or piece of the puzzle. In order for the team to receive full credit, each individual must have his or her piece of the puzzle complete. This teaches social responsibility because each student in the group will be depending on others to do their part of the project. The important outcome is to develop a vision that an individual is more valuable when fulfilling a role as part of a group rather than working alone in isolation. Therefore, societal responsibility is a theme that permeates throughout the whole neighborhood, including the techno-school. Community and school spirit are generated through a constant stream of caring, not only for one's own sake but for that of others in the neighborhood.

*Techno-faculty engage students in virtual reality*

Learning in a setting that reflects *virtual technology* requires students to use their imagination and creativity for making logical decisions. The techno-school will incorporate at least three dimensions of technology. The first dimension of technology is *multimedia* and the making of learning more of a visual process. According to Fred T. Hofstetter (1997) of the University of Delaware, the ability to use multimedia will emerge as a life skill, and those individuals both young and old who do not know how to use multimedia will become disenfranchised. What is being suggested here is that it is important that residents in the renewal community do not end up watching life go by instead of living their lives fully. Personal computers will utilize CD-ROM technology for assisting students in self-contained neighborhoods to gain access to information throughout the world.

Combining CD-ROM technology with access to the Internet (information superhighway) will extend the students classroom beyond the walls of the classroom. Students will be able to download information for integration into project work. Classroom teachers will be able to download curriculum delivered from sources all over the world by means of the Internet. Traditional classroom lectures will give way to interactive learning sessions with teachers becoming mentors rather than dispensers of information. Emphasized will be the advancement of oral and written communication skills, human relationships, and creativity.

A second dimension to school use of technology will be the installation of a *high-tech library* that will enable both students and residents in the community (especially those who may not be able to afford a pc in their home) to gain access to videos, graphics, art, drama and other forms of media from all over the world. Within the school library will be a *Community Research Center*. A variety of data bases will be available to students and community residents. The techno-school library will serve a dual role as both a learning and recreational center for students and their parents. For example, library pcs can be used for searching for information about a particular sport, hobby, or just for fun. They can also be used for upgrading one's workplace skills, for career counseling, or for changing a career path.

A third dimension to technology is merging workplace skills with those required for home maintenance as part of the program delivered in a *technical and vocational* program. Therefore, technical learning will attempt to combine job and home skills as part of relational learning formats. The learning how to use household technology will assist individuals (both young and old) to increase the value of their future homes by showing them how to wall paper, paint, lay carpet, fix leaky faucets, and certain other around the house activities. These courses, however, will also have students apply similar vocational/trade skills in preparation for employment, such as repairing a pc, maintaining electrical systems, or monitoring heating and ventilation systems. In this regard, the adoption of *tech prep* formats which are currently available in many public schools in the nation will also be appropriate for the renewal community. Connecting public schools grades k-12 to local community colleges will be a very important aspect of public education in the community. *Tech prep* agreements between public secondary schools and community colleges will assist in guiding students to the next level of learning.

The fourth and final theme of the techno-school School is *occupational preparation*. Emphasized here will be highly interactive learning formats such as internships with business, apprenticeships upon graduation, and cooperative work experience while attending grades 13 and 14 in a local community college. The techno-school with its techno-faculty will attempt to provide school credit for a variety of work experience prior to graduation. While the intent is for all students to enter into grades 13 and 14 (free of tuition), there will be an incentive of receiving pay while learning to earn. Also, the technology used in business will complement that use in the school, which will assist in keeping the lines of communication open between businesses in the community and teachers in the new wave school.

At the conclusion of the k-14 educational program in the renewal community is a *guaranteed job*. If the student is unable to find employment at the conclusion of the k-14 program, he/she will be permitted to receive additional training free of charge. This accountability is crucial to keeping curriculum and instructional strategies contemporary. Also, businesses will be held accountable by demonstrating, advising, and team-teaching with school educators on a continual basis to assure that the program is working.

## Housing with a flair

Without affordable housing, there cannot be a real community. Being homeless in such a rich country as America is a national disgrace. Some individuals still believe that the homeless are all drunks, physically handicapped, or mentally incompetent, and are thus beyond help. To the contrary, many homeless individuals have jobs, but they do not make enough money to pay for housing. Homeless individuals often have been actually working most of their lives. However, when they do lose their jobs, they lose their homes; and when they lose their homes, they often lose their families too, (Kozol, 1995).

Housing in the renewal community will be *self-managed and self-governed*. In other words, there will be a governing committee who carefully screen individuals seeking admission. The selection process will be geared towards creating a multicultural community. It will however attempt to balance the socioeconomic levels of families by having a representation of residents from varying economic success. Therefore, the renewal community is not primarily for AFDC families, but its makeup will be quite diverse. However, there will be a conscientious attempt to blend the less fortunate into the fabric of the neighborhood, from the homeless to the affluent.

For example, both the unemployed and employed homeless may receive some attention for admission in the community. Their children need to be in school, have their immunizations, and be able to interact in a socially uplifting environment. The community center which combines health care with general physical and mental fitness will provide a mechanism for getting these individuals to value work as well as to participate in the community. The continuous education of community residents will give heads of households the *drive* to take them to the next level. Another significant group of individuals that will be helped are the individuals who are not on welfare but are a little above the poverty line. These individuals often are neglected in the economy, but they also need to get back on their feet. This will allow these individuals to build a small savings in order, if they decide, to also buy their own home. Finally, those individuals relying upon welfare, whether unemployed or employed, will be helped by this community housing system. These individuals are in this situation because their current salary does not enable them to pay rent or buy food. This housing system will provide rent to own options for all residents (not just those less fortunate) as long as they abide by their social obligatory contracts.

*Residency Options*

The option to purchase their own residence will be made available to those who may decide that the community is their home, and they would like to live there for an extended period of time. Once an individual has obtained full-time employment, the option to apply their present rent to a home purchase comes into effect. The maximum time to rent may be established at 5 years. After the 5-year period, the family must make a decision as to whether to purchase the present residence or find a home elsewhere. The critical parameter here is that sufficient housing must become available to new residents on a systematic basis in order to meet the needs of other families.

A number of other alternatives may be offered to community residents. Supplemental housing vouchers could be used to assist families for upgrading their residences. If, for instance, a person wants to upgrade the home in any way by painting or putting in new carpet, then a voucher (subsidy) could be provided to pay for part of the cost. This gives individuals incentives to take care of the property. These supplemental vouchers could be distributed at the first day of rent with the stipulation that at the end of a 2-year period, part of that voucher could be cashed in and applied toward a mortgage payment on a residence or to cover partial costs for repairs or home improvements.

Similar supplemental residency vouchers may be increased if students meet school attendance requirements, if families participates in seminars aimed at improving self-image, social responsibility, and career advances, and if residents extend their assistance to others through community volunteering efforts. The ability to accumulated housing vouchers through behavior that enhances the environment in which residents live and work helps community residents to achieve the American dream, reducing over a period of time the need of government assistance.

For those who assume leadership in a housing cluster by means of self-management models, additional voucher subsidies could be provided for exemplary service. For example, if residents become active in a neighborhood watch program, volunteer for assisting others in emergency situations, or become part of neighborhood clean-up projects, then residents could receive additional subsidies. However, each subsidy would be provided on a volunteer basis, and the accounting would be certified by a community services group housed in the community center of the renewal society.


**Public service with a new twist**

When one thinks of government, one may think of authority, management, overseer, supervisor or someone who has some amount of control over other individuals. However, to have an effective government, it is crucial for community leaders to actually reside in the community. In addition, it is critical for leaders to create a spirit of volunteerism in which community residents assume control over their own destinies by taking on responsibilities that typically have been assigned to government service agencies.

Expecting community residents to serve on specially formed councils to solve community problems will become a fundamental expectation. Self-management  involves serving on arbitration or mediation panels to decide action to take on criminal complaints, local disagreements, and the future direction of the community. Therefore, the renewal community is an attempt to empower community residents to solve their own problems, leaving local government to attend to only basic town needs (such as police, fire, street repairs, etc.).

The government will consist of a chief administrator, residents elected to a variety of local councils and commissions, and representative of local civic groups. The central government will be kept to a minimum size with a reliance upon commissions to plan and decide on community needs. Residents who abide by their contracts with the community will be eligible to vote in local elections. Those who break community rules as determined by their peers will be required to serve their communities or be asked to leave. Enforcement of community laws would be the responsibility of the local police force.

To keep everyone informed and communicating, there will be *town hall meetings* once a month. These meetings will serve to bring individuals up to date on current events and also to allow the townspeople to voice their opinions about certain laws, regulations, or stipulations that they feel need to be renewed or enhanced. This will also give the townspeople a chance to give comments or suggestions about how the town can be run more efficiently. These interactions will give the people voice and get them involved in the community.

*Reducing crime*

So the million dollar question arises once again. "What can we do to stop or reduce crime?" Many stereotypes of criminals seem to foster the perception that they are alcoholics, drug addicts and individuals living in poverty. How can these and other individuals be brought into the community and live together in unity? First, take away the things which are said to create an atmosphere for violence, such as alcohol, drugs, and gambling. Therefore, the renewal communities will not permit bars, casinos, or 'x-rated' entertainment. All leisurely activities will be family centered with an emphasis upon community functions (parades, concerts, etc.) and family-oriented establishments. Individuals who violate community standards will be required to submit to counseling at the town center or to move from the community.

Crime prevention again will be based upon local community control of their neighborhoods. *Neighborhood watch programs* operated block by block or unit by unit by local residents will complement the police force. Individuals identified as breaking local community laws and standards of behavior will be required to state their defense before local councils. Except for violent crimes, residents will be expected to perform civic assignments to work off their punishments, rather than being incarcerated.

A critical aspect to self-management is to utilize an evening curfew that applies to all children under eighteen and to individuals who have committed crimes in the past. This curfew will require children to be in their homes by 11:00 p.m. Neighborhood watch is another way to help individuals stay out of trouble while protecting the rights of all residents. Most individuals feel that if someone is watching, a crime is less likely to be committed. What will be stressed in this community is basically family and social interaction. As a result, business hours will be slightly decreased to give employees more time to be with their families. This will encourage parents to spend more time with their children. It is important to have the community perceived as being family oriented--and

31

not totally commercially oriented. Retailers and other businesses in the renewal community will have their hours of operation restricted with *all* establishments required *to close at least one day a week.*

The major deterrent to crime in the renewal community is the ability to access a well-paying job. Job opportunities are basic to crime control. For example, job opportunities will exist for those interested in working for the local government as a police person, civic official, or a government service provider including legal, sanitary, and recreational support. Companies which anchor the commercial sector of the renewal community will also provide job opportunities. Having the vast majority of residents employed in jobs with a future will likely negate many of the causes for residents committing violent crimes.


## A retail sector with vision

The community will contain mainstream shopping that is built into the residential segments of the neighborhood. The retail sector will create a small town image featuring many different kinds of stores. In order to have a community for people who may not have vehicles, the main street will include grocery stores, department stores, pet stores, and clothing stores. To keep prices competitive, co-op food stores and others will be a mainstay in the retail sector. It will be the primary objective of town councils to put into place mechanisms that result in prices being the same, if not cheaper than, the prices in the surrounding areas. Neighborhood co-op ventures will be permitted for provide basic family needs such as a food co-op, a bank co-op, a clothing co-op, and perhaps a general variety store.

In addition, it may be feasible to permit other kinds of stores to offer their goods and services. Therefore, competition for goods and services will not only be local but also regional. Residents of the community will still be able to shop elsewhere (outside the renewal community) placing sufficient power in the hands of consumers for keeping prices comparable for merchants in the immediate vicinity of their homes.

A *reciprocal volunteer transportation system* will be a necessity. This voluntary system allows individuals who have access to automobiles to volunteer to drive others who do not have transportation to locations both in side and outside the community. In return, these volunteers will receive a voucher for free services that they may use in the future as other needs arise. This concept is that of a *service exchange bank* where residents can build on accounts for free services which may be 'cashed in' at future times. In this example, a *service exchange bank* keeps track of who has transportation credits, along with volunteer services done by individuals in the community. For example, if individual A volunteers to give individual B a ride and individual A somewhere down the line needs a baby-sitter, that person has a certain amount of credits to choose a baby-sitter, free from the volunteer program. The credits add up according to the number of hours of volunteer time that is put in by a particular individual. Whatever service one voluntarily provides for another, this person will in return receive a service from the same or another individual depending on need. The principle being stressed is the principle that 'if you do good to others, good things will come to you.'

## A commercial sector with a commitment

You may ask yourself, where is the money going to come from to create the renewal community? What about overcrowding? What incentives will businesses have to train and hire the residents of the renewal community? What type of business will this community attract? As with anything new, there will be many questions and no doubt many criticisms.

The most important question to be addressed is, 'What types of businesses will be willing to establish residency in the community?' In areas such as Delaware, Maryland, Pennsylvania, and New Jersey, there will likely be businesses such as banks, insurance companies, and real estate agencies. However, in Texas, the occupations will relate to those such in electronics, crafts, or trades such as plumbing or carpentry. In Florida, there will be businesses that require individuals who are skilled in the telecommunication and tourism industries. In areas to the far west such as California, businesses to anchor a renewal community may include electronics, computer repair, or banking. Each community will attract those kinds of companies that offer the kinds of goods and services typically found in that region of the country. It is important to note that there is no one company model/service/product that meets the needs of all regions of the country. Each community will be somewhat tailored made to fit into the style of that region.

Where will the funds come from to establish these communities? The money to set up these programs will come partially from those businesses that are seeking profits and partially from government. There are many incentives for the government to participate in these services. One incentive is that the government will receive more income through taxes when residents are working. The more individuals are working, the more money government receives. The second advantage for government is the more businesses increase the standard of living for these individuals, the lower the cost of Medicaid. This welfare program at the present time is costing the Federal government over $66 billion in 1996. However, with reduced welfare roles, general welfare costs will be substantially reduced to state and federal governments over the long-term. Food stamps, AFDC payments, supplemental social security, unemployment compensation, etc. should also be reduced as families become independent of the reliance upon the traditional 'safety net.'

Moreover, the companies that volunteer their expertise to local schools by providing cooperative work experience, apprenticeships, and internships for the students in grades 12-14 will be able to assure themselves of qualified workers. These business representatives, serving as mentors to the youth in the community, will be in a position to exert a leadership that is so desperately needed in our public school systems. These business persons will themselves become indirect teaching institutions as there is no better place to get trained for employment than by actual working in a company.

Therefore, funds will be generated from three sources: one is government grants to design and renovate military complexes; a second from businesses who may be able to reduce their costs of operations while at the same time create a whole new breed of customers; and three, the renewed families who eventually will find themselves in a position to pay taxes back into their community for supporting the services required to keep the community progressing in an appropriate direction.

Another important question is what incentives will there be to attract companies who are willing to take on additional responsibility of reforming welfare in this country as well as training employees utilizing innovative educational designs? There appear to be several incentives. Initially, each business will be provided with a *tax incentives* similar to those provided in the past by many states and local communities for sports' arenas to house a professional team of some kind. The government will be able to provide these economic incentives by directing existing expenditures away from Medicaid, food stamps, etc., to redesigning military bases for commercial purposes. In addition, families who are now receiving a variety of welfare subsidies will eventually become taxpaying citizens, thus participating themselves in the development of their own communities.

Another incentive for business to become involved is the likelihood of expanding the market for their products and services. How? Think of the new purchasing power of large numbers of additional consumers coming on board who have traditionally been 'standing on the sidelines.' To a company, these new wage earners represent additional customers, and a corresponding profit! Another incentive relates to *lower medical costs* that businesses will incur. Because of the preventive care programs and the Wellness Center which keeps individuals in good health, a business can reduce operating costs, especially those related to fringe benefits.

Finally, an important incentive relates to companies creating a strong national image for attempting to solve a persistent problem in the

American economy; that being, the exorbitant welfare costs that are burdening both states and the Federal government with significant funding responsibilities. By seizing the opportunity to demonstrate a way to overhaul welfare programs in the country, business leaders will reap substantial rewards through national recognition of their effort and also by setting an example of how a partnership between business, government and consumers can make all parties a winner. Business can earn greater profits by reducing operational costs; government can gain additional revenues for increasing services to the residents in the community; and consumers can enhance their standard of living by obtaining jobs that lead to a career. This partnership demonstrates a *social responsibility* among all and relying upon the 'power' of the free market system for setting direction for welfare reform.

## Conclusion: creating a mainstream society

What is proposed here is an innovative approach to helping others in time of need. Getting individuals off of the welfare cycle and into the mainstream of society is an accomplishment that benefits all members in our society. What differentiates this country from others is the economic freedom afforded its citizens, in that decisions may be made independent of government authority. By holding out the American dream to all citizens (the purchasing of a home), families and their children will experience ownership, something that is vital for creating personal wealth. By attaining employment, role models become much of the landscape for children. By creating an atmosphere of social responsibility, communities can be reformed into a small town environment where destiny is controlled by local leadership and local participation.

The 'healing of America' focuses upon recreating a spirit of individualism, accomplishment, productivity, and societal bonding. The healing process must come from within, rather than from the impersonal nature of large bureaucratic governmental programs of the past. The healing process must result in accomplishment with the realization that families can become independent of social workers and outside intruders. The healing process must have a long-term effect upon the attitudes and values assumed by a new generation of workers. The healing process begins with bringing together business, government and families on welfare with the goal of enhancing what is great about the American experiment; that is, opportunity to instill in each citizen a sense of pride. Earning while learning is only appropriate if at the end of the process is a guaranteed job. However, the healing process in American also requires safe communities, educated children, healthy citizens, strong families, and spirited volunteers.

Renewal or power communities will not come about easily. The reallocation of public resources, a serious commitment on part of the business community to reform welfare, and a willingness to experiment with new kinds of standards and expectations are all required. While the initial funding for redesigning the renewal communities will be substantial, the willingness to take a risk and strive for a totally new approach to society building may result in a new beginning for many families caught in a vicious cycle of unemployment and despair. Of course, no experiment can guarantee success. However, putting forth a bold attempt at job creation and family renewal represents what this country is all about. Without boldness, would we have electricity, jet airliners, or telephones? While all these experiments resulted in great advancement in the American standard of living, each inventor had his doubts. Each inventor was labeled as being out of his/her mind, and each inventor started with little or no financing. Well, now is the time to begin a new venture that no doubt will shock some but to others may provide a second opportunity to enhance their standard of living.

# 2 Creating a mega community with small town passion

The solution to welfare reform must include an emphasis upon the entire individual and the whole family rather than on simply targeting employment as the key component in such a strategy. The replicating of those attributes which brings families together as part of a community with passion is critical to raising the standard of living of those consumers who are in need of a second chance at life. Based upon a study completed by the Roper Center for Public Opinion (1997), a family-friendly community is one that has an absence of crime, low rates of drug and alcohol abuse, good public schools, first-rate health care, and a clean environment. Based upon demographic portraits of 301 metropolitan areas included in the Roper survey, the top ten communities in which to live are:

| | |
|---|---|
| Sheboygan, WS | Kenosha, WS |
| Fort Collins, CO | Bremerton, WA |
| Pittsburgh, PA | Burlington, VT |
| Charlottesville, VA | Spokane, WA |
| Boston, MA | Hickory, NC |

What do these communities have in common? They all have a small town passion while providing 'mega' services to their residents. For example, in Sheboygan, Wisconsin, residents claim that it is easy to get a job and to obtain day care services for their children during the workday.

In Kenosha, Wisconsin, youth groups go about the community removing graffiti from buildings. Volunteerism is an integral part of community life in this small town. In Fort Collins, Colorado, there are considerable activities scheduled for youth during the day. A variety of cultural events and sports are close to the homes of residents. Finally, in Bremerton, Washington, public safety and excellent public schools are top priorities.

What the Roper survey suggests is that family-friendly communities can be created anywhere if people work at it. The best places to raise a family are neighborhoods where residents are willing to cooperate with one another. A family-friendly community is one where neighbors can count on one another in time of need. The model neighborhood to reform welfare suggested here assumes that families can and do shape their own communities, and former AFDC families if given a second opportunity are very capable of replicating these kinds of communities. In other words, it is the good feeling about one's community that generates self-esteem--and not simply feeling good about the workplace.

In the Roper survey, parents were requested to use a 1-10 rating scale to rank a variety of features associated with an 'ideal community' for raising a family. In Table 2.1 below, the top three features of such a community are low crime rate, low drug/alcohol problem, and good

Table 2.1
Features considered important by parents
when raising a family

| Feature | *Mean Score |
|---|---|
| Low Crime Rate | 9.7 |
| Low Drug/Alcohol Prob. | 9.6 |
| Good Public Schools | 9.5 |
| Quality Health Care | 9.3 |
| Clean Environment | 9.2 |
| Affordable Cost of Living | 8.9 |
| Strong Economic Growth | 8.8 |
| Excurric. School Activities | 8.7 |
| Access to Colleges | 8.3 |
| Many Activities for Youth | 7.8 |

Source: Roper Center for Public Opinion, 1997
*Note: 10 rating = extremely important

public schools. These three features are also the target of the model communities that could evolve from federally held facilities and land. Three of the ten features of a family-friendly community relate to the importance of education. In the Roper study, good public schools, extracurricular activities, and access to colleges were identified as very significant features. In regard to welfare reform, the chances of turning around the lives of heads of households of AFDC families will likely increase significantly if equal educational opportunities become commonplace in the renewal community.

## Balancing work requirements with reality

The major thrust of current welfare reform is to get the head of every family on assistance off welfare and into work within two years or lose all benefits now currently being received. Lifetime benefits traditionally associated with many public subsidized welfare programs are basically to be limited to some time period, but states have the prerogative to set even stricter time limits if so desired. While the intent of such welfare reform is notable, reality suggests that cities across this country where large pockets of families on welfare exist will not be able to absorb thousands of welfare mothers and fathers Complicating this need to find employment has been past public policy which has encouraged the development of suburban communities and workplaces resulting in millions of jobs leaving inner cities and moving to the outskirts of city boundaries.

It has been reported that over 25 percent of all households in the cities of Detroit, Chicago, Philadelphia, and New York were receiving welfare benefits. It takes a growing economy to absorb new entrants into the workplace, but the likelihood of the present service-based economy providing sufficient jobs at living wages is up to debate. Although there may be an excessive demand for jobs for which welfare recipients may qualify, wages are not likely to increase due to competitive pressures from international trade. With the elimination of the economic contract between workers and management that existed in the past and in its place the emphasis upon providing only a wage that the market determines, head of households will be at the mercy of cost minded corporate giants. Some may find jobs, but a considerable number will be 'left out in the cold'.

## Empowering residents through a commitment mentality

Therefore, it is time for a new model of hope to enter the welfare reform movement, a city with passion. At the heart of this model city is the importance attached to *empowerment.* The model of hope organizes many different kinds of families into a social arrangement where a *commitment* is fostered between businesses that anchor the community and households in the neighborhood. The basic foundation of the model city is the reallocation of existing military resources for enabling families to restart their lives in a new environment that focuses attention upon those things that keep families together, such as self-respect, integrity, civility, ambition, and role modeling.

The model of hope as suggested here can evolve from different segments of a community, depending upon particular traditions, customs, and values associated with a specific region. For example, the core of all activity about which neighborhood activities evolve can be health care, education, entrepreneurship, or public service, to name a few. Therefore, what is suggested here is that not all model neighborhoods of hope must be designed in the same way. Whatever is identified as a core represents the spirit and vitality of the community. Everything emanates from the core of the community. Some examples of alternatives are provided here.

*An entrepreneurial spirit as the core*

For those in poverty, entrepreneurial endeavors provide a way out with more opportunities for self-employment emerging each day. The telecommunication's era has resulted in vast new opportunities for income through business ventures created on the basis of the imagination and ingenuity of persons. The creation of the family business as a retailer in a local community or a family-based franchise associated with a large corporation is a path open to families of low-income. Since the model of hope requires a thriving retail sector where shops provide the basic services required by the community, the opportunity to become an entrepreneur is great.

What would be required to make an entrepreneurial core the centerpiece of a neighborhood is not radically different from that of the past. For example, local universities and even the local public education system could take on the responsibility of organizing seminars, workshops, and formal courses on how to start a new business. Children in public schools would have their curriculum revolve around entrepreneurship as students learn to read, write, do math, and adapt technology to a retailing sector.

It has been estimated that perhaps only 5 to 10 percent of welfare recipients will opt to take on the risk of creating their own businesses. The problem with running a small business is having the knowledge and ability to manage many responsibilities associated with such ventures. However, the mega communities with a small town passion provide an excellent opportunity for such ventures if 'seed money' is made available for training and implementation. In this regard, Community Development Corporations (CDC), a mechanism already utilized in many urban centers, can be adopted for a similar purpose in the new model communities of hope. Amy Kay (1997) of the Aspen Institute states that Community Development Corporations have doubled since 1992, indicating that they provide an alternative that has some merit. In Figure 2.1 below, the number of CDCs has increased from 108 in 38 states in the United States to 248 in 44 states in 1996. As of 1994, the Aspen Institute calculated that 208,000 people had received loans, training, or technical assistance from such programs.

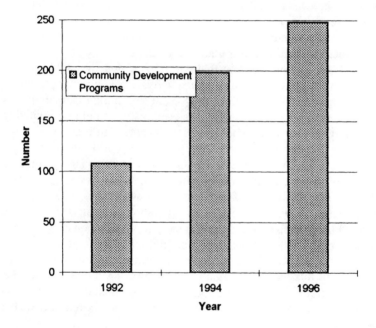

**Figure 2.1 Community development programs, 1992-1996**
Source:     The Aspen Institute, 1996

The strategy for assisting those families who are in poverty or close to poverty through small business venture programs originated from countries in the developing world such as El Salvador and Bangladesh. Using 'seed money' generated from both the private and public sectors, women have been targeted for such ventures with the objective of

41

assisting them to become independent of public subsidies. Correspondingly, in the United States, there are 'pockets of poverty' similar to those in developing countries. Having such financial and training assistance made available to AFDC families can also come about through an expansion of Community Development Corporations (CDC) that target small business development in the model communities proposed here.

One of the primary problems of AFDC families is that they lack both initial funding and the necessary collateral to gain access to the loans required for starting a small business. However, through a Community Development Corporation, it may be feasible to adopt a *group borrowing mechanism* whereby groups of borrowers can guarantee each member's loan, thus providing peer pressure for repayment of these loans. Such an innovative mechanism could be put into place that enables AFDC families and others to venture into small business as part of their American dream. The premise of a Community Development Corporation is to use private-sector principles within the framework of a public sector (such as a community) for solving problems that government alone has not been able to in the past. A glowing example of how private-public sector principles work is the success of the Bedford Stuyvesant Restoration Corporation in Brooklyn, New York, where a CDC has been instrumental in revitalizing a community that has large numbers of low-income families.

To assist in developing an entrepreneurial spirit in a renewal community, a health center can provide medical insurance through a 'group entity' rather than by store by store. A day care system could also revolve around the needs of residents who work long hours in the retailing sector. A system of public transportation that caters to residents who would likely shop within short distances from their homes could also be implemented. Although the details are not set in stone, it is up to the imagination of the leadership in the community to devise strategies for accomplishing this outcome. Again, by empowering residents to devise their own destinies, a competitive spirit that has been characteristic of the free enterprise system (and is the envy of the world) is released in the model community.

Entering into the entrepreneurial ranks provides parents with opportunities to become role models for their children. It also provides moments for educating their children about important principles of the free enterprise system as well as the specifics of creating their own businesses. Children can also become part of the family business depending upon their age and interest. However, exposing children to the benefits of working for themselves and seeing their parents succeed directs their attention to the rewards of working hard. The skills parents can transmit to their children are immeasurable, but the opportunity to become self-reliant and independent is important for the next generation of workers to witness.

Single-parent teenagers as well as older adults can all join in partnerships as the technology now available makes creating a new business easier and more practical. For those with weak business skills, entrepreneurial training will be a necessity. However, the direction one takes depends upon personal ambition. Joining different kinds of work teams through entrepreneurial ventures can help heads of households overcome their own weaknesses. The time is now for families to gain a new perspective about future jobs and the need to go on their own. Being pressured into a low-level service sector job as a fast-food cook, a maintenance assistant, or a hotel service worker (cleaning rooms, laundry, and general household maintenance) is a thing of the past. The time has come to elevate the visions of families of poverty, and a new outlook may be required.

*The health care center as the core*

In the model of hope, the health care center could possibly become the core of the community. In this instance, business, public education, and the retailing sector may all revolve around a community health and fitness center. The public school curriculum can focus upon the importance of staying healthy. Students will learn to write, read, do math, and apply technology within the context of the hospitality, leisure, and health industries. The health center would rely a corporate giant in the health care field to anchor the business sector in the community. The hospitality and physical fitness center combined with a health care facility could provide many opportunities for employment.

Retailers would provide shoppers with places to purchase and /or rent health care equipment. In addition, the retail sector could offer an assortment of restaurants that cater to those seeking improved menus reflecting fitness and health. The public service sector, in this instance government, could devise physical fitness oriented playgrounds for children and similarly designed parks for adults. Special bicycle and running paths could be designed to enable individuals to maneuver throughout the town. The primary means of transportation would likely be bicycles or simply walking to get to retailers and places of employment. Even public security could emphasize non-motorized vehicles that protect the environment. Again, such physical fitness oriented communities can be designed with varying emphases and based upon the premise that residents are empowered to determine the parameters within which family members are to function. The contracts between the health care and physical fitness center and neighborhood residents in the renewal community form the basis of all town activities.

The fastest growing segment in society is the baby boomer, who will be entering into later years of life by the year 2005. Because of this expectation, a community could be established around public service including volunteerism whereby residents develop a support system that caters to the needs and desires of older residents. Since older residents require transportation, medical care, physical therapy, home care assistance (cutting lawns, cleaning the house, etc.), and entertainment, such a town can be organized along developing a support system of caring. Since men and women today are expected to live into their 80s, and since many of the poor have difficulty planning for their retirement with sufficient funds available to purchase food, drugs, and medical services, such a community centerpiece may be appealing to both the young and old.

Having a core of community service, neighborhood schools would focus upon preparing students for employment in health care, recreation, and service occupations that cater to the needs of the elderly. The health care sector would focus upon the special needs of the elderly and the retail sector in providing services required of those over 50. Closely aligned to the profit sector of the community could be a neighbor-to-neighbor program whereby many everyday needs can be fulfilled by volunteers. Establishing nonprofit organizations for serving community residents also create jobs for town residents. The health care facility could become the coordinator of a services volunteer program. Again, the public sector could assist local nonprofit organizations through grants to provide such services as meals on wheels now available in many middle-income communities or transportation through care-van services to residents homes. Such a community focus reflects the movement towards civility and those occupations that enhance the quality of life.

The public schools could emphasize the arts whereby students receive exposure to varying aspects of the entertainment industry. The local theater could be directed towards entertaining older adults who are in need of recreation and diversion from their daily routines. Such theater could include joint performances between students and older adults in the community who have ample time to practice for such ventures. Retired residents with experience in producing and directing plays can assist local educators in this regard. The result would be the creation of a bond between the old and young as they learn to work side by side.

A complementary component to this model is the inclusion of the 'traditional' public service sector as a core for community activity. In this regard, public service focuses upon preparing individuals to enter government at the local, state, and national levels. Learning how to plan, organize, and implement public programs to enhance the welfare of society is important to both empowering and directing residents to accomplish society goals. In such a community, public education would be geared towards preparing students for entering into civic oriented occupations such as town planners, public auditors, public defenders, security and public safety, etc. Entering public service can be demonstrated as an admirable objective with such 'public servants' becoming role models for our children.

*Education as the core*

Another strategy for the renewal community could be an emphasis upon educational services to residents. A k-16 educational system could become the core of the model of hope. In this instance, educational programs may focus on coordinating community activities from educating youth and adults for jobs in a community to enriching residents through exposure to the arts. One outgrowth of such an emphasis could be attracting a business anchor that required employees with highly developed technical skills. The reliance upon larger more established companies in the business sector could be a boom to making higher paying jobs available to residents who may not be accustomed to such an opportunity. Therefore, the educational programs in the public schools could be tailored to preparing students as well as retraining adults for jobs in computer technology, programmers, and repair technicians.

The public school system can hold seminars, workshops, and programs designed for creating a community whose residents are seeking a baccalaureate degree. Branches of a community college or local university can be established in the model neighborhood. The public sector may design a support system that enable residents to have easy access to local schools. The health center could be located in the same facility as the public school. The retailing sector could provide shopping of more technical stores such as pc technology, educational materials and software, books and entertaining, and perhaps travel services to museums, etc.

In public education, the curriculum would emphasize the computer sciences whereby students focus upon careers of a technical nature. Math and science become the core of the curriculum in which reading, writing, and the arts support the major thrust of the curricula. The intriguing element here is that the model of hope can be designed for residents with traditionally low incomes, signaling to the public that all citizens in this nation can set high goals for themselves and their children. Similarly, in this regard, expectations of community residents will be that children and adults may opt to become teachers at the local public school or faculty at a community college or a university. With the number of children given birth in the 1980s coming along, the demand for public school teachers is expected to increase significantly well into the 21st century.

An example of the kind of ingenuity that could be adopted in a renewal community is that of the Coleman Elementary School in the city of Baltimore. This school is located in a low-income neighborhood and operates on a year-round calendar. It has working relationships with many local businesses as well as endorsing frequent contacts with parents of the children who attend the school. The philosophy of the administration of the Coleman School is that it must become an integrated services school in that it extends its programs and services to the residents of the community in which it is housed. The school calendar includes what are referred to a enrichment 'intersessions' that students volunteer to attend. It is during these sessions that students go outside their curricula and become part of innovative learning projects.

Education in the renewal community is also to be integrated into all aspects of the local neighborhood. Such a school calendar could be a year-round program of study with opportunities for students to engage in volunteerism during different phases of study. Elementary, middle-school, and high school programs could all reflect a similar philosophy permitting students to build upon previously learned concepts. The key to success will be a mentoring program whereby community residents agree to become learning assistants not only to their own children but to at least one other child who attends the neighborhood school. Shared mentoring will become an integral part of community life, as residents share their experiences with the next generation of leaders. The mentoring strategy is based upon an acceptance of the philosophy that many people are anxious to do more in their neighborhood if given a chance to 'channel' their energy into meaningful contributions.

In the renewal community of hope, there will be no reason why residents cannot become part of a small town passion that is proud of passing on the rich traditions of their culture to their own children as well as other children with varying backgrounds. Becoming a culturally enriched mega community will enhance the lives of its residents. A model of hope can incorporate such expectations into its design considerations. It is the parents in the community that bring sustenance, structure and discipline to the next generation of leaders. Being taught to believe in themselves is vital if children are to create visions that will eventually become the foundation for enhancing the quality of their lives. An integrated educational system is a very important part of this adventure.

## Legal framework for handling crime and complaints

The inner city where a substantial number of AFDC families reside has been the breeding ground for gangs and violent crime. Not a day goes by without reading in the newspapers of a drive by shooting or a drug related murder or a liquor store or grocery store robbery. The inner city is also the home of a great number of poor and those on welfare. One solution for reducing crime in neighborhoods has been to pressure welfare recipients into jobs with the expectation that the crime problem will go away. Crime has not disappeared and it won't. Present welfare policy is not working. Crimes in communities relate to misdirected anger among segments of neighborhoods, and thus is a human problem. In order to reduce criminal behavior, proposed solutions that suggest a 'band aid mentality' through a quick-fix, short-term perspective are bound to fail. What is required is a comprehensive, long-term venture where resident accountability is a fundamental aspect of a second chance at life.

Less violent crime is reported in the more affluent areas of the city and the corresponding suburbs. Although violent crime can occur any where at any time, its occurrence is less likely in neighborhoods where people are generally employed and the community is in control of its residents. Is the answer to make everyone wealthy? No! Providing financial subsidies in the hope that more money in the hands of consumers will act as a catalyst to get people to become more independent does not work. An example is subsidized housing where large numbers of dwellings remain in disrepair. The residents don't save and invest. After a couple of years the housing becomes run down and fades into just another slum. Politicians have learned through much frustration that one cannot solve the welfare problem by throwing money at it. Attitudes and expectations of those individuals in need must change. In this regard, AFDC families must want to change to make a better life for themselves.

The basic assumption behind the model community proposed here is that people want to be given a chance to make a decent life for themselves. They want to work and provide for their own families. Yes, they want a chance at the good life, the golden ring, but they are not asking that it be handed to them. They are willing to work for it if given a fair chance. They can't do it by themselves, but they can do it together. Collectively as a community, residents can strive to make a better world for themselves and their neighbors. The model community is for those individuals who are presently frustrated about the state of their lives and want t do something about it.

Having said this, it must be recognized that crime, even violent crime, may occur in the model community. For example, murder is the most violent of crimes. However, it is often committed against members within the same family. Husbands murder wives and wives murder husbands.

Brother is often pitted against brother, sister against sister. Robbery and theft (although those resulting in murder are rare) are often committed by the most desperate of individuals. However, no longer do we have the romantic villain of the Old West, such as Jesse James or Billy the Kid. Dead and gone is Ma Barker, Bonnie and Clyde or Pretty Boy Floyd. When Willie Sutton was asked why he robbed banks, he quipped, 'cause that's where the money is'. Modern surveillance technology has become so advanced that it will soon relegate such criminals as a thing of the past. The take is small and to risks too high. How is the model community to deal with new forms of criminal behavior as they emerge? Reviewing the basic assumptions of the current American Justice System will help us adopt a different kind of model for the renewal community.

*The present adversarial legal system*

There are two basic systems of justice. One is the federal system, consisting of the district court system. United States district courts have original jurisdiction over all crimes occurring on federal property or those classified as federal crimes by law. Original jurisdiction refers to trial court. Cases are tried on *information or indictment*. The United States is always the plaintiff and a legal officer representing the United States files a paper called *information* which becomes the basis for the claim in a criminal trial. Alternatively, the United States Attorney or other competent legal officer calls together a panel known as a grand jury. The grand jury reviews the facts of the case and hears testimony. The grand jury examines evidence as presented to it by the United States Attorney and decides whether or not there is sufficient evidence that a crime was committed and the accused committed that crime.

Individual states follow a process similar to that of the federal court system. However, the states usually have two courts of original jurisdiction. There is the misdemeanor court which handles 'small crime' or felonies which are not serious. There is also a state superior or circuit court which handles more serious felonies. The juvenile court which handles youthful offenders less than 18 years of age is usually a part of either the superior court or the circuit court. In most misdemeanor courts there is no right to a jury trial. However, cases are presented before the court within 60 to 90 days after they have been 'papered.' In most superior or circuit courts at the state level, criminal trials occur between four and six months after a case has been 'papered,' or after the state grand jury has rendered an indictment. In all cases, the plaintiff is either the United States at the federal level or the state or commonwealth at the state level. The assumption is that the crime committed by the accused is a crime against the people.

48

Our basic system of justice is an *adversarial system.* There is a prosecuting attorney and a defense attorney. An administrator of the trial is a judge, and a jury decides matters of fact and law in a criminal case. Unanimous jury verdicts are the rule. In our adversarial system, the prosecuting attorney is obligated to introduce fact into evidence that will tend to prove the guilt of the accused defendant beyond reasonable doubt. The defense attorney's job is to prevent the introduction of evidence on those matters which are improperly introduced by the prosecutor. This is to assure that the defendant gets a fair and impartial trial. An example of improper evidence might be evidence prejudicial to the defendant and not relevant to the proof of guilt of the defendant. In some cases, the evidence being offered was improperly obtained or the evidence being offered is tainted in some manner. It is also the defense attorney's job to introduce evidence that is favorable to the defendant.

In a trial the prosecuting attorney begins the trial by calling to the witness stand individuals sworn to tell the truth for the purpose of introducing evidence into the court record. The prosecutor believes these witnesses called will testify to facts and documents which tend to prove the guilt of the defendant. After a witness testifies for the prosecution, he/she is cross examined by the defendant's attorney. After the prosecutor has put on his entire case and has rested, defendant can put on his case if he so elects. Defendant's attorney calls witnesses on his behalf and after they have testified, the prosecutor cross examines them. Cross examination is an extremely effective adversarial tool because it challenges the witness to clarify statements he made under direct examination and can show undue bias or prejudice on behalf of the witness.

In the event that the defendant is determined to be guilty, the judge imposes a sentence according to the law. The sentence of the defendant depends on two factors, punishment and rehabilitation. In assessing punishment, factors are taken into consideration such as the severity of the crime, the injury to society, violence and mitigating factors. Rehabilitating factors might be whether or not the defendant is a first offender, whether he or she is likely to commit another crime, the remorse of the defendant and restitution to the victim for any injury received. If incarceration is called for, the defendant after sentencing is remanded into the custody of prison officials.

*Revising the legal system for the renewal community*

In the renewal community, the residents are subject to the same laws, rules and regulations as the state. If appropriate, the model community could get the state to amend its charter granting partial autonomy to the model city to enforce its own criminal code. Precedent is found in the manner of the relationship between the District of Columbia and the Federal Authority. In certain instances, the City Corporate Counsel's office prosecutes offenses for certain crimes and misdemeanors on a much less harsh basis than the Federal Authority. Also, the concept behind the model neighborhood is for a different kind of legal system that stresses to the criminal the need to moderate and conform to the expectations of residents for the good of the city. The model city wishes to modify the existing criminal justice system to enable an individual to adapt his behavior towards productive efforts to assist the model city in achieving its goals. In order to given criminals a second chance, present criminal sanctions and punishment required by law and administered through traditional federal or state court systems might have to be revamped.

People who have come to live and work in the model community have done so because they want to have a second chance at life. They have volunteered. They have come to embrace a new way of life and have adopted as their own lifestyle a philosophy espoused by residents in the renewal community. This philosophy is embodied in the Rules and Regulations of the model city. One set of expectations requires all residents to participate in crime prevention and community safety. All residents of the city are to meet twice per month by predetermined neighborhood boundaries and attend at least two town meetings of the city council. Neighborhood crime prevention groups and legal advisory committees will permeate throughout the model city. There will be a responsibility for each resident to assume a mentoring posture in terms of guiding youth and other neighbors into appropriate behavior patterns that benefit the whole community.

By keeping alert as to the 'pulse of the neighborhood', residents will be expected to be actively involved with and alert as to the welfare of their neighbors. In this regard, many social events will be scheduled through the calendar year for the purpose of enabling residents to intermingle and discuss issues as they arise. It is the camaraderie generated among residents in the model city that deters crime. For example, residents must volunteer to help with city wide events such as Fourth of July parade and picnic, the homeless food drive, the bloodmobile, United Way campaigns, and other worthy events In order to avoid the emergence of slum housing in the model city, all residents must maintain their property in architectural conformity with their neighbors. Such a practice will prevent locations within the community from becoming opportunities for committing crime. While not mandatory, all residents are encouraged to be good neighbors, to get to know those around them and to socialize with them.

All residents who have children in school must participate in PTA and PTA functions and volunteer in the classroom once per month. Since the local public schools double as meeting places for neighborhood and city-wide events, the school is the natural focal point to kick off many if not all neighborhood activities. Every resident is therefor responsible for the physical appearance of the school and its well-being as a center of learning and community activity. Again, by directing the attention of neighborhood youth towards positive elements in the community, the result should be a deterrence to crime. The same thing it true for adults who are likely to avoid criminal behavior in a community where neighbor looks after neighbor.

Since pride in ownership and in a neighborhood are essential to the success of the model city, every resident is responsible for the welfare of everyone else. Diligence and teamwork are the watchwords for a better tomorrow. What are we to do with those who break the rules? The current system in place needs to be changed or modified to comply with the aspirations of the community of the model city. That being said, a criminal defendant should always be given the right to a trial if so desired. That may be in the best interest of the defendant but not necessarily in the best interest of the community. In the event a resident abuses his rights and privileges by breaking a law rule or regulation, he or she must atone by giving back to the community the equivalent of what has taken from it. As a practical matter, the more serious crimes can't be handled in this matter. Such serious crimes must be referred to state or federal law. However, intervening steps may be adopted by residents of the model city to deal with more serious crimes if all parties agree. Since the model city is based upon the service to the community, remedies must adhere to this principle.

*A different kind of judicial environment*

The model community is a city of, by and for its residents. Since the residents have an obligation according to the rules and regulations of the city to participate in its political affairs, they also have an obligation to participate in its judicial affairs by being members of a judicial panel. The authority of the community is brought to bear on the offender be he an adult or a juvenile. The focus of the community is that its residents conform to the behavior adopted for the good of all in the community. Just as a new child in school must adopt his dress code and manner to that of the other students in the school in order not to offend classmates, each resident must conform the rules and regulations of the community or face a reasonable penalty imposed by members of the community.

The model city faces new challenges and must adopt new methods to deal with those who break the law. The accused in the model city can elect to admit personal wrong and meet with a board of five persons, three from the neighborhood and two from the city at large. The panel shall be monitored by an attorney who shall serve without pay as part of his or her community obligation to mediate and monitor the meeting. The offense shall be read as well as any mitigating factors. In order to regain the confidence of other residents, the self-admitted perpetuator of a community crime can agree to a community service obligation rather than paying a fine or going to a prison. The commitment for community service shall be discussed and agreed upon by majority vote of the panel. The accused shall upon completion of his or her community service shall report on the experience which shall be used to assess the effectiveness of that panel and future panels. Two years after successful completion of the community service commitment, all mention of the incident shall be stricken from the records. The emphasis of the model city on correcting criminal wrongdoing is not to disparage the individual but to attempt to assure the individual that it is the behavior that is unacceptable not the individual. It is the behavior that the model neighborhood is attempting to mold through a 'second chance'.

If the accused disagrees with the terms of the commitment or restitution, he may appeal to a three judge panel those parts of the decision of the panel with which he disagrees. Such appeal must take place by notifying the mayor of the model city by certified mail within ten (10) days from the date of the rendering of the decision of his intent to appeal the decision. The actual appeal must be presented to the mayor within thirty (30) days thereafter of each of the exceptions. The exceptions can only be made as to the commitment for community service or the amount of restitution and for no other reason (by election of the accused, the fact of wrong doing is not an issue).

One kind of criminal behavior that can easily undo all the good of an innovative judicial program is domestic violence. How can the model city interfere in the lives of members of any family? Is alternative dispute resolution and mediation effective in these instances? Alternative dispute resolution and mediation of disputes have been used as tools to aid the court system in several states. Their adoption has met with significant success. The disadvantage is that they can prolong litigation and discourage litigants from a final settlement of disputes. However, the advantage of alternative dispute resolution and mediation is that it can reduce or eliminate the violence from domestic disputes. Such programs are to be instituted in the model neighborhood. The assumption is that because the model city encourages interaction with neighbors and community, the parties to a domestic dispute are less likely to use violence because their lives are not entirely private. Because domestic violence has an adverse effect on the community, neighbors and friends can be expected to intervene before a domestic dispute becomes violent. One or both parties can turn to a neighbor for solace and protection. The parties are then directed to the HMO for psychological and family counseling and in most cases the dispute will likely end there.

Family disputes of a more lasting and permanent nature will be turned over to mediators and arbitrators where the dispute is reduced to a simple monetary adjustment of support and an equitable division of the community property. Again the neighbors (and not close friends to the parties involved) are part of a mediation panel arbitrating the dispute. This is appropriate since every resident in the community realizes that they could be sitting on 'the other side of the fence' and are certain to come to a just decision. Such a decision can be used by either party to the dispute and entered into as a final order of a court of competent jurisdiction for final divorce, property disposition and support decrees. While such a decision is taken by such court as 'presumptively correct,' exceptions to it can be argued and litigated in that court.

The model city is a team concept. In football, for example, there is an offensive team, a defensive team and special teams. The offensive team tries to move the ball towards the opponent's goal to score points. The defensive team tries to prevent the opponent from moving the ball toward its goal. The special teams handle kickoffs, kickoff returns, punts and punt returns. Members of each team work as a unit to get the entire job done. Each member must be able to depend on the other member not to be out of position to make the play or defensive scheme work. Each team member relies on the others to do their respective jobs. Similarly, the university football team, an industrial team and the community town all have to work together and trust one another to make the system work for all.

In a criminal case, how exactly does the mediation work? First the mediator obtains from the proper authorities a statement of facts concerning the incident and the rules, regulations, statutes and laws alleged to have been violated. The mediator reads to the respondent (defendant) and the panel consisting of town representatives the statement of facts and explains how the alleged law was broken. The defendant first is asked whether or not he/she agrees to the statement of facts and law. Here the defendant may make any amendments necessary to the statement of the mediator, and the statement is adjusted to the point where both the mediator and the defendant can agree. Then the defendant in this instance is required to submit himself to the jurisdiction of the panel. The panel makes a determination whether a wrong was committed and, if so, to what degree has the community been damaged.

If a wrong was committed with no damages, the matter is closed. However, if any damage to the community is determined, the panel examines the evidence and assesses the nature and extent of the damages. The defendant has the opportunity to introduce at this point any mitigating factors which would tend to reduce the nature and extent of damages. The town panel then makes its decision as to the findings of fact and law and as to the kind and amount of restitution taking into account the nature of the offense, the extent of the damages, mitigating factors and the position and wealth of the defendant in the community. The decision of the panel is binding on the respondent and can only be appealed to the circuit or superior court having competent jurisdiction if such finding is clearly arbitrary and capricious or excessive. In no case shall incarceration of the respondent result from this procedure except in case of alcohol or substance abuse where inpatient treatment is clearly indicated and substantiated by at least two board certified physicians who have examined the defendant. Also there must be unanimous consent by the panel that such in patient treatment is in the best interest of the respondent and the community.

The whole idea here is that the people of the community work with these offenders to get them to modify their behavior to the standards of the community. Community involvement is continuous, providing empathy and compassion for those who may require a special support system to re-enter the mainstream of the neighborhood. However, the ultimate punishment for those who cannot or will not conform their behavior to community standards is exile from living in the community. While the individual will not be dismissed from employment, this resident may be denied preferential treatment in regards to receiving community services available to other law-abiding citizens.

For example, if a non-resident wishes to apply for an advanced position such as a supervisor in a business which anchors the community, all candidates will initially be evaluated for the supervisory position based upon the same criteria. However, preference will be given to that individual who is a law-biding resident of the renewal community if equal skill levels have been determined among the candidates. In addition, residents who abide by community standards will be provided a transportation discount card for a bus, taxis or rail transportation to get to and from work. However, access to other city services such as entertainment and sporting events will be more expensive to those without a residency card. The residency card also can be used as a low interest credit card for food, goods and services and cash advances. Those who continually perpetuate crime upon neighborhood residents will be restricted in their use of 'free community' services as they make retribution back to their town in the form of service or fines. Such restrictions will be gradually repealed as those individuals earn community trust through their commitment to earning their way back into the mainstream of the neighborhood.

The juvenile community criminal system shall also try to guide misdirected juvenile behavior to that which adheres to community expectations. As part of their commitment to 'rehabilitating' juveniles, the focus of the renewal community will be upon education and retraining. Parents generally will be expected to serve as mentors to those individuals

54

in need of role models as they make their way back into the mainstream of community activities. Parents of juveniles judged as violating community standards will be required to participate with their child in educational activities in the local public school that are designed to prepare that child for employment or to advance to a post-secondary educational institution. If a child continues to display disruptive behavior in spite of the attendance of his or her parents, he will be placed in a school outside the model city until he becomes sixteen years of age. At that time he may be exiled from the community if a panel finds as a fact that his presence in the community is detrimental to the welfare of its residents.

For juvenile offenders in the high school years over age 16, peer pressure will become the tool for regaining respect in the neighborhood. With the aid of teachers, counselors and recreational supervisors, evidence shall be presented regarding the juvenile in the community before a panel consisting of two members from the offender's high school and two adults from the renewal community. The panel will decide whether or not the juvenile offender was involved in the incident and what damages were caused by his/her conduct. If there is no majority decision concerning the findings and recommendations of the panel of four, then an arbitrator will make the final decision. Once damages have been assessed, the panel or arbitrator shall decide what restitution shall be made and what can be done to modify the behavior of the juvenile. An arbitrator many also be given the responsibility to evaluate decisions of the review panel of students and adults as it relates to fairness. The juvenile must also agree to the decision of the panel or the arbitrator or face expulsion from school. In the event expulsion is inappropriate and the juvenile refuses to take part in the process, then a formal legal process according to state law will be initiated.

The idea of the model city is to keep criminal management as low key as possible, and therefore local crime will not be highly publicized in the media. By having a community where everyone is acquainted with their neighbors and where neighbors are familiar with what is occurring on the town streets, the closeness of the community will assure conformity to acceptable standards of behavior. By having a model town that features passion and understanding, the element of commonalty should result in a high degree of solidarity and thus impact on bringing a new dimension to the legal environment of the renewal community.


## Controlling guns

The issue of gun control needs to be addressed in the renewal community. Research appears to support the contention that permitting citizens to carry concealed handguns reduces crime. Based upon a 1997 study by

John R. Lott and David Mustard of the University of Chicago (1997), 31 states that permit citizens to carry concealed handguns have seen their violent crimes declined. Lott and Mustard found that permitting citizens without criminal records to carry concealed handguns deters violent crimes. They argue that if all 50 states had permitted law-abiding citizens to carry concealed handguns in 1992, there would have been 1,570 fewer murders, 4,177 rapes eliminated, 60,363 fewer aggravated assaults, and 11,896 robberies eliminated. However, it is also important to note that Lott and Mustard indicated that auto theft and larceny rates rise when state permit concealed weapons among its citizens. In other words, states that permit concealed legal hand-guns can expect a 5 to 9 percent drop in violent crime but a 2 to 3 percent increase in offenses such as stealing.

Whereas control is more of a state and national issue rather than one that can be dealt within a local town, the issue of gun control still needs to be addressed. The evidence also indicates that the public use of guns in 'the heat of the moment' is rare. Therefore, the use of a legal handgun following an auto-accident, etc., is rare although this does not offset the use of such guns within households during family arguments and other encounters with friends and neighbors. The key inference here is that *legal handguns* appear not to be the primary concern of citizens in the United States. However, the illegal handgun is another matter.

Violent crimes committed with handguns upon community residents must be deterred. Therefore, the public schools, town meetings, and neighborhood camaraderie must all intertwine in order to get the message across that using guns as part of criminal behavior will not be tolerated in the renewal community. Those criminal acts which involve the use of handguns must be avoided. The message to the residents in our model city about the consequences of carrying concealed weapons must be continuously communicated to both the youth and adults. Community safety must be a top priority in the model city is to be successful. However, to counteract trends toward violent behavior, it is the solidarity of the neighborhood that must stand in the way as a barrier to exhibiting irresponsible behavior. It is only by residents helping other residents and being aware of what is going on about them will a deterrent to violent crime come about. Therefore, residents of the renewal community must be sensitive to issues surrounding handgun control, but it is their presence and oversight everyday that is likely to have more impact upon the safety of their neighbors than laws prohibiting concealed weapons.

## Reinventing housing

Home ownership remains the essence of the American dream. In 1940, American communities consisted primarily of renters where only 40 percent of housing was owner occupied. In 1994, the rate of home ownership has increased to approximately 64 percent. The term home is also taking on a different perspective. For example, the traditional separation between home and work is now becoming more blurred. For example, home businesses are beginning to become part of the norm in American communities. Home-based commerce enables individuals with modest means to enter into business as an entrepreneur without the need to gather together a large amount of money. In addition, there is a 'home school revolution' where homes are being converted into satellite school rooms whereby parents take control of the learning of their own children. The reality is that homes are taking on different purposes, signaling a need for perceiving a home quite different from that of the past.

Traditional zoning laws must be avoided in the renewal community if the concept of community integration is to be successful. For example, the renewal neighborhood desires residential housing to be interspersed among corner stores, dentists, restaurants, coffee shops, and other useful establishments. Since the main street of the newly created small town serves as the hub of activity for neighbors, it is important that residents become visible in their communities. The development of office parks or shopping malls which are customarily separated from the community by means of set aside land is to be avoided in the renewal community. What is suggested here for the model town is a pattern of 'walkable', mixed-use neighborhoods where a variety of housing in interspersed among retailers.

Different kinds of housing for residents can also be become part of the renewal community. As is the case in Britain and Australia, a supply of low-cost housing can be erected without the need of a large public bureaucracy or public funds. To make them slum proof, the renewal community would require all housing to be owner-occupied. This in fact substitutes the landlord for community police in terms of ensuring that community residences remain in good repair. With the homeowner having to be present in the residential building, there is an automatic built-in quality control factor which preserves both the health and environment of a community. With such a policy, accessory apartments could be accepted as a new form of housing for residents of the renewal community. Accessory apartments provide living space for families adjacent or attached to a principal family residence. The income derived from rents helps owners pay off their own mortgage as well as make home living more affordable. At the same time, it provides a low-cost housing opportunity for those not prepared for home ownership.

Living above stores, owning a residence within an office building (on a different floor), and sharing parts of residences in the form of common areas are all ways to generate reasonable housing. Whereas zoning laws in many communities prevent this kind of housing, the renewal community would favor such a development. The accessory apartments described above could be adopted by grandparents who may desire to live with their own children, and thus be available for tending to day care responsibilities of their grandchildren. Cluster housing interspersed among small business retailers is another form of generating low-cost housing. Similarly, duplex homes whereby parents live near their children will be welcome.

Efficient land use is another aspect of the housing policy for the renewal community. The model city proposed here would restore citizen rights within reasonable limits to determine the use of the land as they see fit. For example, lots larger than a half acre for a residential housing will not be required. The objective of the housing policy is to enable residents to avoid having to use their automobile to shop or to make time consuming trips to work. The primary reason for a rejection of housing would be proof of damage to the environment of the community or individual health. A policy similar to that of Germany could become part of the model city. In Germany, planners impose no restrictions on where and how homes are built. However, Germany does monitor population density by limiting the number of homes build on an acre. Such a policy has merit for the model city proposed here.

A rethinking of public policy towards housing is already becoming a reality. Some of the new ideas already being implemented can be expanded into the renewal community to assist residents in becoming homeowners more quickly. The need here is to generate public-private partnerships in which low-interest mortgage money is made available to residents seeking a second chance at life. For example, in the Cabrini Green complex in Chicago, Illinois, failed high-rise buildings are being replaced with mixed-income housing which is to attract middle-class professional residents. Set aside funds accumulated though Community Development Corporations can make this happen in the model city just as well. In addition, the $3.5 billion current Low-Income Housing Tax Credit program could be adapted to residents in the model city for generating diverse housing.

### Reconfiguring a power neighborhood

The best foundation for a strong community is frequent and cordial contacts among residents. Daily interaction is the basis for reducing crime, conflict, and anguish. Having model towns where residents can use their sidewalks rather than automobiles enables the emergence of a collegiality where the human spirit can easily be lifted. The *power neighborhood* is one in which residents can create a closeness that fosters trust and understanding. Within this framework children can be expected to grow and mature realizing the importance that is attached to being neighborly where friendship, informal cooperation, and mutual aid are the 'heart and soul' of social and economic power.

The physical layout of a neighborhood can have much to do with the psychology or mindset of town residents. The physical attributes can either provide opportunities or obstacles for bringing residents together for a unified purpose. Although neighborhoods can vary in population and density in terms of housing, they can also vary in the way streets, sidewalks, housing, traffic, and retailers are organized. The planned model community proposed here suggests that a majority of the population in a neighborhood reside within a 10 to 15 minute walking distance to its center. In this regard, workplaces, stores, community events, and public schools should all be within a two-mile radius of one's home. The streets of the neighborhood should be laid out in a network design whereby residents can get to their destinations by varied routes. Buildings in the model community should all face the sidewalk and should not reflect a difference in income levels of the residents. It should be impossible to determine the kind of family living in any housing in the neighborhood.

There should be a mixture of buildings in that large, small, duplexes, shops, restaurants, and condominiums are interspersed around a public square. In this instance, schools, public meetings halls, theaters, churches, and other public civic buildings should be placed on a public square where residents can easily become visible to their neighbors. Open space for parks, playgrounds, and outdoor entertainment should be located near the public square. Common areas for public gardening, group farming, or other communal projects should also be aligned to the public square.

The model city must enable residents to conduct most of their daily activities within walking distance from their residence. The essence of the model community is the ease with which neighbors can meet and exchange thoughts without fear of intimidation. Having sidewalks lined with trees and other picturesque plantings creates a comfortable environment for generating camaraderie. Having lower-income housing looking like its higher-income neighbors avoids the segregating of families by socio-economic status. Providing housing above retail establishments can reduce construction costs for erecting home environments. Streets in the neighborhood should be designed around the rights of the pedestrian rather than traffic. Off street parking should be required, preferably at the rear of buildings. Isolated parking lots between buildings should not be permitted.

The designing of entirely new communities using readily available military bases is an intriguing idea. Creating communities of between 5,000 and 15,000 residents with well defined residential, transportation, and commercial pathways provides a challenge for community architects.

In 1997, it has been estimated that there are over 100 such communities currently in the planning or construction stage. States that appear to have adopted planned communities such as the one proposed here include Virginia, North Carolina, South Carolina, Alabama, Tennessee, Colorado, and Florida. Two examples of such planned communities from which much can be learned are Harbor Town in Tennessee and Celebration in Florida. Each of these communities emphasize sidewalks, parks, and an assortment of other gathering places. Harbor Town features narrow streets, residences in close proximity, and front porches. Harbor Town is a 130-acre model community design by RTKL Associates of Baltimore and was begun in 1989 on Mud Island in the Mississippi River. Celebration is Walt Disney Company's vision of the model community near Orlando, Florida. Built around a lakefront main street, Celebration consists of approximately 4,500 acres consisting of 8,000 residents to accommodate approximately 20,000 residents. The project is estimated to cost some $2.5 billion. Therefore, as architects gain experience in how to construct such communities, redesigning former military bases as part of a vision for helping AFDC families gain control over their lives appears to be closely aligned with today's realities.

### Conclusion: committing to a new wave community

Rethinking of public policy is now required. While presently there are small pockets in American cities where private-public partnerships have been formed to tear down old high-rise public housing and in its place construct townhouse communities, a different kind of housing policy may be more in need. In this regard, much remains to be done. City schools are being repackaged as 'theme schools' in an attempt to attract suburban youth into city environments. Charter schools have been formed whereby the leadership of such schools is provided by the business community seeking ways to implement innovative educational strategies.

However, whereas these educational and public housing projects do have some merit in many of our larger cities, they are not sizable enough to have an impact on the national welfare problem as a whole. The tearing down of hundreds of failed high-rise apartments and replacing them with mixed-income housing is certainly a step in the right direction. However, renting a townhouse instead of an apartment appears to be no panacea. What is missing from these attempts is residential empowerment; that is, enabling individuals to gain control over their own lives. Gaining access to better housing is a worthy goal, but gaining access to better jobs with better wages cannot be ignored.

Pumping life into communities requires more than access to better housing. For long-term purposes, it requires access to better jobs, jobs that residents know they can obtain. Competing on a playing field that is not level places many families in poverty at a disadvantage. Competing for jobs with students graduating from better schools, having a heritage of ownership, and enjoying access to private transportation, children of poverty are often at a disadvantage. In order to level the playing field, children of poverty require an equal opportunity to engage in the competitive process of well-paying jobs. They need better schools, access to transportation to get to places of employment, and motivation to own their own homes. The level playing field in this instance is the neighborhood that provides the support system to help solve those problems associated with growing up.

We are entering an unprecedented era where work as we have known it in the steel, automobile, rubber, and chemical industries no longer exists. It therefore seems that dramatically new systems for employing and compensating people are now required. While we must continue to revitalize cities anywhere we can, it is also important to reallocate available resources to quicken the pace of revitalizing the lives of many American citizens in search of a future. While some analysts suggest a greater portion of the federal budget should be redirected from the upper- and middle-income entitlement programs such as social security, Medicare, and housing mortgage tax write-offs, others argue for less drastic changes to help those families in need. Correspondingly, what is being suggested here is that it may not be necessary to reallocate huge amounts of moneys from one class of citizens to another. A better alternative may be to redesign social policy that enables individuals to set their own destinies through equal opportunity. An additional side benefit is that these individuals become tax paying citizens which can result in the generation of additional public funds to reimburse local government for generating the renewal community.

The way to pump up the vitality of a community is to put into motion a 'wave of opportunity' for residents to reap the benefits of prosperity. This can only be accomplished by residents working in productive jobs that bring respect and dignity to one's life. Feeling good about yourself is a prerequisite to feeling good about your community and the future of your children. When given an alternative, citizens in this country have always adopted freedom as their choice of action. Being free to decide one's future is the basis of each of the models suggested above. Exhibiting the element of freedom by participating in a different way how business organizations are structured and the way public decisions are made results in a new form of 'democratization'.

The intriguing aspect to designing new planned communities is the symbolism attached to 'a land of opportunity'. Restarting the lives of families in poverty through a voluntary program whereby the image of community is portrayed every day results in a sense that achieving the

American dream is possible. Arranging residents in a 'close knit manner' sets the stage for accomplishing this objective. By focusing upon the socialization of families and generating 'social capital' as the centerpiece of welfare reform, conformity to community standards becomes a reality. By networking community public education, health and recreation, public security, and retailing into a planned community, each sector feeds off the other.

By designing complete communities around one particular anchor, whether business or public service or education, a rallying point for generating solidarity emerges. The case in point here is the in a democracy, it is the will of the people that is reflected in the decisions made to plan and organize. While a planned renewal community may not be for all welfare recipients, it is an alternative that fosters a shared vision by all who reside in such a neighborhood. The layout of the actual community reflects the overall philosophy of welfare reform signaling to residents the significance of collegiality.

In this regard, there are three principles that must be adhered to if a planned community can lead AFDC families out of pubic welfare programs. First, each model city requires a core of activities about which residents can evolve as they attempt to enhance both the quality of their home life as well as their work life. Secondly, all aspects of a planned community must lead to societal integration in that residents have a stake in its outcome whether a parent, a worker, or a resident. In this regard, assuring public safety while at the same time having compassion for those who exhibit criminal behavior reinforces the second chance at life theory which is the foundation of welfare reform. Thirdly, a planned community must be an attractive and well-designed for residents with varying economic resources, since diversity is a community strength and not a weakness. The critical element here is committing to a social contract which binds families to the ideals and objectives of a renewal community.

Once these three principles are adopted, and as long as the spirit of the new wave community is perpetuated, models of hope can take on varied forms. In addition, the size of a model community can be relatively small to serve a community of 5,000 residents to one of 15,000, depending upon the military site to be used. The costs associated with establishing a planned community will also vary depending upon the ingenuity of the planners and the partnerships generated between the business and public sectors. The conceptual basis for creating a mega community with a small town passion is only subject to the creativity and imagination of architects, city planners, welfare reformers, and other advocates of enhancing human kind. While the model city focuses upon the utilizing of soon to be closed military bases, other open spaces may be adopted.

Finding suitable land is not the problem. The problem is a nation's will to initiate a comprehensive approach to welfare reform, one with a vision.

# 3  Show me the money: reclaiming the marketplace and workplace

An increasing number of American families appear to be under siege, especially those presently on welfare. American families generally have ridden a roller coaster since the concept of a new commonwealth of states was finalized in 1787. Over these years, many families have seen their economic welfare enhanced while at the same time others have struggled just to survive. However, no matter what the socio-economic status of the family, all had to endure through emotional wars including the Civil War, WWI, WWII, the Korean War, and the more recent Vietnam War. In addition, the American family has had to struggle through the turmoil of the a rebellious youth in the 1960s, the searching for equality among the roles of females and males in the 1970s, and the emergence of drugs, guns, and family violence in the 1980s.

## The great divide

There has been an increasing gap between incomes generated by those families in the upper and middle classes and the *underclass* over the past two decades. According to Stephanie Coontz (1992) in  *The Way We Never Were: American Families and The Nostalgia Trap,*  since 1986, each year has resulted in the income gap getting wider and wider. In 1980, the average chief executive officer (CEO) of the 500 largest companies in the United States earned 30 to 40 times as much as the blue collar worker. However, in 1994, the average CEO earned 187 times as much. Conversely, the real wages of the high school graduate are considerably lower today than those earned in 1963. Since many of the working poor have only a high school diploma or less, a working parent does not keep a family out of poverty.

During the 1980s, the rich/poor gap widened in 43 states. The proportion of low-wage earners in the population has accelerated over the past decade. Much of the blame for the decline of wages among low-income families has been attributed to the decline of organized labor, the oversupply of low-skilled immigrants, and parental irresponsibility. However, no matter what the reason for the expanding 'great divide', the fact remains that this great income dispersion between the rich and poor affects all Americans, since those who are unable to find work (or are able to find work at dismal wage levels) will no doubt leave a legacy of crime, drugs, and abuse.

Economist Paul Krugman (1997) attributes American income inequality to technology while Lester Thurow (1997) suggests the global economy as the culprit. However, the intriguing aspect here is that both technology and the global economy have resulted in two power shifts in the workplace. Employees have lost negotiating power, especially in view that labor unions have lost members in large numbers over the past decade. In this regard, labor has also lost political power in that at least one party, primarily the Democratic Party, traditionally represented labor and particularly blue-collar worker jobs where welfare recipients often seek employment. Now, both the Republican and Democratic party appear to be representative of small and large business. With the labor movement at a standstill and with no powerful force protecting either the white collar or blue collar worker, the ability of those heads of AFCD families to overcome discrimination and other barriers to employment lessens. Show me the way to make money is the 'cry' of those on welfare. Show me the money is a reality check for welfare reform. Where the average worker in 1996 received a meager 3.3 percent raise in salary, top executives enjoyed double-digit increases often approaching 20 percent. Even corporate profits in 1996 increased by an estimate 11 percent. With trends like this, and no one representing the common worker, the impact of such extreme earnings distribution is bound to continue to have a negative effect upon welfare reform, particularly in terms of finding long-term employment.

*The working poor increases*

According to Diane Crispell (1996) in *American Demographics*, two in three poor children have parents who work but whose earnings are not sufficient to lift them out of poverty. In 1994, 38 percent of all poor children in the United States lived in a working-poor family whose parents actually worked 50 or more weeks per year. However, Crispell further reports that another one-third of poor children lived with parents who worked less than 50 weeks per year. The result of this phenomena of not being able to work for a *living wage* has approximately 5.6 million children living in working-poor families in 1994, up from 3.4 million 20 years ago. These children in working-poor families represent approximately 8.2 percent of all American children.

In this regard, Crispell reports that most working parents of poor children have low levels of education which explains in large part their low earnings. Seventy-three percent of these parents never attended college. In addition, the proportion of 'traditional' two-parent families with both biological parents of children living in the same household continues to fall to only one in four. It is projected that this ratio will increase to one in five by the year 2010. The Census Bureau in 1996 projected that the number of single-parent families will grow at an average rate of 14 percent between 1995 and 2010. Since many children in poverty live with single-parents, this trend does not bear well for any foreseeable significant change in the living conditions of families in poverty.

Impacting upon the 'great divide' between the rich and poor is the burden that many single-parents place upon themselves and their children by perpetuating illegitimacy. Charles Murray has called illegitimacy the major social problem of the decade, (*Phi Delta Kappan*, March 1995). Stepfamilies are said to leave children worse off than single parenthood because children are at risk of abuse or neglect by adults who lack a biological investment in them. The obstacles to overcoming the 'great divide' are perceived as insurmountable by many families in poverty, suggesting that a new look must be taken as to assisting families to learn how to fend for themselves. Our Model provides incentives for assuming individual responsibility in this respect.

The evidence appears to be overwhelming that single-parent families today are six times more likely to be poor than two-parent families. This is caused by low wages traditionally paid to women and to real wages of those with the high school diploma or less decreasing since 1970. Single-parent families are also more likely to fall into poverty because of unfair divorce laws for dividing of property, or inadequate enforcement of child support agreements. In addition, poor parents are twice as likely to divorce than the more affluent, and teens who live in families in poverty are six to seven times more likely to become unwed parents themselves. Some individuals argue that childbearing is a goal of many teenage mothers since it creates something of their own, which is important in a life where very little is owned.

The "great divide" can also be seen in how society perpetuates inequality in public subsidies. Past public policy has generally encouraged a form a "reversed socialism" for the rich leaving many families in poverty to fend for themselves. For example, 75 percent of social welfare spending typically goes to those families who are *not* poor. The average person with an income over $100,000 receives cash benefits-- such as social security or subsidies to grow wheat--of almost $6,000 a year which is about the same that many families in poverty earn in an entire year. When tax benefits are entered into the equation, the inequities between the rich and poor become greater. The federal government typically spends at least four times as much on housing subsidies for the middle-income American that it does for the low-income. For example, in 1991, households with adjusted gross incomes of more than $100,000 a year received $11.2 billion in government housing subsidies, compared to approximately $3.9 billion of the low-income, (Waldman, 1992).

The 'great divide' continues. In 1994, taxpayer will spend $25 billion for food stamps compare to $29.2 billion on subsidies to agribusiness. Then there is the so-called *Aid to Dependent Corporations.* In 1994, the federal government deliver an estimated $51 billion in direct subsidies to business along with another $53.3 billion in corporate tax breaks. Ironically, the difference between providing welfare for the poor and that for the rich is that the *handouts for the rich* are not stigmatized as they are for the families in poverty, (*Phi Delta Kappan*, March 1995).

One of the tragic outcomes of income disparity between the rich and poor is the collapse of the belief of AFDC families that the free enterprise system is best for all. The loss of this belief reflects a lack of control over their daily lives as families attempt to manage their financial affairs. The result is the cynical 'me-first mentality' which presses materialism, selfishness, and disregard for consequences of one's actions. New sets of attitudes strain relationships among family members where reciprocity is not commonplace. In its place is a household of disassociated members who live in defacto arrangements where each individual seeks his own identity through personal strategies.

**Gaining control over family finances**

Most suggestions for reforming welfare include proposals for moving recipients from public assistance into the workplace. The assumption is that once welfare recipients are off welfare and employed, they will be able to manage their finances and support their families. However, Marlow, Godwin, and Maddux (1996) suggest that the kind of job obtained may not pay sufficient wages to get families above poverty levels. In addition, families in poverty may not know to utilize effective money management practices, if even they were fortunate enough to obtain a better paying job.

Santiago (1996) suggests that there has been very little interest in welfare reform for putting into place incentives which guide welfare recipients into good financial management. To Santiago, there are both *internal and external barriers* that discourage welfare recipients from instituting effective money management practices. For example, externally, earning extra money through a second place of employment or gaining access to a better paying job often disqualifies heads of households from receiving public support in the terms of health care, income supplements, or food stamps. Even though earning additional wages through hard work is a beneficial practice, public policies in place have historically provided disincentives to work. Although these external barriers are expected to be reduced or eliminated as welfare reform is implemented, the need for finding employment in jobs where substitute benefits can be obtained is critical. Finding a job is just one part of the puzzle; securing a job that provides sufficient health care, dental care, and disability benefits is another. The moving of a *safety net* from the public forum to the private sector is an admirable objective of society, but it is also one that requires close monitoring to assure families attempting to move out of poverty are able in fact to care for family health care needs, especially those of children.

Internal barriers to effective money management also exists (Iane, 1987, Langer, 1983, Lewis, 1968, Petigrew, 1980). Heads of households of families in poverty generally perceive any attempt of managing their money according to accepted practices in financial planning as futile. Their top priority is tending to the needs of food, clothing, and shelter for their children. However, there is often just enough money in hand to worry about nothing more than paying off everyday bills such as electricity, telephone, and heat. What is left over for as food and health care needs is often marginal. Therefore, earning constraints is the primary internal barrier to effective money management.

Conversely, a study completed by Marlow, Godwin, and Maddux (1996) at the University of Georgia confirms that many welfare recipients perceive themselves as actually possessing good financial management skills. In Table 3.1 on the next page showing data derived from interviews of 35 families on welfare in the states of Georgia, welfare recipients believe they generally have considerable control over their finances. Given the popular stereotype that welfare recipients have feelings of hopelessness and little control over their finances, these findings may be somewhat of a surprise. The Control Index calculated which attempts to quantify the degree of control these families have over their finances was 19.75, clearly indicating a vote of confidence in their own ability to manage their finances.

**Table 3.1**

**Feelings of control over money matters**

| Control over: | Percentage | | | |
|---|---|---|---|---|
| | None | Not Much | Some | Much |
| 1. the amount of $ you have | 6 | 29 | 37 | 29 |
| 2. increasing income | 17 | 23 | 34 | 26 |
| 3. decreasing expenses | 15 | 21 | 27 | 38 |
| 4. saving money | 9 | 9 | 38 | 44 |
| 5. getting out of debt | 14 | 9 | 23 | 54 |
| 6. getting extensions on bills | 18 | 27 | 44 | 12 |
| 7. family discussions of $ | 27 | 21 | 21 | 32 |

Feeling of Control Index: Mean = 19.57 (Range: 7 - 28)
Source: University of Georgia, 1996

When the same 35 families on welfare were asked about the worthiness of setting financial goals and other aspects of money management, similar findings were again found. In Table 3.2 below, the six questions asked were summed to form a Financial Futility Index to quantify family perceptions over possible financial concerns. For every item about financial futility, fewer than half of the sample responded that they agreed with the statement. The resulting index of 2.5 supports the contention that financial futility is much less than expected.

**Table 3.2**

**Financial futility of welfare families**

| Possible money concern | % agreeing |
|---|---|
| 1 Credit is necessary to buy something over $100 | 49 |
| 2. Financial goals are out of reach for us. | 37 |
| 3. We do not have enough money to try to budget. | 49 |
| 4. Someone else always needs money, so if I set some aside, I would just have to give it away. | 20 |
| 5. It is unnecessary to set financial goals because we could never accomplish them | 26 |
| 6. It does no good to save for the future | 26 |

Financial Futility Index = 2.15 (Range 0-6)
Source: University of Georgia, 1996

In the same study, when the 35 families on welfare were asked about their current financial planning and saving behaviors, the results again indicated these families were not much different from those who may be more affluent. In Table 3.3 below, the welfare families interviewed indicated that they are capable of planning and saving their money according to specific needs. While a vast majority of families on welfare

## Table 3.3
## Financial behavior of welfare families

| Behavior | Rating Scale | | | | |
|---|---|---|---|---|---|
| How often do you . . . . | 1 | 2 | 3 | 4 | 5 |
| | (% by category) | | | | |
| 1. have a plan for spending your money? | 11 | 11 | 9 | 9 | 60 |
| 2. manage your money so you have  enough to last until your next paycheck? | 26 | 3 | 14 | 20 | 37 |
| 3. set aside money for a future purchase | 3 | 14 | 9 | 17 | 57 |
| 4. spend more than you make? | 29 | 11 | 11 | 6 | 43 |
| 5. set aside money to pay current | 3 | 23 | 14 | 11 | 49 |

(Rating Scale: 1=never, 2=rarely, 3=sometimes, 4=frequently,
                              5=almost always)
Source:  University of Georgia, 1996

(60 percent) indicated they have a plan for spending their money, there seems to be considerable follow through on their plans when paying off bills. It is interesting to note that even though these families considered themselves active in developing spending plans, 49 percent indicated that they also have a tendency to spend more than the family earned (43 percent almost always and 6 percent, frequently). There appears to be some discrepancy as to how effective is that financial planning conducted by welfare families.

These findings do however suggest that what families in poverty may need are educational programs that prepare heads of households to better manage their money. Although the problem of money management may not be as severe as is typically portrayed through stereotypes of such families by the general public, there still appears to be some concern about the effectiveness of financial planning. On the other hand, there is a need for information as to what financial assistance is available and what are the eligibility requirements. The sensitive issue here is that many welfare recipients perceive themselves as capable of fending for themselves in the marketplace by devising strategies that meet their immediate goals. Any plan to assist them in this regard must be carefully developed in order not to insult their intelligence. However, what is missing is knowledge as to what kinds of assistance are available for guiding present welfare recipients into a long-term strategy of saving and investing, (*Advancing the Consumer Interest*, Fall 1996).

Therefore, the focusing upon specific characteristics of welfare recipients and attempting to provide training to strengthen weaknesses in present money management practices would likely to only result in resentment. In this regard, welfare recipients do not exhibit a high sense of futility about managing their finances. While their planning and saving behavior may be not considered traditional in terms of the middle-class values, welfare recipients do generally put money away to pay bills, do not borrow money recklessly, and are capable of establishing savings accounts of approximately $500 per year. Therefore, rather than focusing upon teaching welfare recipients how to enhance their budgeting skills, a more useful strategy might be providing information on the benefits of investing over the long-term, using credit wisely for gaining access to home ownership, and protecting their assets through sound insurance policies.

There appears to be a great awareness of what it takes financially to survive on the part off welfare recipients, but not much attention is currently being devoted to the future. Although low levels of education and changes in family composition often result in poverty, low-income families are very capable of becoming independent financially. However, with single-parent females heading up many of the AFCD families, long-term financial planning is not a priority, however, surviving is. The consequences of not addressing long-term goals results in families without vision and hope. Setting family goals, whether they be to enroll children in college, purchase a residence of their own, or plan for retirement, puts into place the mindset of fulfilling dreams, and that is what the democracy and the free enterprise system is all about.

*Women in need of a secured future*

Because women generally take more time off work for child care, live longer and make less money than men, they need to devise strategies that prepare them for the 'unexpectancies of life' whether they be sudden unemployment, divorce, or death of a partner. Leaving retirement planning to their spouses, or ignoring long term goals in single-parent families is not wise for women. In order to care for not only themselves but for children, women must learn to save and invest more than men, says Christin Cook (1996) of Merrill Lynch. According to the Merrill

Lynch Baby Boom Retirement Index, a single man making $30,000 a year without a traditional pension must save $11,881 by age 35, $56,583 by age 45, and $168,627 by age 65. However, a single woman in the same situation needs more than double that amount by age 35 to $31,357, by age 45 to $95,395, and by age 65 to $378,300, *(Sunday News Journal, 1996)*.

The reasons women must become more aggressive in their financial planning is that they have a tendency to live longer than men, have lower wages than men, and have interrupted careers. For example, women born in 1950 will likely live to an age of 87, compared to 81 for a male. According to a 1995 U.S. Labor Department population survey, women earn 76 cents for every dollar earned by men. And finally, a female taking one year off to tend to children will suffer dramatically in terms of long-term financial planning. If a 35-year old woman contributed $1500 annually into a 401(k) plan with an employer match of $1,500 per year at 8 percent rate of return, that individual would accumulate $509,774 during an uninterrupted 30-year career. However, if that same female took just one year off, especially during the early years of work, that nest egg would decrease to $467,847, some $41,927 less.

While those in poverty may not find themselves in a position to place $1500 per year into a retirement plan, the consequence of not being able to put any money aside has a significant effect on the welfare of women in this country. The consequences of ignoring the future because of pressing daily financial needs leaves but one alternative, a reliance upon a public subsidy of some kind. For example, social security has been targeted by many families for the primary means of financing one's old age. However, a typical social security check for the average American family generally results in receiving income placing one in poverty. Therefore, to become more secured, the need to think long-term is now more prevalent then ever. The reality for females heads of AFDC families is that they (with increasing responsibilities) are likely to be susceptible to additional financial stress as they are required to obtain employment. This is especially true for females who have traditionally been subjected to workplace discrimination in terms of treatment and pay. Maneuvering through an economy where interruptions to a consistent income are likely requires different money management strategies not familiar to many females on welfare.

The *glass ceiling* is a metaphor that depicts the frustration and obstacles faced by both females and minorities as they attempt to develop careers within a company structure. Women and minorities make up approximately 57 percent of the labor force in 1996; and by the year 2005, it is projected by the Bureau of Labor Statistics that they will be 62 percent, (Adams, 1993). What is troubling is that corporate giants have been downsizing and restructuring to compete in a changing global economy of the 21st Century. Whereas career advancement is a concern for many, just getting a job is just as important for others. And once a job has been obtained, women often find their careers shunted into support or staff positions that will not provide them with the experience they need to advance in a career. Women and minorities are now faced with a new set of *invisible choices* that often lead to dead-end jobs.

*Consumer education comes center stage*

Three areas that AFDC families require assistance is credit management, investing, and financial assistance. Since families on welfare are also entering into a workplace that encourages ingenuity and creativity while at the same time inviting uncertainty and surprise, different kinds of financial strategies must be adopted. Financial planning becomes an important piece of the puzzle as families attempt to become independent of public support. Taking center stage in the renewal community will be a continuous stream of consumer education programs for both adults and students. The workplace may no longer be considered a reliable source of steady income. Other strategies related to spending, saving and investing, must be adopted to overcome the uncertainties of the workplace..

*Spending management*

Gaining control over general spending and that associated with credit cards are two critical aspects of money management. As the public safety net disappears, a private safety net generated by families themselves must be put into place. For example, let's look at the budget of a family of three, formerly on public welfare, with a monthly take-home pay of $2000.

### Monthly Expenses

| | |
|---|---|
| Rent . . . . . . . . . . . | $750 |
| Food . . . . . . . . . . . | 365 |
| Telephone . . . . . . . | 100 |
| Transportation . . . . . | 100 |
| Clothes . . . . . . . . | 100 |
| Electricity/water . . . . . | 65 |
| Medical Care/Sundries . | 100 |
| Credit Card Payments . | 400 |
| Allowances . . . . . . . | 20 |
| | ------ |
| Total | $2000 |

The irony of such a family budget based upon $24,000 take-home pay is that it includes no allowance for saving and investing. These two aspects reflect the primary reasons for budgeting in the first place. In the current digital economy, wealth is being transferred from the worker to the investor as witnessed by the steadily increase in the values of stocks over recent decades. Therefore, in order to reap the benefits of the prosperity resulting from the technological revolution we are now also witnessing, families on welfare must adopt innovative strategies for sharing in this newly created wealth. In this instance, it is critical for families to adopt a strategy of getting more 'spending value' from their earnings in order to have funds available to invest, a formidable challenge to say the least..

Three areas in which funds can be reallocate are shelter, the telephone, and credit management. Gaining access to different kinds of housing could reduce rental by as much as 10 percent, releasing somewhere around $75 for savings and or investing (please refer to our budget on the previous page). With today's competition in telephone long-distance and local rates, additional savings of approximately $25 could be a reality. Families often have credit debt above the recommended 15 percent of take home pay. In this instance, the percentage of debt is 20 percent or $100 over what is recommended. Therefore, if the credit amount was reduce to $300, another $100 could be released for savings and investment.

What makes it difficult to reallocate funds from spending to saving and investing is the number of 'infomercials' being disseminated by means of television, radio, and the Internet. With the business community adopting a two-tier marketing strategy, they are be seeking consumer's attention along a two-dimensional grid. Targeted are the more affluent, middle- and upper-class families and at the same time the lower-income, blue collar worker. For example, companies are tailoring their products and services to two different Americas. With the two ends of society becoming more alienated from each other, products and services are to be marketed in corresponding more segregated ways. Telephone services, access to the Internet, denim jeans, restaurants, and banking services are being marketed to appeal to low-income consumers differently from others. In the department store era, we have seen the emergence of two kinds of retailers; on one hand K-mart, Wal-mart and Caldor appealing to low-income consumers and the more upscaled Nordstorms, Tiffany's and Sachs the other. Whereas both kinds of retailers are doing quite well, those department stores in the mid-scale such as J.C. Penney's, Gimbels, and Woodward & Lothrup are struggling to survive.

Combining this dual marketing with the telecommunication's industry, consumers can be reached in their homes, automobiles, sidewalks, and the workplace.    Companies can now access the top and bottom portions of their market with ease.  With this ability to intrude into each person's private space whether through the personal computer, telephone, or television set, more frequent contact with consumers for 'enticing' purchases is inevitable. The temptation to spend will become more likely as sophisticated images with amazing charismatic sensitivity may 'strike' at any time during the day.

With the push to spend and to use the credit, smart, or cash card, consumers will have to become more disciplined in their reactions to the marketing schemes of the corporate community.    Consumer education must emerge as the antidote to the  urge to mass consume products and services of which many will no doubt add very little to enhancing one's standard of living.    Therefore, while preparing to reenter the workplace may be a challenge in itself, the learning how to get value for money in the marketplace is another, especially for a group of individuals who have not be so vigilant about spending strategies in the past.

Therefore, the art of spending is likely to become even more important if welfare recipients are to make their way off of public welfare programs and into a state of independence.    The trick is to bargain through negotiating  and not simply being receptive to superficial advertising pitches that appeal to only the senses and not to a rational purchasing strategy.  In today's highly competitive market, more families will no doubt be unable to afford those products that were once seen as a birthright of the middle class--the new car every other year, new clothes for each season of the year, and the annual two-week vacation.  Many consumers have cut back in areas where prior generations would not have considered skimping on in decades past.

Ironically, this shift in consumer spending strategies has created a lucrative opportunity for marketing specialists to provide low-end goods and services that are palatable to the low-income consumer while at the same time offering more customized versions to those with middle-class aspirations. With marketing personnel realizing that low-wage earners do control a large mount of disposable income, they are moving into an underserved minority that now may be considered a group with clout and choice.

Calendar-wise shopping is another aspect of spending management that will be emphasized in the renewal community. Below in Table 3.4 is a calendar-wise shopping plan which will be an integral part of the renewal community.    Considerable savings can be achieved by simply purchasing goods when they are traditionally on sale.  A generally accepted practice on the part of many businesses is to discount their merchandise at exactly the same time every year.  For example, appliances are frequently heavily discounted during the month of January each year.  On the other hand, during  June and July, floor covering and heating fuel are the cheapest.

76

Consumers can also save considerable amounts of their income by purchasing a majority of their clothing during the summer months. Businesses generally adhere to these practices as a result of tradition as well as economic senses. As noted here, timing of purchases is extremely important. The battle for implementing such a plan is the conflict between time and convenience.

In this regard, consumers generally overspend on the bulk of their purchases because time is more important than money. When getting the greatest value for money is an integral part of consumer spending strategies, timing is a critical. Seasonal discounts and consumer expectations will merge into a purchasing strategy that protects the residents from price gouging. However, lower prices and more frequent sales by local merchants will no doubt be encouraged by technological advancement in the marketing and distribution of goods and services in the years to come. This expectation will be capitalized upon by residents of the renewal community as the theme of getting value for your money

## Table 3.4
## Calendar-wise shopping

| January | February | March | April |
|---|---|---|---|
| Appliances | Air Conditioners | Shoes | Fabrics |
| Carpets/Rugs | Cars (Used) | Garden Spls. | Hosiery |
| China | Curtains | Infant Cloth. | Paints |
| Men's Overcoats | Housewares | Luggage | Shoes |
| Furniture | Toys | Skis | |

| May | June | July | August |
|---|---|---|---|
| Handbags | Bedding | Appliances | Carpet |
| Jewelry | Clothing | Sportsware | Tires |
| Outdoor Furn. | Rugs | Sum. Cloth. | Bedding |
| Auto Access. | Shoes | Elect. Equip. | Coats |
| TV Sets | | | Sch. Spls. |

| September | October | November | December |
|---|---|---|---|
| Bicycle | New Autos | Men's Suits | Shoes |
| Fall Fashion | School Spls. | Winter Cloth. | Quilts |
| Hardware | Silver | Appliances | Coats |
| Lamps | Major Appl. | Blankets | Autos |
| Autos | Autos | Used cars | After x-mas sales |

Source: Florida Today, 1997

77

is adopted by the public schools, the retail sector, and town council meetings.

Therefore, financial management is a critical aspect of any welfare reform program if AFDC families are going to participate in the new wealth currently being generated by the knowledge economy. The renewal community provides ways for residents to reduce their expenditures for basic items such as food and housing. As indicted earlier, to enhance one's quality of life and corresponding economic standard living, it will be necessary to invest. Therefore, getting a job with a living wage is important, but it is wealth creation that will lead to enhancing one's quality of life. The renewal community is designed not only to get people to work, but to get residents to adapt to a new set of purchasing strategies to counteract a whole new set of temptations to spend. Consumer education is to be a continuous and integral function of the renewal community, one not taken lightly by both educators and the residents.

*Investing in America's future.* Increasing personal savings rates as well as expanding investments into stocks and mutual funds are two attractive alternatives readily available to all consumers. At the end of 1996, personal savings represented 4.9 percent of disposal income, up from 5.0 percent in 1988. However, these rates are much lower than the 8 to 9 percent range in the 1980s.

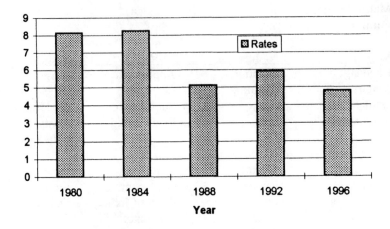

**Figure 3.1  Personal savings rates by year**
Source:      U.S. Commerce Department, 1997

Whereas families where one or both parents have been working have had opportunities to reallocate part of their earnings into a systematic investment plan, wealth creation becomes an integral part of their financial planning. A similar strategy must be made available to former AFDC families. The renewal community is specifically established for this purpose; that being, finding new ways to reallocate consumer earnings for generating a new form of income security.

Mutual funds are the 'new kid on the block' for many investors. Mutual funds come in all different sizes and packages. Depending upon an individual's risk tolerance and investment objectives, investing in mutual funds is coming routine for many American workers. The diversity afforded by such investments enable heads of households to streamline their investments according to specific goals and risk tolerance.. There are mutual funds for just about any investment strategy.. Through a systematic plan of investing of a portion of each month's earnings, the average worker can take advantage of the compounding of interest or dividends received as a by-product of such endeavors. In this instance, workers can earn interest upon interest over long periods of time by pooling their money into ventures for sharing in the prosperity of a nation.

The era of putting money away in a personal savings account or a Certificate of Deposit for creating wealth is a thing of the past. With yearly inflation rates running between 2 and 4 percent since the late 1980s, it is important for workers to make investments where the rate of return is between 7 to 10 percent yearly. This is the part of welfare reform that must be addressed. Getting families who traditionally have not invested in their country because they simply did not have the funds to do will no doubt be a challenge. However, investing in one's country contributes to the mindset that reflects upon a basic economic premise; that being, sharing in the wealth that is created by its workers.

*Getting financial help for personal ventures.* One area of extreme importance is that of guiding children in the direction of getting as much education as possible in preparation the higher paying jobs in the workplace. In this regard, with college tuition rising into the stratosphere, getting financial assistance for our next generation of leaders will be paramount. Of course, good grades, consistent school attendance, involvement in extracurricular activities, and voluntary participation in general community service projects will help in getting students accepted to college. However, paying for college and other related costs may be another matter.

Education will be taken seriously in the renewal community. Parents must be consistently involved with their children on an everyday basis. The premise here is that once children know their parents are concerned with their lives and that they are to be constantly involved in important events in their young lives, the result will be a family bonding that brings comfort and trust. When it comes to reaping the rewards of hard work in their schools, the payoff is that children can see the value of their effort. In the renewal community, reliable and trustworthy 'search firms' must be ready to assist parents and their children in seeking out scholarships. While customarily search firms charge fees anywhere from $10 to $500, such a service should be financially supported by the local school district in the renewal community.

Ways to assist children in getting financial aid for possible college is guiding them into challenge courses, participate in internships, and to complete an independent study project outside of their normal public school curriculum. Attending summer leaning campus is another way to learn about financial scholarships. Another way to inform parents of alternatives is to access the Internet in the local school library. Currently, that National Association of Student Financial Aid Administrators has sponsored a home page called *http://www.finaid.org*. Getting community residents wired to their local schools to access the Internet will be a top priority in the renewal community.

The creation of a Community Development Corporation for generating partnerships between the private and public sector will be a must for the renewal community. Businesses brought in to anchor the commercial sector of the renewal community may also set up programs that 'guaranteed' payment of college tuition if students meet a specified criteria. What is suggested here is that a comprehensive support system funding be readily available for graduates of the local high school who intend to go to college. The success of a renewal community will be its ability to educate its residents--both old and young, and keep them up to date in terms of skills and knowledge. Not becoming discouraged is paramount if children are to persist in their effort to move their families to the next level on the socio-economic stratum.

Correspondingly, 'micro-financing' of small business ventures is another important aspect of the renewal community. Historically, it has been rather easy to help start a new small business by using funds offered by a state economic development corporation or some other generous benefactor. However, it is more of a challenge to assist an established business *to expand* and advance to a new level of performance. What has generally been the practice of the past cannot be allowed to be part of the renewal community. Currently, an Aspen Institute report indicated that there are about 266 micro-enterprise programs in operation today. However, most of the support previously given to these small businesses consisted of 'start-up' business training and a grant of a few thousand dollars. Also included in such a financial package is a credit line of between $25,000 and $50,000. The limitation of such financial assistance is not providing additional moneys for expansion. The problem to the obtaining additional funds is a lack of experience on that part of new

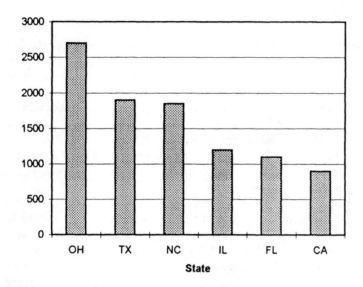

**Figure 3.2    New small business ventures:  1994-1996**
Source:        Site Selection Magazine, 1997

small business entrepreneurs for getting loans from a local bank. Therefore, as part of the financial assistance package available to entrepreneurs seeking to set up a business in the renewal community must be a new kind of alliance particularly with a state economic development office to get access to larger sums of money.

On the positive side, the Aspen Institute (1997) also reported that out of 405 randomly selected recipients of grants for such small business ventures, 83 percent were high school graduates of which 78 percent were female and 62 percent were members of minority groups. In addition, 56 percent of those individuals who started a small business relied solely upon small grants from a micro-financing group, and 78 percent of such businesses survived at least two years. Since it is the small business that hires most of the new workers in this country, a special effort is to be made in the renewal community to assure that there is an equal opportunity for all residents to initiate a new business venture. Having courses and seminars available through the local public school will also help those in need of specific information as to how to go about starting one's own business.

### New era managing the family resources by the Internet

Traditionally, a family of four with an income at or below 200 percent of the federally defined poverty level, or approximately $28,704, has problems paying the rent, mortgage, and utilities. They also often have difficulty getting adequate health and dental insurance. For a family of four who is at the official poverty level, the income amounts to only $14,375. Moreover, these problems are even more severe. At both levels of poverty, people are primarily dealing with their basic needs related to finding food, shelter, home repair, health are, and clothing. These families do not typically have the time nor energy to get involved in other things like community activities or education, two important aspects of the model city being proposed here.

Based upon a survey of 1207 randomly selected low- and moderate-income households by the University of Delaware, problems related to housing, transportation, and purchasing furniture and appliances were frequent problems. In Figure 3.3 below, data related to problems identified by households living in an urban center of Wilmington, Delaware, reveal the need for legal services, reading and writing programs and victim's assistance are considerable less.

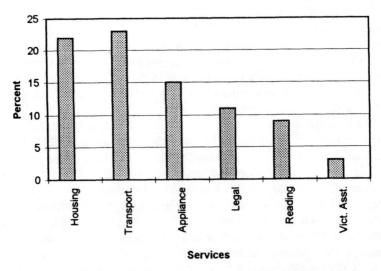

**Figure 3.3 Service needs of low- and moderate-income households**
Source:     University of Delaware, 1996

In the same survey, data was gathered relating to needs of youth living in these same households. A portion of the data collected was analyzed according to those households with someone age 17 or younger residing. Responses of those participating in the telephone segment of the survey are summarized in Figure 3.4 below. The data reveals that gaining support from the other parent and finding wholesome activities for children to participate in were the two most frequently faced problems. Over 10 percent of those respondents in the telephone survey indicated that finding day care, poor school performance, help with parenting, trouble with the law, and dropping out of school were frequent problems in their households in regards to raising their children.

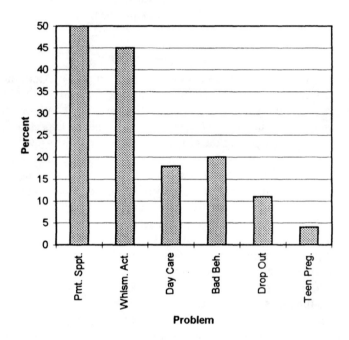

**Figure 3.4  Problems with youth age 17 or below residing in households**

Source:  University of Delaware, 1996

In order to assist families in the renewal community, time management becomes a very important aspect of being capable of solving family service needs and coping with the problems of raising children. The renewal community enters the electronic age by making concentrated effort to wire residential homes and public institutions in the neighborhood to the Internet. At best, the public library, school, museums, and other public facilities must provide free access to the Internet for those who cannot afford to have their homes connected. The key to getting residents connected to the Internet will be the job placement combined with aan infrastructure that ties into the local public school system. The Internet is expected to be an integral part of the lives of the American family in the model city; and as it generates its momentum, the reality of its impact will be immense. Three aspects of the Internet that merits consideration for the renewal community are shopping, education and job training.

*Shopping online*

Electronic commerce is quickly becoming a reality. In 1994, electronic commerce was simply a dream, something to look forward to in the distant future. As of 1997, it is estimated that ove $200 million in electronic commerce is being conducted, with the amount expected to grow geometrically every year in the near future. The key to the growth of electronic commerce will be assuring the public that consumer transactions conducted over the Internet are secure. The sending of money or money equivalent electronically without interruptions over the Internet has been the one element that continually holds back electronic commerce in the past. But with the private sector expected to generated new software packages to protect both retailers and consumers from having money stolen during the transmission process from purchaser to seller, this reservation among consumers will no doubt disappear. With heads of AFDC households expected to be working 40 to 45 hours per week once full-time jobs are obtained, there is little time left to manage household affairs. The reduce time associated with shopping online and the convenience of having goods and services delivered directly to ones home provide an alternative for parents that cannot be overlooked.

The use of the Internet is of particular value to the female head of AFDC households who is now being targeted for full-time employment. However, if we look at how her typical week will likely be if she obtains employment, we can see that time becomes a valuable commodity. Based on research by the DuPont Company on 18,000 employees, the need for flexible work hours, support for child care and public referral programs becomes much of a need by the single parent female working full time. As shown in Figure 3.5, both single-parent females and women in dual-earner families working for a large corporation such as DuPont spend over

84

45 hours per week in job related activities plus an addition 8 to 9 hours getting to and from work. However, only two hours per week are spent in volunteering and community work. In addition, a hefty 21 to 24 hours per week are devoted to child care tasks with another 18 on general household tasks. While work has its bonus in generating income so one can become independent, it also has its consequences especially as it relates to the essence of the renewal community where social capital is treated equally to economic capital.

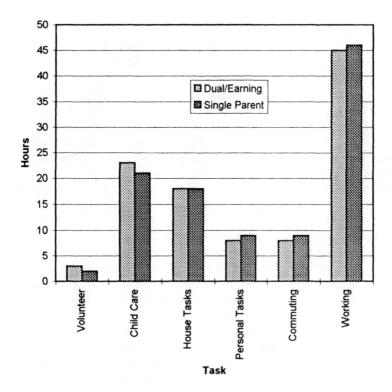

**Figure 3.5    How employed women spend their time by week**
Source:          DuPont  Study, 1996

Changing work styles are  changing family household management styles. Using the Internet to reduce the time to gain access to those goods and services required for nurturing children is becoming more feasible.

Denying residents of the renewal community access to such a time saving device would simply acerbate those problems that have always hindered AFDC families, such as not having access to information for making wise purchasing decisions. The result has been AFDC families being subject to extensive fraud and deceptions. The renewal community will remedy this by taking the initiative to 'wire' residents and public facilities quickly. The Internet will become the backbone of the community. Shopping online cannot be overlooked, and its ability to change lifestyles must be considered if residents will gain value for their money earned through the demands of full-time employment.

*Online education and job training the norm*

Time is also more of a factor job training. With a continual need to upgrade job skills, retraining is likely to become more commonplace as heads of AFDC households attempt to hold on to their jobs. In addition, keeping children 'learning active' may become a reality if they have access to innovated and challenging educational software which can be downloaded to homes. A whole new learning environment is now available to those who have access to the Internet. Online education can consist of simply learning how to do math by enrolling one course, or becoming involved in a sequence of courses leading to a certificate or a diploma. Similarly, an adult can enroll in a job-training workshop or seminar, or an entire program at a local university possibly leading to a 4-year degree.

The key component here again is 'time-saving learning'. Having to drive to a local learning facility and spend sitting time in a classroom will become the relic of education. For the working adult where time is the most valuable commodity of life, leaning outside of the public educational institution whether the local school or a community college will become commonplace. Interacting electronically with both a teachers and classmates will bring a new form of networking for residents. Bringing the outside world into the household will enable children and adults to see how complex problems can be solved through team efforts. Managing education now takes on a new perspective, one that should assist families in maintaining their skills at a level that are in demand by the business sector in the renewal community.

In terms of consumer education, there will be ample software packages to download for assisting families to manage their income and expenditures. With the financial planning software packages user friendly, any one can reduce their time in caring for their finances. Keeping records has always been a problem for most families no matter what socioeconomic class. However, online assistance for learning how to keep records, file income taxes, and develop personal balance and income statements will enhance the chances of families to succeed in maintaining their independence. Regaining control over money is critical if AFDC families are to be able to achieve their dreams. Connecting AFDC families to the Internet is a top priority of the renewal community.

*Linking nonprofit and governmental agencies electronically*

With the renewal community being established in the information age, public access to information is extremely important. Since information is the strategic commodity of the 'knowledge economy', there is also added importance to accessing data about community family support systems as businesses attempt to assure that their worker's needs are being met. Attracting qualified workers is important to those businesses that anchor the renewal community, so anything the public sector can do to assist a retailer or other company in this regard will provide a competitive edge.

Therefore, the renewal community will feature a *renewal.net* electronic network which will link neighborhood nonprofit and public sectors organizations for the purpose of disseminating information to residents quickly and at low cost. The only item a resident will require is a personal computer with a modem. Again, for those residents who are unable to afford such a connection, the public library and other public buildings will provide free access. The *renewal.net* will feature at least four kinds of services for helping residents manage their financial and other family affairs. One feature will be email for enabling residents to communicate with neighbors and business throughout the model city.

A second feature will be *an electronic public newsstand* where agencies can disseminate information to the public as to available services. There will also be a *town chat* component whereby residents can join in electronic conversation about their needs for assistance. A final component of *renewal.net* will be a *help service* where community residents can go for assistance in learning how to access the community network as well as linking to the World Wide Web. Since technology can be confusing, the model city will have a community group who will be available for advising residents through the problems that arise when learning how to use a personal computer.

While the electronic family support system may be targeted for connecting social agencies to families in need of assistance, the *renewal.net* can also include an *electronic commerce* sector in which local retailers go online for marketing goods and services. Moreover, such a connection could expand the marketing of goods and services by local merchants to a national or international audience. Therefore, by going online, both residents and retailers are provided an opportunity to join in the 'knowledge economy' through the Internet, an aspect that should especially raise the hopes of heads of AFDC families who desire to become an entrepreneur. Getting back into the mainstream is an important aspect of the renewal community.

## Using temp agencies to get back into employment

A 1990 Census Bureau survey indicated that the nation's temporary labor force could be more than 19 million workers, or 16 percent of the U.S. labor market by the year 2000. In 1995, companies spent $4.9 billion to hire temporary workers, more than doubling what they paid in 1991, according to the National Association of Temporary and Staffing Services. The U.S. Bureau of Labor Statistics estimates that temporary help agencies will continue as one of the top 10 growth industries through the year 2005. This trend is driven by corporate downsizing and restructuring as companies attempt to increase productivity without having to resort to hiring workers full-time.

Whereas temp agencies have been traditionally helpful to retirees and homemakers who simply desired to work part-time, they now are being looked at as an alternative for finding full-time employment. Although companies are hesitant to hire full-time employees on the spot, they are willing to hire temporary employees for short term project work. However, temporary workers can become full-time employees if employers desire to expand operations and in need of additional staff. Thus, temporary work is an excellent way for residents of the renewal community to generate contacts for possible full-time positions since they gain experience working with different kinds of companies. Temp agencies also provide training for their temp clients, and this is another way for welfare recipients to upgrade their skills without having to put out personal funds.

## Mentoring, an idea whose time has come

Companies are taking a particular interest in developing a networking strategy that assigns mentors to new employees for the purpose of assisting them 'learn the ropes' about management. In the past, women and minorities have had trouble finding role models in business in order to learn how to get ahead. The renewal community takes mentoring to the next level. Businesses who anchor the renewal community will be expected to create a *board of mentors* who are available to assist residents with their financial responsibilities, spending strategies, and careers. Mentors can come from both inside and outside of the renewal community. Mentors can come from professional societies, school alumni groups, local retailers, and non-profit organizations.

The idea is to have a group of mentors available to help residents with specific needs. The purpose of a strong mentoring program is to create a bond between residents and those individuals who have proven records of success. The mentors become role models not only for adults but for children in the neighborhood. Having a community advisory board of mentors can also provide the expertise so desperately needed as residents attempt to redefine their futures.

## Eliminating the training gap

According to Richard Leone, president of the Twentieth Century Fund in New York, American workers face staggering job and income losses in the coming years as a result of the upheavals from new technology, a restructuring a companies, and the global economy. As welfare reform continues to be a political salient issue, the complications of attempting to employ thousands of new workers at a time where companies are downsizing, restructuring, and not committing to full-time employment are very real. Accompanying work-force cuts is uncertainty and stress. Leone states that there is a $120 billion training gap which is the difference between the estimated $40 billion currently spent by the private sector for training and the $160 billion needed if all companies are to enhance the capabilities of their existing employees.

If show me the money is a rallying point for residents of the renewal community, then an aggressive training program will be a must. Looking at this situation from a *macroeconomics* point of view, several changes are now in order for healing America. First, a series of federal tax credits to help businesses that anchor the renewal community to pay for increased education and training programs would serve as a catalyst. Similarly, federal tax deductions for those residents who seek to upgrade their own skills individually through private training programs could also boost such efforts. Thirdly, private-public partnerships could be created that permit small businesses to join together for generating less costly group training of workers or attracting larger amounts of funding than could be obtained on their own. This alternative may require a change in current federal law about permitting small companies combine in common business needs. Finally, unemployment insurance system can also be modified to enable resident to upgrade their skills without losing their current benefits during the time of retraining.

On the *microeconomics* level, the renewal community will attract private job training companies that form formal contracts with businesses for upgrading job skills. However, such job training must guarantee placement at its conclusion. Being privately funded, it could supplement job training offered by the public school system in the community. Private sector training would likely be of short-term duration, between 3 and 6 months, and be designed to equip residents with those skills specifically required of those businesses which anchor the neighborhood. The target for the job training programs will be those weaknesses that have been identified as deadly to those seeking employment; those being, lack of work ethic, lack of dependability, and a bad attitude.

Participants in such programs will focus upon overcoming their own resistance to authority, the displaying of distracting facial expressions, (smirks and slouching), and overt remarks of disgust. Reducing gestures of defiance which undermine the building of trust between employees and employers will be emphasized. In addition, by having strict standards for success, participants who pass out of the training programs can be automatically employed by businesses who are seeking qualified employees. However, graduation from such programs will not be automatic. Participants will have to earn their graduation and subsequent placement onto the job.

According to Wilson in *When Work Disappears* (1996), only 12 percent of the employers in the Chicago area surveyed indicated that lack of entry job skills was a primary problem of inner-city applicants. The major concerns for such employers was that applicants were immature, undisciplined, and unmotivated. Therefore, job training in the renewal city will take on a different orientation than that familiar to public sector programs where passing is almost always automatic. In the renewal city, standards will be rigorous, but graduation will merit immediate recognition of success by full-time employment.

**It takes a better parent to build a community**

There is great importance in making children feel valued and respected not only by parents but other residents in the community. In the renewal community, a parenting movement will be undertaken through churches, schools, recreation centers, and town meetings. One of the primary goals of the renewal community is to increase the numbers of children who are humanely raised. With effective parents, children will be guided to learn while in school, to engage in civic activities, and to assume a social responsibility for others. They can be taught to avoid teenage pregnancy, drugs, committing violent and non-violent crime, and becoming suicidal. Sexism and racism will be reduced. The renewal community will not let parenting occur by chance.

The catalyst for developing parenting educational programs will be a town council consisting of residents serving as a support group. In many instances, heads of households do not have sufficient funds to get to a psychologist or other kinds of professionals for advice as to how to correct misdirected behavior of their children. However, changing behavior of children often begins with changing behavior of parents. Being a perfect parent is not what parenting is all about. What is top priority in the renewal community is a systematic plan for getting parents involved with the lives of their children. Teaching parents life skills which they can relay to their children is most important in the renewal community.

For example, money management is extremely important to both parents and their children. Breeding a reader is fundamental to getting a child geared to meet the rigors of public education. Assisting children understand what courage means by mean of identifying heroes and other role models helps youth to think of their futures. In this regard, helping children work with a mentor for achieving their dreams goes a long way in building self-esteem.

Assisting parents raise their children must be a community-based objective. Any success of the renewal community will be determined by how its children grow and mature. By reducing sexism and racism at early stages of life, the chance of developing a truly integrated community where trust forms the basis of all action becomes more likely. However, leaving parents isolated within the confines of their homes will not likely result in such an achievement. Parenting education is what will provide the catalyst for expanding the visions of parents and their children. Creating a climate where commitment is expected will result only after children become aware how self-discipline, education, and civic responsibility impact on their chances for success. Balancing work and leisure with child rearing through effective time management practices is at the essence of parenting. Learning how to raise children in a working environment whereby 40 to 50 hours a week may be spent in a location away from home is a challenge. In the renewal community, work domination is not the intended outcome. Balancing commitments through parenting education is one way to begin.


## Reclaiming the America marketplace and workplace

Maureen Milford, a staff reported for a local Delaware Newspaper, puts it best when she writes that nearly one-half of all women experience discrimination while 36 percent said they did not feel respected (News Journal, 1993). To many, the workplace is still traditional and patriarchal with many obstacles remain in place for women. This perspective is based upon what some label as the reneging of corporate giants to adhere to a social contract with the worker. Implied in this economic contract has been an historical commitment that a worker will receive fair treatment in return for his or her services. In return for providing skills and being loyal to a company, the worker will receive a wage that is a reward for devoting one's life to enhancing the profitability of that company. Therefore, in the model city, there is to be a reciprocity between the worker and business executives. Part of this bond between labor and management is an implied understanding that workers are to share in the financial benefits that they made possible by making a company prosperous.

By adopting the strategy of downsizing and restructuring, corporate giants have decided to exploit the worker by either outsourcing functions to 'cheap' labor found in other countries, mostly in less developed than that of America, or importing 'cheap' labor (immigrants).This exploitation of capital, in this case labor, has been elevated as a primary strategy to assure that every business quarter results in a profit. The result has been an angry and frustrated worker who has seen opportunities within the corporate structure disappear. This change in economic philosophy on part of business executives has been particularly hard on single-parent families and especially those families living in poverty. The result has been male earnings becoming stagnant since the 1990s while female earnings have adjusted upward ever so slowly. In 1983, females earned 64.9 percent of males while in 1992, the difference had narrowed to 74.2 percent, (New Journal, 1996).

While two-parent families have been able to hedge somewhat by putting a second wage earner into the labor market, the single-parent head of household has suffered disproportionately. The kinds of work which remain have been in the service sector and in mostly part-time jobs that pay close to minimum wage and offer no benefits, no retirement pensions, no opportunity for advancement, no loyalty between management and the employee, and no power. For those in poverty, the likelihood of relying upon work in the private sector for generating sufficient resources to get one's family out of poverty gets less and less. In addition, many of the small businesses that were available to hire residents no longer exist. It may be suggested that all business today is basically big business. For example, agribusiness corporate giants are replacing the small farmer, K-marts are replacing the local small retailer or corner neighborhood store, and McDonald's and Wendy's, etc., are replacing the local small town restaurant. The ability for those heads of households to live full and free lives is perceived as non-existent for many.

What our model suggests is that it may be time to rewrite the script of life for families who find themselves subjected to a new wave of obstacles. The key to getting out of poverty is work at a wage rate that results in raising family standard of living. However, if corporate giants are reneging on the economic contract with the American worker, how can we turn things around and provide a new set of opportunities? There is a need for a new model to institute a new kind of free enterprise system whereby the American worker has a say in how business and the surrounding community evolves. The model city in this instance consists of partnerships between parents, schools, businesses, and social agencies in the community. Each segment feeds off the other.

The whole community is based upon contracts in place where the rules of the game are set initially for all residents. The economic compact emphasizes the American tradition that as many residents as possible should share in the prosperity which emerges when loyalty and respect become the norm. It is a general feeling among those in poverty that government basically taxes too much, spends too much, and interferes too much in their lives. In the model proposed here, government plays a secondary role while the resident of the community is encouraged to the reinstitution of those American traditions which have made this country as great as it is. At the heart of the American tradition is volunteerism, commitment, loyalty, and self-respect. The objective of the model is to reclaim America for the working family.


## Conclusion: mastering spending and earning potential

Women are making slow headway toward parity with men in the workplace, but this is a small consolation to single-parent female heads of households where living in poverty is an everyday reality. Suzanne Bianchi and Daphne Spain in *Women, Work and Family in America* report that between 1970 and 1995, the share of women age 25 to 54 working outside the home increased from 50 percent to 76 percent, with the biggest gains in employment shown by married women with children. Even though the wage gap between males and females has generally been narrowing over the past 25 years, much of this gain has been due to stagnate wages for men. While adding value to work is expected for all employees, adding value to purchases carries a similar expectation. With wages continuing to be rather stagnant in the coming years and with a continual discrepancy between wages paid between male and female workers, there is merit for spending earnings with greater care.

Becoming money smart is now a necessity. Fraud and deception are part of today's marketplace. However, to counteract such unproductive behavior, citizens of the renewal community will be attacking traditional purchasing strategies by adopting a more communal style of spending. Timing will be introduced as the critical element to purchasing. Purchasing commonly required products through group spending will be more commonplace. Attracting retailers and business anchors who promote generally accepted community standards that enhance the quality of life of residents is critical. Correspondingly, show me the money reflects the ability to get a job with a living wage, the spending of wages in efficient ways to get added value with every purchase, and the reclaiming of both the workplace and marketplace that generates trust and cooperation.

In order for show me the money to become a reality, residents of the renewal community must accept three valuable responsibilities. The first is to participate in rigorous job training programs by challenging themselves to persist and never give up no matter how difficult obstacles to employment appear to be. Secondly, residents must hold local merchants and businesses that anchor their neighborhood to the highest standards of ethics and performance. Becoming alert when purchasing products and services is important to getting value for money spent. Participating in the American dream by investing in its future through sound financial planning strategies is the third and most important piece of the puzzle of show me the money. Putting all these pieces together into a financial management strategy helps families take a giant step toward independence. However, financial independence will only come about through hard work, persistence, and drive.

# Part Two

## A DESPERATE NEED FOR TRUE

## WELFARE REFORM

# 4 Families of poverty in disarray

The American family comes in many styles including single, unmarried and widowed without children, single parents, step-parents, homosexual couples, teenagers raising children, and the more traditional biological two-parent model. In addition, according to the U.S. Bureau of the Census, families have been getting smaller and smaller since 1970, (Thompson, 1996). For example, in 1970, one of every five households had five or more persons whereas in 1996, the number has been reduced to one of every ten. In 1970, approximately 40 percent of households consisted of children with both parents present whereas in 1996, such families account for only 25 percent. In addition, in 1970, individuals living alone represented one of every six households whereas in 1996, they make up one of every four households. It appears that the family in 1996 is smaller with fewer children and more likely to have only one parent present.

According to Yagaoda and Westheimer (1996) in *The Value of Family*, the two most vital qualities for nurturing a family are 'love and commitment'. However, in this regard, some families have not been as fortunate as others. Some families are subjected to unusual pressures resulting from their inability to become a stable unit while functioning within the parameters of a democracy. While it is difficult to identify the one primary reason for this failure of not being able to achieve a standard of living that reflects the expectations of most in one of the richest countries in the world, the fact remains that a considerably large number of individuals are unable to succeed both at work and at home.

Society depends upon the passing from one generation to the next a set of values that depicts what America is all about. Values important to American traditions have been those such as education, commitment, work, sharing, helping those in need, and respect for individual rights. In addition, the passing on of past customs and mores is critical to taking society to the next level. Not repeating the mistakes of the past relieves

97

future citizens of historical failures, permitting time to design better ways to solve problems as they arise.

Immigration, a mobile labor class, and a fast-changing global economy have resulted in a substantial number of children in poverty. Many 'professionals' who attempt to assist families in need have traditionally focused upon the theme of 'child saving'. Examples of societal attempts to help children in families of poverty have been the abolition of child labor, advocacy of compulsory education, day care, food stamps, and a variety of public health services. The debate for assisting children in need has generally evolved around the merits of public agencies primarily at the state and local level. A second debate has focused upon how to develop a social support system that may be appropriate for keeping biological parents together. A third strand of the debate has been how to integrate the non-profit sector (through public service obligations on the part of every citizen) into a strategy of mentoring our children. Protecting our children continues to be the rallying cry of welfare reformers who continue to suggest innovative ideas about the benevolence of the State as the primary catalyst for protecting the rights of those less fortunate.

**Shifting demographics**

Since the 1970s, there has been a surge in the rate of divorces and out-of-wedlock births for those parents of families in poverty. An outcome of these two trends is the emergence of large numbers of families with a single parent as the head of the household. By 1989, slightly more than half of all families in poverty were headed by a single women. Single-parent families have one of the highest poverty rates of all family types. Dissolution of marriage is another demographic that correlates closely to families in poverty. Whether because of abandonment, separation, divorce, or death of a spouse, marriages dissolved with greater frequency since the 1970s. This trend of family dissolution has serious economic consequences in that it has a tendency to drive households into 'instant poverty'.

*Surge of children in poverty*

With the surge of divorce and out-of-wedlock births has come an increasing number of children living in poverty. Akerlof of the University of California at Berkeley and Janet Yellen (1996) of the Federal Reserve's Board of Governors argue that the marital contract between parents and children has changed so dramatically that it actual spurs illegitimacy. Their studies conclude that the availability of the birth control pill and the legalization of abortion has weakened the female's ability to gain a commitment from the biological father. They suggest that young women who engaged in pre-martial sex have traditionally been able to obtain a promise of marriage from their partner. This trend toward a non-commitment on the part of both parents has resulted in a large number of children being born and raised by one parent, changing the expectations of parents as to what roles are to be played by each parent. Female-headed households typically have the highest poverty rates of all family types as alluded to earlier in our discussion, (Hira, 1996). This trend has serious economic consequences for children in that it results in placing a substantial financial burden upon those heads of households least capable of supporting others. As illustrated in Figure 4.1 on the next page, one child in five under age 18 currently lives in poverty.

A significant aspect of family life is the role parents play in rearing their children. When we further examine the makeup of the contemporary family, children appear to be facing a rather different set of parental relationships than prior generations. According to figures gather by M. Fanco Salvoza from National Parenthood Initiative, approximately 14 million lived in mother-only households in 1990, (Father Figures, 1996, p. 5). The number of children who do not live with their biological fathers has also been increasing over the past decades. In 1960, the number of single parent families resulting from divorce was approximately 800,000. The number in 1996 was just under 1.2 million. In addition, the children in these families spend on the average 6 years in a single-parent family. Compounding the circumstance that children are more likely to be found in single-parent families is the fact that approximately 1 million babies are born to unwed women. Unfortunately, the statistics also depict a large portion of these babies born to mothers under age 20. A final disturbing statistic is that in 1996, two-thirds of the 10 million women with children in father-absent homes receive no child support from the biological fathers, (Father Figures, 1996, p. 5).

*Mobile families*

Another intriguing characteristic of families is their mobility. Factors contributing to this mobility are usually economic in nature. According to Hira (1996), individuals often move to take advantage of job opportunities. However, there is an important social consequence to this new phenomenon. Many children lose regular access to the extended family. Hira suggests that the extended family has less opportunity to perform an important function of transmitting value from one generation to the next. Grandparents, sisters and

99

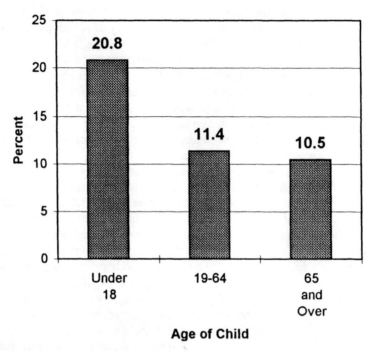

**Figure 4.1  Percentage of children in poverty by age group**
Source:      Census Bureau, 1996

brothers, and other primary family relations are being displaced through geographical separation resulting from a need to obtain employment. In their place is an institutionalized environment consisting of public day care centers, place of employment child care facilities, and private church support groups. Therefore, the roles played by family members, in addition to two parents, are being displaced by an economic reality

Providing for both the economic and emotional needs of children is quite demanding in a family where one individual has responsibility for both. Bane and Ellwood (1995) state that meeting the needs of child care while attempting to hold a full-time job makes it difficult to cope with child rearing crises such as taking care of a sick child, being available for school holidays, and making visits to a physician. Therefore, without the support system of the extended family, children are placed in a position of witnessing their parents struggle through everyday responsibilities, resulting in great uncertainty when relying on them to solve daily problems. A lack of success here lays the groundwork for failure as these children eventually assume similar roles as head of their own families. The role models may become detrimental to creating the kind of nurturing necessary in order to connect children to events that are important to their young lives.

Bane and Ellwood suggest that the critical element in enhancing child welfare is having a family support system in place that can handle the idiosyncrasies of everyday life. The ingredient that has to be replaced because of the dissolving of the extended family is a spirit and camaraderie that comes about from the 'bonding' of parents and children. The kind of family system now required may be considered by today's standards informal, but it represents a spirit of bonding where individuals, not organizations, care for one another, where self-initiative becomes expected within a community, and where neighbors must fulfill the responsibility of helping others in time of need. Historically, it has been the local community and the family social support system that has helped families through those difficult times that keeps families together. This has been part of the American tradition, and one that presents the greatest of challenges as new family management systems emerge.

*Deadbeat fathers*

Then there is the issue of deadbeat fathers. Searching out and finding deadbeat fathers is not exactly the best role model for parents to set for their children. Of the 10 million women with children in father-absent homes, a substantial number receive no support from the biological father, (Salvoza, 1996). Family expectations are part of a 'giving and receiving' model in which individuals balance their personal and family lives by demonstrating to their children that each person assumes a variety of roles throughout one's life pattern. When one parent is not perceived as giving, a narrow perspective of life is developed. The expectation in society is for parents to stay together so they can benefit from the advantages of the free enterprise system. The strength of the American marketplace has been the freedom to choose from alternatives as one purchases goods and services. It has been a similar expectation that united families situated in a free enterprise system can better enhance their welfare by making their own choices without government interference, an outlook that differentiates the U.S. from other economic and political systems throughout the world.

*Surrogate families*

The traditional two-parent family is now evolving into a family in disarray for many households in poverty. This somewhat dysfunctional family is the result of many years of a welfare system with good intent but also with a predominance of misdirected policies. In 1995, the FBI reported that there are approximately 25,000 gangs consisting of between 300,000 to 500,000 members. These gangs may be considered surrogate families in that they set the rules and corresponding behavior that dominates relationships. Such rules are likely to take precedent over those set by parents of children. Gang violence simply reflects the lack of stability that some individuals have in their lives every single day.

Michael Hedges of the Scripps Howard News Service reports that teenage girls committed a quarter of all juvenile crimes in 1995. More than 700,000 girls were arrested pushing their crime rate up faster than that of teenage boys. In 1983, about one in five arrests of teenagers was classified as a female; in 1995, it is now one in four. Since 1983, the rate of female juveniles arrested rose 23 percent, more than twice the rate of boys arrested, which rose only 11 percent. One factor attributing to such a rise in female crime is the increasing number of female gangs that have emerged since 1980, (Poe-Yamagata, 1996).

The forcing of families of poverty into one model for everybody is not what this nation is all about. What has resulted is a series of strong emotions and resentment from those who have been repeatedly subjected to the rigid practices and policies of governmental agencies. Forcing members of a family to meet the expectations of an outside group suggests a degree of elitism, a perception that places responsibility and leadership outside of the immediate family, specifically, the parents of a household. Another result has been many of our youth seeking 'other role models' or surrogate families such as gangs who can bring some direction, success, and bonding into their lives.

With families straining at their seams, and with role models being removed to a position of subservient to an outside governmental force, the thread that holds families together is 'frayed' and at the point of breaking beyond repair. Members of families generally desire to set their own future, to determine what is best for them, and make choices that meet their needs. Families do not desire to be forced into accepting low-paying jobs, into specific job-training programs out of desperation, or into participating in mediocre health care programs for members of their families. Members of families do not desire to be forced into living arrangements where their safety may be sacrificed. One result of this discontentment is the formation of 'complementary families' such as gangs where a new set of parameters are put into place for our youth. When expectations within one family framework cannot be achieved, then another will emerge to supplant the first.

*The diversity of poverty*

It is important to be reminded here that families on welfare do not reflect a dominance of just one culture, nationality, or race. These families represent the diversity of our society. For example, approximately 40 percent of welfare recipients are white; 40 percent, black; and 17 percent, Hispanic. The average family size of welfare recipients is approximately 2.9 persons with most living in urbanized areas. The number of families receiving aid has increased 163

102

percent from 1970 to 1973, from 1.9 million families to approximately 5 million. Since 1960, the share of white children born out of wedlock has soared six-fold to nearly 20 percent, and the black illegitimacy rate has tripled to 66 percent. The high rate of poverty and related social ills that plague many of this nation's families does not focus upon any one segment of our society, (Hoffman, 1996).

Most experts agree that the welfare system of the past has many flaws. Saul Hoffman (1996) of the University of Delaware suggests that the safety net in place has resulted in additional pressures to divide families rather than to bring the together. Hoffman argues that welfare benefits have been readily available and perhaps more generous to singe-parent families than married-coupled families. Hoffman (1996) further points out that the welfare system generally encourages the breakup of a married-couple family. For example, if a father cannot find work, his mere presence in a household may stand in the way of a family receiving welfare benefits.

In addition to a rise in divorce rates, Hoffman points out to the rise of births to single women, especially teenagers. For example, in 1991, about 6.2 percent of American teenage women gave birth. This is about twice as high as the birth rate in the United Kingdom and about seven times as high as in France. In addition, about two-thirds of such births are to unmarried teenagers, most of whom later seek welfare benefits. In addition, many single-parent teenage mothers who do obtain welfare remain in poverty. The rate of child poverty in the United States has risen from 15 percent of all children in 1970 to 22 percent in 1990. Hoffman (1996) points out that this is the highest rate in the developed world. For example, only 10 percent of Canadian children are in poverty and only 5 percent of Swedish children.

*A surge of immigrants*

In 1997, it is predicted that legal immigration will surge to 854,000 with an additional 300,000 entering this nation illegally. The number of immigrants are expected to increase by 100,000 annually over the next decade. By 2050, it is estimated that there will be nearly 400 million American citizens in this country, including a larger new wave of immigrants. Therefore, the diversity of the American family is expected to continue. Some 785,000 resident aliens collected U.S. Supplementary Security Income (SSI) in 1995, and around 550,000 drew checks under the Aid to Families with Dependent Children. The cost to American taxpayers, not counting non-cash aid such as food stamps, was more than $5 billion in 1995, (Pearson, 1996).

These immigrants come to this country with their vision of the American dream. They come in search of a destiny not only for themselves but for their families. Language is a key issue for these immigrants. Although many immigrants do not speak English when they arrive in this country, most seek out strategies to 'blend or melt' into the American mainstream. What is specially significant to immigrants is their perception that learning to speak English is to their economic benefit. For example, a study of Southeast Asian refugees in Houston, Texas, found that those persons who could speak English fluently earned almost three times as much money as those who only spoke a few words. Ninety-percent of Hispanics, according to a recent Latino National Political Survey, placed language development as vital to enhancing one's financial success in this country, (Chavez, 1996).

Chavez and Miller also point out that the work ethic of today's immigrants is just as strong as that of the Irish, Italians, and Polish of past years. According to the 1990 census, foreign-born males have a 76 percent labor-force participation rate, compare to 74 percent for native-born Americans. Hispanics have the highest rate of any group, 83 percent. In this regard, immigrants often start on the lowest rungs of the economic ladder and move up. Typically, their household incomes reach parity with a native-born American after about ten years. In addition, immigrant-owned businesses are frequently found in the inner city, thus becoming a revitalizing force. Examples of this are the turnaround of parts of New York City, Newark, and Washington, DC. The stability of the family has had a positive effect upon the ability to start of new place of business. In this regard, only 6.6 percent of foreign-born are on welfare in 1995, compare to 4.9 percent of native-born Americans.

The expectations of immigrants have generally been to seek strategies to 'melt into the mainstream' of the American marketplace. The obtaining of the American dream is perceived as being accomplished by devising strategies that focus on family strengths and support systems. Family bonding is extremely important as parents and their children establish small businesses in the communities in which they live. It is through the informal support systems that many of these families make their way as a private entrepreneur. It is through the information support systems that many immigrants get themselves educated for the purpose of working in corporate America. Therefore, many immigrants and their families are good examples of how letting the energy and imagination of individuals 'run free of one model support-syndrome' result in vibrant and cohesive communities and families. In addition, the establishing of successful role models provides a better transition for passing on important values and beliefs to children.

Of particular interest to Americans is the number of Mexican immigrants that make their way into the United States each year. Many U.S. citizens perceive Mexican immigrants as remaining in the U.S. for long periods of time because they are attracted to the U.S. by extensive welfare and social programs that are not available in Mexico. However, according to a study completed by the Public Policy Institute of San Francisco, most Mexican immigrants are young and single. They only remain in the U.S. for short periods of time as they customarily return home when their savings have been accumulated. The institute reports that only 20 percent of all Mexican immigrants stay in the U.S. for more than five years and concludes that Mexican immigrants will generally return their homeland if wages are too low, rather than seeking welfare.

Therefore, social welfare programs have little effect on migration decisions of Mexican immigrants in particular, (Reyes, 1997). Of course, basing future immigration habits based upon historical trend may be challenged since immigration continues to play a significant part in employment trends, particularly in the Southwest part of the U.S. In terms of welfare reform, federal restrictions on access to social programs by legal immigrants have been significantly tightened.

**An emerging underclass**

In the 1970s, Time magazine announced the *emergence of the underclass*, a term associated with an increasing number of families primarily found in the inner cities. A critical point made in this piece was the fact that such a bleak environment nurtures values that are at odds with those of the majority. It was also inferred at that time that this new underclass produces a highly disproportionate number of this nation's juvenile delinquents, school dropouts, and welfare mothers. The emergence of the underclass was considered a metaphor for a social transformation that draws the attention of society to a 'glitch' in America's showcase to the rest of the world. According to Mickey Kaus, author of the *End of Equality* (1992), the continual presence of the underclass poses a great challenge to the public sphere and social equality.

The major issues of the underclass debate relate to how public institutions such as schools, social welfare agencies, and religious organizations can assist families in their struggles to survive in a community which appears to be hostile at times. Questions that were proposed during the 1970s remain today. The answers to these questions are crucial to enhancing family welfare for many Americans attempting to raise their standard of living. Does public welfare destroy the will of heads of household to work and therefore erode family stability? What is the role of culture (defined as the influence of sets of attitudes, values, and group behaviors) in changing the perspective of family strategies for enhancing their own welfare, rather than depending upon public welfare programs for leading them out of poverty? What is a family's responsibility to make contributions that benefit society as a whole? How can a family perform its vital functions in neighborhoods that may reflect high levels of crime, low school attendance, pre-martial pregnancy, and a spirit of desperation and lack of pride? What is the capacity of public institutions to counteract the weaknesses of both families and neighborhoods for bringing about a revitalization of communities in need of stability?

*Families move to isolation*

Compounding the problems of children in families of poverty has been the emergence of three transformations that have led to the 'postindustrial society'. A most significant transformation has been an economic one in which manufacturing as the core of the American economy has now been replaced with information production, with the result of higher-paying, lower-skilled jobs typical of the industrial era disappearing in favor of those characterized as lower-paying, service-oriented in nature. A second transformation is one of demographics in that communities consisting primarily of European ancestry have been replaced with African-Americans, Latinos, and other immigrants who have traditionally been at the lower-end of the socio-economic scale. The final and most significant transformation is that of spatial in which large numbers of families migrated to suburban communities which resulted in a heightened segregation in many inner cities. According to Katz (1995) in *Improving Poor People,* these three transformations have combined to create not only a new urban form, but a new kind of urban family, one that has difficulty making ends meet.

The 'depopulation' of American cities and the 'deindustrialization' of the economy have placed additional burdens upon the inner city family-- as well as many in the rural areas. These two processes have isolated large numbers of families from the mainstream of the American culture. What has resulted is a variety of sub-cultures which reflect families with varying values, beliefs, and customs. With cities having difficulty cultivating a sufficient number of jobs for its citizens, the expectations for improving living conditions of residents are lowered for those possessing marginal job skills. According to Katz (1992), poverty now increasingly exists within a context of hopelessness. Children of these families are also likely to perceive poverty and dependence upon government as reality since they see their parents isolated in communities where jobs and a living wage are not available. With heads of households being chronically unemployed for long periods of time, children are connecting their own poverty with poor schooling, lack of opportunity to escape from the inner city, and isolation.

Joblessness, inadequate education, and poor health intensify the need to come to a consensus as to how to reverse the negative aspects of past public policy. In many communities where there are large pockets of families living in poverty, public schools do not educate their children, the local police do not prevent an escalation of crime, violence, and the use of illegal drugs, and the health care system does not tend to the needs of 'expecting mothers'.

Although there are some differences that distinguish white from black families, the issue of poverty is not basically race related. Similar pressures over the past several decades have reshaped all families. The issue is not what has happened to the black, white, Latino, or underclass family, rather it is an understanding of how to change present circumstances in order for these and all other families to maintain their pride. The diversity of poverty and the reasons for poverty should not distract us from the ultimate goal of society; that is, to redistribute society's opportunities through a system that protects the rights of all families. The issue of families in poverty is a people issue, an equity issue, and a destiny issue.

*Proliferation of female-head households*

Since the 1960s, women's opportunities in the labor force have expanded considerably. African-American women who had been virtually excluded from well-paying jobs in the 1950s, have been the greatest beneficiaries of expanded work opportunities. According to Mark Stern (1993), during the 1960s and 1970s, African-American women's average earnings and those of black men and white women converged. He goes on to suggest that there also may have been two contradictory effects upon the household. Stern argues that improved female opportunities may have negatively impacted upon the male heads of households in terms of reducing their incomes. Jobs which were exclusively held by male heads of households are now subject to wage competition by females. Kathryn Neckerman (1993) goes one step further in suggesting that the resulting gender conflict in families of the urban poor through the enhanced opportunities of females to obtained higher paying jobs may have increased their willingness to escape from unsatisfactory marriages or to avoid marriage altogether. Neckerman concludes that women's economic emergence may have contributed to the proliferation of female-headed families, and notably in urban communities.

Although the rise of wages was an important contributor to perhaps leading to a decline in families in poverty since the 1960s, women's work specifically has been a powerful force in the realignment of the family's decision making process. Whereas women in families prior to this time period relied upon the male household head to provide a living wage, changes in the employment sector over the past three decades have added a new dimension to this phenomena. With women now getting into more of the mainstream of employment, the roles of females and males have directly been affected. A resulting possible decline in the wages of males have been counterbalanced by the increasing wages now being obtained from women in the workplace. According to Stern (1996), family strategies during the 1970s relied more upon extending the roles of both male and female wage earners for enhancing family living conditions. Moreover, the expansion of the economy over the past several decades has permitted more than one family member to seek full-time employment to compensate for slower growth of wages.

Stern reminds us that the current irregularity of employment, economic dislocation, and urban restructuring is taking its toll on all American families. It is also important to note that the families at the 'bottom of the socioeconomic ladder' struggle more than others, thus generating a whole new set of problems even when there are two wage earners. The classic situation in the 1990s is that with women wages leveling off and male wages actually in a state of decline, the increased opportunities for female employment has now resulted in additional pressures for change in public policy. The capability of two-parent families, let alone a single-parent household, to provide for a stable family environment is being challenged.


**Disruptive public welfare policy**

Public welfare as we perceive it today originated in 1935 as Aid to Dependent Children (later Aid to Families with Dependent Children). This legislation was part of President Franklin Roosevelt 's program to raise the standard of living of thousands of families attempting to make their way out of the depression. Its original purpose was to assist mothers who had become widows. However, after World War II, the Aid to Families with Dependent Children was revised to help unmarried or separated women with children. As time progressed, the AFDC program began to take on a new dimension by setting criteria for participation. For example, a 'suitable home' clause was introduced into AFDC regulations to control the sexual behavior of women. In this instance, females were required to maintain a separate household for their children, preferably one with the biological father. However, another AFDC regulation denied a female financial assistance if a man other than the biological father was living in a household. In the 1980s, AFDC was again revised by cutting off aid to a household if a woman with a child lived with working relatives or friends. In this instance, AFDC failed to recognize the increasing number of families who respond to hard times by forming extended households, (Katz, 1993).

As a primary program that applies to the poorest of families, AFDC recipients are subjected to a stigma in that they are relying upon public funds for survival. Families in poverty have noticed that the benefits received from AFDC are notably lower than that of Social Security, which has been categorized by some as a welfare program that delivers disproportionate benefits to the middle class. Another public welfare program often criticized by the poor is that of the income-tax deduction for home mortgage interest. Other public policies have had detrimental effects upon families of poverty, especially those found in urban centers.

For example, as a result of the Great Depression of the 1930s, the federal government began to underwrite mortgages to help thousands of citizens to either keep their existing homes or to purchase new ones. However, one unfortunate outcome has been the emergence of 'redlining' whereby banks labeled communities as a poor risk, preventing residents to get loans. In this way, the federal government acted as a catalyst for hastening the decay of inner cities. It was easier for families to get mortgage money for purchasing new homes in other neighborhoods, especially in suburban areas, rather than in their own community.

Additional public policies also hastened the decay of American cities and family stability. Mortgages for veterans, the development of interstate highways, and tax deductions interest paid on mortgages all accelerated the growth of the suburbs. The newly organized governments in many of the suburbs had much autonomy in land use, zoning, and deed restrictions that had a tendency to excluded immigrants, poor families, and many minorities. Therefore, the result of past government policies at both the local and federal level has been suburbs drawing tighter boundaries around cities. What has been left in cities are poor residents requiring expensive services but with little ability to pay for them.

*The dependency trap*

As public agencies attempt to keep families together, their past record has been questioned in terms of reality. Bane and Ellwood (1996) both argue that what has resulted through the casework model is a series of misplaced assumptions about how to assist those families in need of financial support. What has actually resulted is a series of rigid and punitive policies that have done more to disrupt family unity than to enhance it. Bane and Ellwood argue that the result has been the emergence of the *dependency trap* in which families receive income maintenance for long periods of time with little hope of ever moving off welfare.

Welfare reform advocates who worry about dependency often refer to perverse values and irresponsible behavior of those receiving welfare benefits. Bane and Ellwood refer to welfare dependency as a habit that robs people of their self-esteem and dignity. The key to getting families out of the welfare habit is enabling individuals to gain control over their own personal lives and situations in the workplace. Bane and Ellwood suggest that as long as heads of households perceive work as minimum wage service to their employers, those families in poverty will not likely change their expectations as to what the future may bring. And in addition, as long as welfare assistance intrudes upon family relationships while stigmatizing families to the rest of society, the dependency trap becomes a safety net that only desperate people will subject themselves to in search for their survival.

It is important to note that under the logo of welfare reform, future welfare benefits are not likely to remain perpetual. A time limit of some kind will be put into place to encourage parents to seek and obtain work. However, the challenge for keeping families together is to find work that has a respectable living wage attached to it. The challenge is also to enhance the expectations of families by assuring that a safety net remains in some form as the marketplace continually evolves into advanced stages of technological development. Therefore, if policies are not put into place to assure sufficient employment for those parents in families below the poverty level, then a new form a dependency may reemerge.

*The scourge of urban renewal*

Urban renewal policies of the past have customarily included the tearing down of community housing but failing to replace such housing with affordable units. Katz (1993) reports that between 1950 and 1960, urban renewal resulted in the tearing down of approximately 128,000 units, may of which rented for an average of $50 to $60 per month. They were replaced with only 28,000 units with an average rental of $195. In place of homes, past urban renewal policy encouraged the redevelopment of central cities with office tower, hospitals, universities, and the facilities that service them. Similarly, the 1956 Highway Act created an interstate highway system in which cities were reimbursed 90 percent to cover construction costs. According to Katz (1993), the new highways encourage movement away from the cities to the suburbs. In addition, they also created barriers between sections of cities, walling off poor families from central business districts.

The punitive elements to past public policy have resulted in families being subjected to increasing number of obstacles in their attempt to remain viable. However, each added another level of burden to already overburdened parents. The effects of such policies are still being felt today. Although there has been a movement to tear down large public housing units and replace with smaller townhouse-oriented communities, the reality is that many families in poverty remain outside the framework of public policy. While some have been helped, others remain destitute. As in Figure 4.2, approximately 20 percent or over 15 million children feel the effects of past public policy failure. These children still cope with hunger, poor housing, illness, accidents, general crime and family violence. Such a continual barrage of helplessness leads to a demoralized generation with an acceptance of passivity as a strategy of endurance.

110

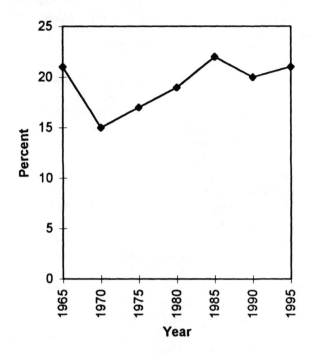

**Figure 4.2   Percentage of children in poverty 1965-1995**
Source:      Census Bureau, 1996

*A driving wedge between families and institutions*

Attacked for inaccessibility, inadequacy,  and unresponsiveness, public
and private institutions have deserted many American families of
financial need.  Families often find themselves in the midst of political
contradictions.  Katz (1995) argues that the only viable institution that
has remained a positive factor for assisting families in need is the church.
As institutions such as local schools, hospitals, and the police are
removed from a community (and in their place regional versions are
created), the basis of creating a wholesome neighborhood also disappears.
An inevitable consequence is a corresponding movement towards a
privatization of crucial neighborhood services as witnessed through the
emergence of private medical outpatient labs, private schools/daycare
centers, and a private security force. Therefore, the stable community

which families seek gradually disappears, and in its place evolves distant replicas of the local community in regional centers far away from the urban resident.

Therefore, as securing an improved quality of life becomes more elusive, those families living in poor neighborhoods have a tendency to collapse. As Katz (1995) notes, without a public sphere of involvement, no policies directed toward family and work can reshape relationships between businesses, residents, and social workers. The result is a cynical withdrawal of families from their communities and the emergence of isolated households all attempting to struggle through life's uncertainties. Families in such communities function is disarray with a lack of control over their own destinies. What is reinforced is a group of 'sub-cultures' perpetuated through violence on the streets and gang allegiance reflecting another kind of family where few rules exit. Therefore, institutional withdrawal and collapse not only rob families of the services they need, they undermind the foundation that sustains a viable public life and a societal spirit. The lives of everyone are diminished with little hope of change in existing living conditions.

Without the reemergence of local institutions, a new strategy is required for dealing with crime, poverty, ignorance, and disease. Moreover, existing welfare policies have mixed goals of reform, deterrence, punishment, and compassion. Moreover, families often may find it difficult to maneuver within a system in which consistency is non-existence. With so many differing signals, families tend to resort to familiar support systems that may be challenged by the 'political establishment' as inappropriate (eg., non-biological parents, multi-family dwellings, and surrogate parents such as grandmothers, aunts, uncles, etc.).

Therefore, the failure of public institutions touches all Americans in some form. However, such failure appears to impact on poor families with greater force than more affluent Americans. Poor families have great difficult purchasing private schooling when public education fails or purchasing private security systems when the public police cannot deter crime and violence in a neighborhood. The cumulative failure of public institutions challenges the essence of society where growth and some degree of prosperity are expected by all. There are certain basic public services all Americans are entitled to, and without the equal distribution of those services, some segments of society will suffer. Those families of poverty continue to suffer from a lack of consistent support that matches the values, customs, and beliefs of recipients.

## Domestic growth and continued family despair

There has been an assumption that economic growth is directly related to reducing levels of poverty. As the theory goes, as a country produces more goods and services each year, it creates additional wealth. With this additional wealth, a country has new resources available in which to address societal problems related to poverty. Therefore, it is simply a matter of spreading the wealth to those in need. It made common sense for government to simply tax the incomes of those who are working and who are benefiting from the additional wealth they are creating in order to generate sufficient funds for programs to aid families in poverty. Therefore, with patience and a good deal of persistence, poverty could be eliminated.

In the 1960s, economic growth appeared to be the way out for a society seeking to eliminate poverty from its conscience. From 1960 to 1969, real gross domestic product did grow at an annual rate of 4.1 percent. During this same period, the percentage of all persons in poverty declined by 5.9 percent. However, since 1969, there has been surprisingly little progress made to even reduce the number of persons in poverty further. In fact, during the 1980s when the United States experienced a long peacetime period of economic expansion, the poverty rate for this country remained at 8.2 percent of all American households. As illustrated in Table 4.1 on the next page, even though there was a significant increased in GNP in the past three decades, the reduction in poverty has been negligible.

### Table 4.1
### Effect of domestic growth on income poverty rate

| Decade | Percentage-point Reduction in Poverty for Each 1 percent Increase in GNP |
|---|---|
| 1960 - 1969 | - 0.403 |
| 1970 - 1979 | - 0.220 |
| 1980 - 1989 | - 0.247 |

Source: Federal Reserve Bank, Cleveland, 1996

Therefore, there has been a breakdown in a correlation between an increase in the domestic GNP and poverty reduction. Possible reasons for this breakdown may be related to such factors as demographic shifting, consumption inequality, and lack of education of heads of households in poverty.

*Consumption inequality*

The consumption power of families in poverty also diminished somewhat over the past several decades. Since the 1960s, Table 4.2 on the next page illustrates that for each 1 percent increase in Gross National Product, there was a corresponding reduction in the purchasing power of families in poverty. In all three decades since the 1960s, families in poverty have experienced a slight decrease in their consumption, once again illustrating that they have not been partaking in the aggregate income growth of other families during these same time periods. As we analyze the consumption power of those families in poverty, there appears to be little evidence that a relationship exists between economic growth and consumption ability of families in poverty. It may be concluded that the 'trickle-down theory' espoused by many public officials especially during the 1980s did not become operational for those families in poverty.

**Table 4.2**
**Effect of GDP and personal consumption expenditures
on consumption poverty rate**

| Decade | Percentage-point Reduction in Poverty for Each 1 percent in Reduction GDP Growth |
|---|---|
| 1960 - 1969 | - 0.232 |
| 1970 - 1979 | - 0.236 |
| 1980 - 1989 | - 0.199 |

Source: Federal Reserve Bank, Cleveland, 1996

*Income inequality expands*

The Census Bureau reports that the average income of the bottom fifth of the U.S. population remains below 1979 levels. For example, in Table 4.3, incomes for families in the bottom one-fifth decreased 3.2 percent between 1979 an 1995. However, for those families classified as in the top one-fifth, their income increased by 4.1 percent as measured in 1995 constant dollars.

**Table 4.3**
**Average income by household group**
**(1995 Constant Dollars)**

| Year | Bottom 1/5 | Top 1/5 |
|------|-----------|---------|
| 1995 | $8,350 | $109,411 |
| 1994 | 7,982 | 108,947 |
| 1993 | 8,629 | 105,118 |
| 1979 | 8,473 | 88,536 |
| | % changed | |
| 79-95 | - 3.2% | + 4.1% |

Source: Federal Reserve Bank, Cleveland, 1996

Correspondingly, as wages had a tendency to decrease for those in the bottom one-fifth of households, the number of families without health coverage also increased. The number of Americans lacking health insurance continued to increase with the number of uninsured growing by 9 million between 1987 and 1995.

*Growth in entitlements not the answer*

The era between 1960 and 1980 has often been referred to as the *Age of Entitlement*. This was the time when society expected our social problems to be solved. Government intervention was perceived as the way to get families out of poverty and into the mainstream of society. Our vision consists of a new and better society whereby racism, crime, and poverty would be eliminated. A compassionate government would protect the poor, the elderly, and those who for some reason could not reap the benefits of the free enterprise system. Our expectation was that public policy ensure the rights of all Americans to experience an acceptable standard of living. It was thought that Americans are entitled to share in the prosperity which had resulted from advances in technology and mass production.

The three major entitlements of government are related to social security, Medicare and public welfare subsidies to families with special needs. Even though our discussion here focuses upon welfare subsidies, the entire public safety net for all citizens effects how true welfare reform may come about. For example, whereas total entitlement spending in 1965 amount to approximately $186 billion, that figure increased to approximately $900 billion in 1997. The growth in funding for entitlements sets the backdrop for the discussion on how to reform welfare. Total funding for welfare alone in 1960 was about $23 billion whereas in 1997, that amount increased to $308 billion. Therefore, providing a safety net for those families in poverty has resulted in a program that has increased almost 1,500 percent since its conception in the early 1960s. Similarly, total spending for social security and Medicare has increased substantially, which places pressure on policy makers to examine all three programs for the purpose of reducing pressing federal deficits, (U.S. Office of Management, 1997).

In this regard, in 1965, two-thirds of all federal spending went for programs that were specifically budgeted items such as payment for national defense, interstate highway system, and management of public lands, etc. The other one-third of the federal budget consisted of funding entitlements such as social security, Medicare, and general welfare subsidies to families in need. However, in 1997, the opposite allocations are true. Now, more than two-thirds of all spending in the federal budget relates to funding entitlements whereas one-third of the remaining budget supports national defense, transportation, and other domestic needs. Of course, not only did the proportion of federal funds allocated to entitlements change over the past several decades, the total amount of the federal budget also increased sharply. Based on this trend, many individuals believe that unless we can get control of the growth of the federal government, continued increases in spending will result is a financial disaster with huge yearly deficits leading to higher interest rates, lower business profits, and higher unemployment. Therefore, it is commonly accepted that entitlement spending must be significantly reduced by establishing sensible limits to expectations on the part of all citizens in terms what government can and can not do.

The public welfare system was designed to provide a safety net for those individuals who may be disabled, blind, widowed, injured, or poor. The current welfare system is over 50 years old. However, the growth of entitlements since 1960 has been most significant. The percentage increase in transfer payments to those families in need increased at an annual rate of 6 percent per year during the 1960s and 1970s. However, during the 1980s, transfer payments decreased at an annual rate of 2 percent. Moreover, such programs as Medicaid, food stamps, social security supplements, Aid for Families with Dependent Children, and other income supplemental programs do not appear to have assisted heads of households to find their way back into employment. The shifting of the so-called 'safety net' from one of expanding services to one of fend for yourself has put families in poverty in substantial jeopardy. Whether such a philosophy results in vast improvement in the standard of living of those families in poverty remains to be determined. However, it may be argued that in the past, economic growth did not parallel with similar growth in the income levels of those families in poverty.

What infuriates many Americans is that we have not arrived at this new state of family stability for all. During 1996, the amount of the average welfare check received by each household was $376.47 according to the Department of Health and Human Services. The monthly payments per recipient amounted to $133.55. In terms of aggregate numbers, in 1993, the AFDC (Aid to Families with Dependent Children) paid approximately $23.0 billion to 14.1 million recipients. This is not the total welfare bill for America, but AFDC as shown in Table 4.4 below is one of the largest public welfare programs currently in existence. However, in spite of this yearly commitment to assist others in need, we feel betrayed and somewhat bewildered as our vision of what America should be like has not materialized. There has been a shift in American progress, from one of hope to one of despair. Not being able to achieve our vision of safe neighborhoods with heads of households bringing home an acceptable wage has challenged our basic beliefs in the free enterprise system. Many now challenge its credibility since large numbers of families remain in poverty, living in despair. To the average American, it appears futile to continue with the strategy of the past. Something new is required, and that is what this book is all about

## Table 4.4
### Social welfare spending, 1993

| Type of Program | No. of Recipients (Millions) | Cost (Billions) |
|---|---|---|
| Medicaid | 32.0 | $188.0 |
| Food Stamps | 27.0 | 25.0 |
| ADFC | 14.0 | 23.0 |
| SSI | 5.6 | 22.0 |
| Housing | 5.5 | 18.0 |
| School Lunch | 24.5 | 5.0 |
| Supplement/Food | 1.2 | 3.0 |
| Low Income Energy Asst. | 5.8 | 2.0 |

Source: U.S. House of Representative
Committee on Ways and Means, 1993

*Lack of education really hurts*

The lack of education is a very important part of family instability, especially those in poverty. Since many heads of households find themselves unemployed during different periods of their work life, much may be attributed to their lack of education. Almost 70 percent of those who are unemployed in this country have had only a high school education or less. In contrast, it is shown in Table 4.5 that only 9 percent of unemployed had earned a bachelor's degree or more. Education is a critical component of any strategy designed to assist heads of families in poverty to locate employment with a 'living wage.'

### Table 4.5
### Educational background of the unemployed

| Education | Percent Unemployed |
|---|---|
| No High School Degree | 30.8 |
| High School Diploma | 38.9 |
| Some College | 21.2 |
| Bachelor's Degree | 7.0 |
| Post Graduate Degree | 2.1 |

Source: Federal Reserve Bank, Cleveland, 1996

### Conclusion: growth is not the answer

With the passage of *the Personal Responsibility and Work Opportunity Act of 1996*, the 60-year old New Deal Program of President Franklin Roosevelt to protect mothers and their children suffering through difficult times has been officially abolished. The official contract between the U.S. federal government and the poor is now ending. Therefore, the nation is undertaking a new experiment—one which re-examines a society's compassion for helping others in time of need Typically these people are one parent families living in high crime areas. Because of budgetary constraints, politicians find it politically expedient to advocate reduced payments to these recipients because they are idle and stereotyped as lazy, feeding off the public coffers often by fraudulent or otherwise illegal means. These politicians frequently offer solutions that pressure people to work in menial dead end jobs requiring little or no training or skill in exchange for welfare benefits.

The result of this thinking is that welfare recipients have become the forgotten poor, with no future and no hope. They don't vote, pay taxes or participate in community life. In essence they are the victims of our fast paced society. They have poor living quarters often without heat or hot water or sanitation. They have no jobs or skills. They receive substandard health care or no health care at all. They are either very young or old with no one to care or tend to their needs. They have children that have no hope and in reality will likely continue the cycle of poverty. However, these people are human beings who deserve a chance in our society. They cannot compete with the well-educated who have the wherewithal to care for themselves.

In conclusion, families of poverty remain in disarray. The transformation of the family into a variety of complex forms has resulted in a new set of expectations. These expectations often challenge the need to reinforce past traditions and beliefs. The complexity of individual behavior along with that of a myriad of expectations makes the implementation of public policy even more challenging. Families are confronted with the life consequences of single-parent childbearing and child-rearing, family violence and abuse, and a fast-paced technological marketplace where jobs come and go quickly. The lack of family stability brought on with a lack of workplace stability 'eats at the heart' of a society's soul. When expectations are not clear, when goals and priorities cannot be set, and when disruption becomes the norm, the future may be indeed in doubt, especially for those at the lower socio-economic end of the marketplace.

The conscience of America is now being challenged. The realization that growth each year in GNP does not result in eliminating poverty has resulted in a new kind of public embarrassment. The fact is that we are in a new kind of competitive world market which requires business and industry to keep wages low enough to compete with companies that produce goods and services generated in other countries. This strategy creates job insecurity and does not bear well for welfare reform. Having low level skills in a workplace that now requires workers to use sophisticated technology presents another challenge to get citizens off public subsidy roles and into jobs. The outcome of such a 'harsh environment' is family breakdown and more crime. Civility and our sense of national cohesion continues to fray, and a sense of commonality that binds Americans together gets lost in the vast differences and fortunes among families in America. If the wealth generated by a growing American economy will not trickle down to families at the lowest socioeconomic, what will?

# 5 Harsh realities of the workplace

We are in the midst of a telecommunication's revolution where workplace practices of the past may no longer be viable. What this telecommunication's revolution depicts is the convergence of the telephony, entertainment, and computing industries for the purpose of delivering goods and services to consumers quickly and efficiently. At the heart of the telecommunication's revolution is the movement of information among consumers and producers of goods and services situated anywhere throughout the world. The emergence of global markets has raised the stakes of competition in that rapid changes in customers' needs and desires must be reacted to quickly. The need to employ individuals with the appropriate skills to compete with aggressive companies worldwide is becoming more important with each passing day.

However, those skills which made one employable in the past may no longer be feasible now and in the future. The dilemma facing many individuals is how to retrain themselves quickly in order to find employment. An added ramification to this dilemma is paying for such retraining. Finally, job security emerges as a vital issue as companies react to global pressures by looking at the 'bottom line' as the measure of success. With the disappearance of unions as a unifying force for many of today's low skilled workers, no powerful force is readily available to represent the interest of these individuals. With the termination of the workplace loyalty between employer and worker, employees become expendable as job skills become obsolete and competitive pressures drive decision making towards cost-cutting measures in an effort to fend off rivals worldwide.

### Transformation of the economy

In the past, American youth could literally drop out of high school and drop into a job on an assembly line for the purpose of mass producing automobiles and household appliances, etc. The jobs required little skill since they were repetitive in nature and were part of a 'do as you are told' environment. Trade unions were of great assistance as they protected workers from unscrupulous employers who were pressured to consider the needs of their workers. Wages were generated based on contracts between unions and employers, and a sense of job security prevailed. Therefore, an individual with low level skills could generate a living wage based upon the workplace theory of specialization. Assigning workers specific repetitive tasks which were quite easy to learn resulted in mass production as the basic component of the American marketplace.

With American products the envy of the world during the 1950s, 1960s, and into the early stages of the 1970s, exports flourished creating a transference of wealth from other countries to the United States. With accompanying public welfare programs to help those families in need, the rate of poverty gradually declined over these three decades. Families at the low end of the income scale were able to gain some benefits from the mass production schemes of large corporations. However, during the 1980s, a transformation occurred in the workplace in that trade unions lost members and power. Computer technology emerged and the automation of mass production resulted in downsizing of the workplace.

Mass produced products began to give way to customized products and services. Blue collar workers were beginning to be required to manipulate sophisticated equipment designed to replace the assembly line worker in the automobile, steel, appliance, and other industries. The need to employ an individual with *competitive intelligence* became paramount in the 1990s. The need was to hire workers who could add value to an existing product and service, and to do this quickly. The workplace psychology changed from that of performing repetitive tasks to that of generating the right blends of information to enable management to modify products to meet the changing requests of potential customers. Suddenly, businesses required more technically oriented workers who had command of basic computing skills for not only gathering needed information but also for making decisions crucial to the operation of a business.

### A new workplace configuration

The transformation of the economy has resulted in a new workplace configuration which is now an integral part of what Katz (1993) labels the post-industrialized society. This new era of the 1990s relies upon business using information to enhance quality of products, streamlining operations from product design to dissemination, and holding workers accountable based upon 'the bottom line'. In an attempt to hold production costs down, full-time employment in manufacturing dropped from 27 percent in 1947 to only 14 percent in 1995, (Katz, 1996). On the other hand, employment rates grew substantially in the areas of finance, insurance, and real estate. The result of this switch has been a significant change in the kinds of skills required for jobs in this information age. For example, seeking, interpreting, and reporting information is now critical. In this regard, the proportion of jobs in industries reflecting information process rose to well over 50 percent. Therefore, the consequences of this transformation is that jobs require more education.

With the break up of AT&T in 1984, the field of telephony changed dramatically. Communication emerged as the new critical function of multi-national companies. The ability for management to communicate by interactive audio and video networks among departments located in different countries provides a new framework for operating. The emergence of the Internet and the corresponding information superhighway enabled businesses to market their goods and services to a worldwide audience. It has also enabled businesses to enhance their own abilities to compete by gathering information more quickly for reallocating existing resources for meeting the pressures of global competition. The result has been a general restructuring of large corporate hierarchical structures to a flatter operational base. Decision making has been delegated downward to those who have knowledge as to what is occurring during all phases of the manufacturing process.

*Moving away from individualism*

The workplace psychology has been modified from that of an individualistic environment in which an employee works at a basic task in isolation of other tasks to a teamwork environment where the value of an employee is enhanced by working with others. The emergence of a new workplace design is the result of the need for companies to downsize their staffs while at the same time increase the productivity of their workers. As companies attempted to streamline their operations by redefining job descriptions and realigning decision making, the need to support a fewer number of employees has become very evident. The development of teams who work in tandem with other work teams creates another kind of competitiveness for employees. The level of stress at the work site has also increased due to the necessity to react to market pressures more quickly than in the past. As this transformation occurred, those employees with limited or outdated job skills found themselves either laid off, 'outsourced' to another company, or placed in early retirement. Compounding the problem is that many of the remaining low skill-level jobs now available often pay close to minimum wage, pushing families who may have recently emerged from poverty back into poverty.

*Advancing technology*

Technology is changing the way U.S. citizens live, work, and play. The microcomputer and business software applications have placed a priority upon hiring individuals who are computer literate. Basic business 'clerical' tasks associated with records management (eg., filing, retrieving, and managing information) have now been 'professionalized,' resulting in the need for workers with the ability to use advanced applications software for interpreting data. However, this change in technology has created a mismatch between the skills currently possessed by many heads of households of AFDC families and workforce requirements. The days of autocratic management where employees need only to concern themselves with completing a few repetitive tasks each day have disappeared. Instead of being obedient to a supervisor, employees are now expected to be innovative and self-motivated.

A transformation of the workforce continues as technological advances, labor force shifts, and accelerated demands for current information become everyday events. Employers now expect employees to be able to think, make decisions, and solve problems, (Drucker, 1989). These are job characteristics that have not been traditionally held to a high degree by heads of households of families of poverty. The changing nature of work, especially that of the repetitive kind customarily found in lower-skill office clerical jobs, presents a significant obstacle for those who are not computer literate and do not possess higher-order thinking skills.

The Secretary's Commission on Achieving Necessary Skills (SCANS) reported that tomorrow's employees need to possess a skills set containing five competencies: technology, thinking, interpersonal, information processing, and resource management, (SCANS, 1992). However, the report also went on to alert us that the reasoning and thinking skills now required for employment are where most U.S. employees lack proficiency. The challenge facing this country is not only to upgrade the skill levels of those heads of households in poverty, but also retrain those currently in the workforce, (Joyner, 1996).

*The emerging ghosts of the new economy*

There is a suggestion there may be large numbers of 'missing citizens' who have disappeared from the labor force during the present decade. A Wall Street Journal editorial referred to these individuals as the *ghosts of the U.S. economy*, (Wall Street Journal, 1996). The implication here is that due to a rapid technological change in the American marketplace, many skills held by these individuals are now considered obsolete. Everett Ehrlich, undersecretary of economic affairs for the Department of Commerce (1996) estimates that over 1,000,000 men in their primary working years are likely to have disappeared from the labor force in 1996. He also suggests that this may be a continuation of a past 20-year trend in which the percentage of working men participating in the labor force has been sliding.

Lester Thurow of Massachusetts Institute of Technology (1996) estimates that the missing total of men, in particular between the ages of 25 and 60, may be as high of 5.8 million. If missing women are entered into the equation, unemployment rates may be at least 1 percent higher than typically reported by the U.S. Department of Labor over recent years. Thurow argues that the *ghosts of the U.S. economy* is a group that has received little attention in the past. However, he suggests that their existence must be addressed since many of these individuals are headed into poverty if they are not already there. In addition, these dropouts from the labor force are not good family role models for their children who are expected to become the next generation of workers.

These individuals are considered ghosts since they do not show up in the statistics as unemployed. These individuals also do not show up in the ranks of the unemployed since they are not looking for work. Therefore, these citizens are uncounted for in the labor-force participation rates. They are simply discouraged workers who are just sitting at home pondering their future. In 1995, it is estimated that 838,000 men between the ages of 25 and 54 left jobs and wanted to work, but they have also been identified as persons not actively seeking re-employment. This phenomenon has been referred to as the mass disappearance of prime-age men from the working world, (Thurow, 1996).

There are also other groups that may be considered ghosts of the economy. These include the homeless, recently released convicts from prison, the disabled, and those with severe physical problems (such as excessive overweight or partially blind.) Labor-force participation rates generally reinforce the fact that ghosts with these characteristics may be a fundamental problem of society. As illustrated in Figure 5.1 on the next page, the participation rate for men has decreased from approximately 80 percent in 1970 to approximately 75 percent in 1995. According to Ehrlich (1996), the long-term gradual decline of men in the workplace is one of the barometers of workplace anxiety for men. However, female participation rates have generally increased since 1970 rising from approximately 43 percent to 60 percent in 1995.

# Missing Men in the
# U.S. Labor Force

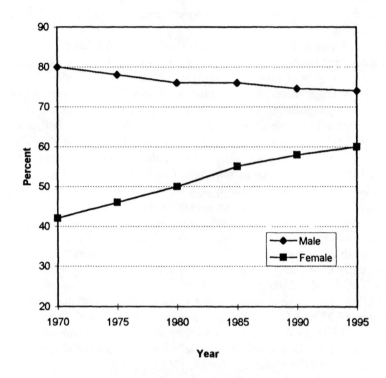

**Figure 5.1  U.S. civilian labor force participation rate**
Source:     Bureau of Labor Statistics, U. S. Dept. of Labor, 1996

Generally, the new economic realities of the workplace require individuals to perceive their opportunities for employment from a different perspective. For example, going back to school to be retrained may not be as useful for gaining employment in today's highly competitive marketplace as many believe. A better strategy for obtaining employment may be that of seeking   temporary assignments through agencies acting as intermediaries.  For example, prospective employers like to preview skills of workers by hiring  temporary workers through temp agencies. By using such a strategy, both the employee and employer gain experience as to how each can assist the other.

According to John Kasarda (1996), the number of jobs available for those individuals with less than a high school degree has dropped significantly since 1950. As depicted in Figure 5.2, the number of individuals between the ages of 16-24 decreased from 5.5 million to 3.5 million for those who had dropped out of school between 1975 and 1995. Those jobs in the manufacturing sector where high school students could do fairly well have gradually disappeared. In place of those jobs have

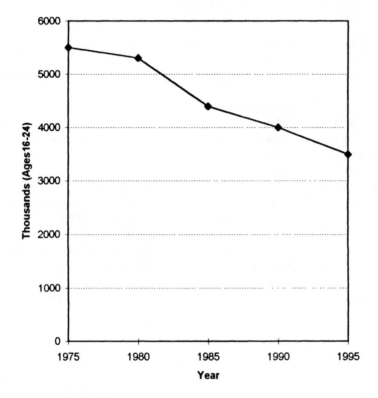

**Figure 5.2 Employment status of high school dropouts, 1975-1995**
Source: U.S. Department of Labor, 1996

been office positions where advanced technical skills are required. The irony of this change in job requirements is that as skills demanded for today's jobs increase, the dropout rate of teenage students hovers around 40 percent in some parts of the nation. A significant portion of these former students end up on welfare as single-parents. This trend is reflected in the reality that a considerable number of heads of households of families in poverty usually have only a high school education or less. Therefore, it can readily be seen why many of these employees of the past are now considered missing from the marketplace. With the likelihood of the business computer replacing an increasing number of workers, there will also be an increasing number of 'missing citizens' from the unemployment ranks. The issue that arises is what happens to the 'have nots' possessing outdated skills and limited access to any alternatives for upgrading their knowledge and capabilities

**The harshness of the minimum wage**

The role that a minimum wage plays in getting those families in financial need out of poverty has been plagued with controversy. The 104th Congress passed a new minimum wage law, increasing it systematically from $4.75 per hour to $5.25 per hour over a series of years. The argument in favor of establishing a minimum wage requirement is that it helps many teenagers and adults currently in low-income families to earn wages that reflect a basic minimum standard of living expected of all Americans. The argument against a minimum wage is that is reduces jobs to those who are in most need of employment since business has customarily reacted to such increases by 'laying off workers' to reduce costs of operations. In addition, because the relative prices of labor and capital influence corporate investment decisions, minimum-wage levels may affect productivity. Ironically, if pay rates actually fall, employers have a greater incentive to buy labor instead of new technology.

As shown in Figure 5.3, the percentage of the workforce earning $5.20

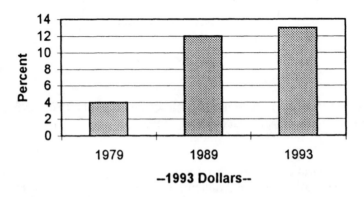

--1993 Dollars--

**Figure 5.3    Workforce earning $5.20 or less**
Source:        Economic Policy Institute, 1996

128

or less increased from 4 percent of the workforce in 1979 to approximately 13 percent in 1993. The result was that there was a boom in low-wage service employment, but productivity also sagged. With the availability of low-wage labor, the need to integrate technology into business operations was not paramount during this time period. It was this same period of time that interest rates went through the ceiling, making it very expensive for companies to purchase expensive technology. The alternate was to purchase low-wage employees, instead.

The dilemma that affects low-income employees is that additional earnings through higher minimum-wage levels will help those families in need advance somewhat; but at the same time, it encourages companies to investigate the merits of adding technology to current business operations. David B. Neumark (1996), a Michigan State University economist, fears that if technology is encouraged to offset the rising price of labor, many low-skilled workers, many of them heads of households in poverty, will never work again. When gross profit margins of business decreased substantially between 1950 and 1980 as shown in Figure 5.4 on the following page, business looked to technology for increasing productivity. It is by increasing output that businesses can take advantage of economies of scale for generating increasing profits. From 1980 to 1995 during a decade of 'downsizing' by corporate America, gross profit margins of business increased from 8 percent to 10 percent of gross revenues, indicating that increasing productivity through technology has occurred. As already indicated, the irony of the situation is that with an increase in technology use, the need for low-skill workers is decreasing. The result is an increase in the numbers of adults at the bottom socio-economic levels, leaving these individuals to fend for themselves with little prospects for employment.

Therefore, the question that remains is whether the focus upon establishing a minimum wage creates more of a distraction from finding better ways to get AFDC families out of poverty. In reality, if someone earns $5.25 per hour, they are likely to earn little more than $8500 per year which is quite below the $15,000 now suggested by the U.S. government as the poverty level for a family of four. In addition, if two parents in one household both work for minimum wage rate of $5.25, the combined total of earnings places that family just above poverty level. Even if the minimum wage is increased to $6 or $7 per hour, the fact remains that achieving a minimum standard of living is not enabling large numbers of Americans to achieve the American dream of being able to meet one's needs without struggling from paycheck to paycheck for survival. The real issue, therefore, is employee displacement by technology and not the minimum wage.

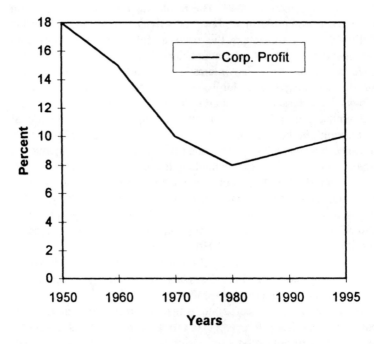

**Figure 5.4   Corporate profits as percentage of revenues**
Source:       Bureau of Economic Analysis, 1996

Coping with complementary expenses associated with full-time employment when one is earning close to a minimum wage is another matter of significance. For example, according to Rich Finely (1996) in A *New Direction for U.S. Welfare*, as individuals become employed, their expenses attributed towards work increase considerably. For example, if a woman generates employment at $6 per hour, her spending per month increases on the average of $75 a month for transportation and $75 a month for social security contributions. In addition, all day child care costs perhaps $200 per month and after school child care costs perhaps half that amount. Based upon research conducted in 1994, Michael Lewis, president of Michael Lewis Enterprises, writes that a two-parent family with two children generally requires around $20,000 per year to cover everyday expenses from food to medical care. Therefore, working at or near a minimum wage is not likely to be the answer to getting out of poverty for many of those families considered to be near, at, or below poverty.

Therefore, the critical issue for the AFDC family is not settling for a minimum wage but getting sufficient schooling and/or retraining required to make an individual marketable. Since about 60 million individuals in this nation find work in approximately 21 million small businesses, the strategy to enhance a family's welfare must be geared to getting heads of households educated. The challenge is to upgrade workplace skills that result in one becoming flexible for being capable of fulfilling several functions within a small business operation. Whereas employees may have a tendency to be specialists in larger corporations, small-time entrepreneurs require a different orientation towards work. Becoming more of a generalist may be appropriate for employment in a small business, but earning a living wage in this kind of environment may result in a formidable challenge to those who are more accustomed to performing repetitive, menial jobs.

**Divisiveness of workplace diversity**

Increasing diversity among members of today's workforce also means increasing opportunities for misunderstanding and conflict. An issue closely related to workplace diversity is the impact immigrants have upon employment opportunities, especially heads of households of families presently living near, at, or below poverty levels. There is a general feeling among those families of poverty that immigrants take jobs, housing, and health care away from them. According to Linda Chavez (1996), president of the Center of Equal Opportunity, Washington, DC., statistics generally disprove this commonly held perception. For example, between 1960 and 1991, the ten states with the highest number of immigrants had lower unemployment rates when compare to ten states with the lowest number of immigrants. Julian Simon of the Cato Institute argues that immigrants actually create new jobs by spending their earnings on the output of other workers. In addition, Simon concludes from his research that the less skilled immigrants take work that Americans generally shun, (Simon, 1996). He refers to the meat packing industry where immigrants work in what is referred to as 'killer floros' where native-Americans refuse to work. However, workplace diversity is changing the labor force patterns of families themselves.

*Work life drives home life*

The changing nature of heads of households of ADFC families over the past decades from a two-parent to single-parent is illustrated in Figure 5.5 on the next page. The reality is that the large numbers of single-parent heads of households have special needs which unmet can easily prevent them from contributing fully to an organization. However, even with more females as heads of AFDC families, companies especially of the small variety, have had difficulty responding with acceptable flexible work arrangements and employee assistance programs to help workers balance work life needs with family responsibilities. The traditional family support system that is critical to heads of households, especially those at the poverty level, is not currently in place due to the mobile nature of siblings and other relatives customarily counted on for child-

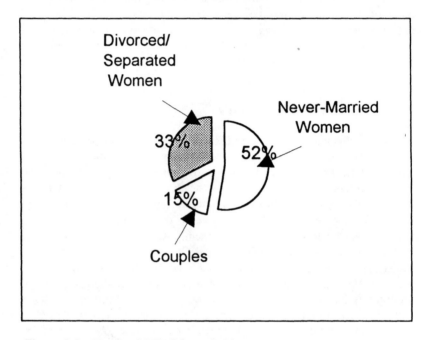

Figure 5.5    Heads of AFDC households
Source:       Hoffman, Time to Reform Welfare, p. 442

rearing assistance. Therefore, even though we accept the premise that employees today are not alike, and even though work can get done in different ways, there remains a hesitancy upon smaller entrepreneurs to change past practices. In our model, it is demonstrated that it is in the best interests of both business and residential neighborhoods to design work policies that are geared to child-rearing responsibilities. The expectation is that individuals will likely become more productive through reduced absenteeism and turnover, will likely have higher morale, and will likely have more opportunity at continued employment over long periods of time.

In the view of Eddie Ferretti (1996), manager of corporate diversity at Nation's Bank, technology enables companies to create innovative strategies for bringing different individuals with differing cognitive abilities, skill levels, ideas, and beliefs to work together to reach a common goal. Technology also requires companies to change the way they look at work processes, where work gets done, and who does the work. Therefore, diversity of the workforce and of available technology is resulting in new ways to organize employees while at the same time meeting the needs of families with varying composition. Larger corporations have responded with a number of strategies to generate important benefits from technological and worker diversity: In Table 5.1, several more common strategies have been identified, and altered versions of these may be applicable to smaller companies. The intent of these strategies is to provide employees with a new sense of camaraderie among individuals with different backgrounds. The result is to *empower* workers to determine what is best for the company and what is best for their families. Getting continual input from workers allows the power of

## Table 5.1
### Flexible strategies for enhancing worker productivity

| Employment Involvement | Accountability |
| --- | --- |
| Task Force | Define/reward behaviors that reinforce diversity |
| Focus Groups | Link diversity performance to company objectives |
| Networking Groups | Tie diversity to team effort and global competition |
| Diversity Councils | Communicate alternatives for enhanced productivity |

Source: Eddie Ferretti (1996), Nation's Bank

diversity to break loose of conventional thinking, and in its place a foundation for advancement through more contemporary work practices

The goal here is to generate an environment where both workplace and family needs are met on an every day basis. The challenge is for employees to learn to value differences among workers in order to develop a sense of trust and confidence. This is more important since many jobs today are beyond the talents and abilities of one employee. Since there is so much information available and so many alternatives for accomplishing work, employees are better off to work in teams whereby particular strengths among co-workers can balance the weaknesses of others.

The result, therefore, is a whole new set of expectations that are based upon the need to create a foundation whereby there is a general respect among employees for one another, an uncompromising integrity, and equality of opportunity. For AFDC families, this modification of the work environment in which self-initiative is expected places heads of households in a new 'arena' where survival is through teamwork and a new kind of bond upon coworkers. With heads of households of AFDC families coming from different cultures, nationalities, racial and sexual orientation, etc., there is a real need today to take such diversity to the next level by blending the many talents of such individuals into an effective unit.


## Adding value to work

The technological workplace is expected to have impact upon family cohesiveness. A central issue to welfare reform is not only the ability to gain access to a job, but to keep a job for long periods of time. Having a consistent income is critical to bringing stability and security to a family seeking to be free of welfare. Balancing family and work is critical to character building. In terms of generating upward mobility, Gilder (1996) writes that the only route from poverty is for individuals at the lower socio-economic status to work harder than those individuals who presently hold positions above them. In order to avoid the probability of having to accept low-paying service jobs (such as janitors, retail clerk, and housemaids which generally lead to nowhere), those heads of households of poverty are faced with in additional challenge of learning how to create *added value to their work* in an information age whereby 'the do as you are told philosophy' is being replaced with 'work with your team'.

Therefore, both workplace and technological diversity has again raised the stakes of competition, not only for producing the best products and services, but for gaining access to higher paying jobs. With most jobs now predicted to require at least an associate degree in a technical area, workplace diversity has placed another obstacle in front of those living in poverty where education has not been a priority in the past. To Gilder, family security is closely tied to family stability which is closely tied to success on the job. It is the pursuit of wealth that typically generates success both at work and at home. Diversity in the workforce may provide that 'spark' that brings families of different socio-economic status together not only at work but in the local community. Getting heads of households of AFDC families to adopt the importance of adding value to work is a significant challenge confronting society. With the emphasis upon upgrading people skills such as communicating and writing (two skills in which many individuals have severe problems), the implication of workplace diversity adds new dimension to the teamwork.

*The permanence of job insecurity*

Job layoffs have become a fixture in today's economy, according to Steve Lohr (1996) of the New York Times. He writes that three-quarters of all American households have had a family member, friend, relative, or

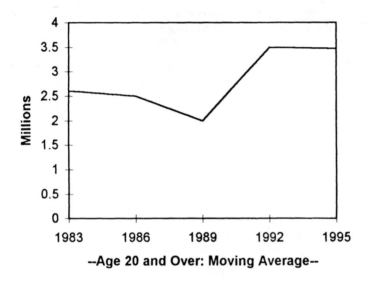

**--Age 20 and Over: Moving Average--**

**Figure 5.6   No. of jobs eliminated by year**
Source:      *New York Times,* 29 December 96

neighbor lose a job since 1980. Even though the evidence suggests that more jobs were created between 1980 and 1995 than wiped out, jobs appear to be less secured now. Lohr concludes that economic insecurity persists and job apprehension is spreading evenly across society at all socio-economic levels. As noted in the Figure 5.6 above, the number of individuals laid off increased during the 1990s from two million in 1989

135

to 3.5 million in 1995. Some believe that the increase in the number of individuals who are losing their jobs is a byproduct of a fast-moving economy. Paul Krugman (1996), an economics professor at the Massachusetts Institute of Technology labels this as 'labor market brutality'. He suggests that job loss is the price society has to pay for having a dynamic economy that in reality creates more jobs than it destroys. In the Figure 5.7 below, the rate of job elimination has also increased from 1.7 percent in 1989 to 2.7 percent in 1995.

One of the outcomes of job insecurity is that even if one finds another job after being 'downsized', employees are likely to become less trusting of new employers, thus creating stressful working conditions that are also likely to impact upon the home environment. Lawrence Katz, a labor economist at Harvard University (1996) writes that 70 percent of Americans today feel that layoffs are not just a temporary problem but a feature of the modern economy that will continue permanently.

Downsizing and the role it plays upon the lives of heads of households must be carefully scrutinized. For example, a sudden change in the direction that a company takes adds insecurity to the worker. Companies

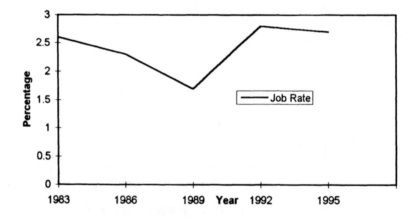

**Figure 5.7**  **Rate of job elimination**
Source:  U.S. Department of Labor, 1996

downsize in order to increase productivity of existing employees, and thus to increase profits. Therefore, the new workplace psychology calls for employees today to be prepared to work in different arrangements. In actuality, the result is that every employee becomes an entrepreneur selling to different employers over time workplace skills that add value to

136

work.   Moving from one employer to another becomes the norm, and for heads of households of AFDC families, job security remains elusive.


## Workspace constantly changing

For example, telecommuting, work sharing, and contract work are three working arrangements that provide a new kind of job responsibility.  Each of these styles reflects an opportunity for heads of households in poverty to become an entrepreneur instead of seeking a low-paying service job which generally has very little security or a future.  The information age has resulted in more individuals working full time out of their homes, working part-time, or working under a special contract with an employer. What is different about these entrepreneurs is that a large initial investment is not required.  There is no need to open an office or store on main street.   What is required is the ability to network and connect to those employers in need of specific skills.

The challenge to present welfare reform efforts is to locate a sufficient number of well paying jobs for those who are required to be removed from public welfare programs within specified time periods.   With the job market constantly changing and with the skill levels required for newer jobs increasing, the likelihood of a AFDC head of household obtaining a high-paying job remains low.  However, when one era comes to an end, a new one emerges.  The workplace psychology of today requires a totally different work orientation than that of the past.   A whole new set of workplace parameters connecting work and individuals into short-term productive relationships places heads of all households at risk.   Finding work in traditional ways may at best result in a low-paying job without a future.  The need is therefore to assist families in poverty to find a niche in the employment sector--and to remain active in it--as they seek ways out of poverty.  Becoming an entrepreneur may be part of our future--not only for families in financial need but also for the rest of us.


## Movement of jobs to the suburbs

The goal of welfare reform is to move millions of people from welfare to work.  However, many families in poverty are largely concentrated in inner cities where good paying jobs are difficult to find.   Past public policy has encouraged the development of communities around cities through the development of an interstate highway system, housing mortgage subsidies, and creative land zoning, among others.   The result of such policies has been accelerated land development which has basically circled many large cities.  Accompanying such development has been the creation of millions of jobs--many in the service sector at banks, restaurants, and retail outlets. Therefore, employment opportunities are increasingly located in the suburbs, but heads of households in poverty customarily do not have affordable ways to reach those jobs.

The American Automobile Association puts the average cost of automobile ownership at $6,500 per year, (Welfare to Work, 1996). That is far beyond the reach of heads of AFDC families. Therefore, without automobiles or affordable public transportation, many jobs, even those in the service sector, are simply not accessible by those in need of employment. Other obstacles making it nearly impossible to get jobs in suburban areas are higher housing costs, lack of family support systems (such as affordable daycare), zoning discrimination and housing codes restricting number of residents per household.. Some communities have instituted subsidized buses and vans to transport city residents to suburban jobs, but such policies appear to be only 'stop-gap' effort, assisting a few where there are many more in need.

The subsidizing of suburban sprawl through the upgrading of interstate highways continues today. The reallocation of huge sums of funds for enhancing mass transit is not likely to affect large numbers of city residents in the coming decades. While some cities have accepted the challenge of developing regional mass transit systems such as St. Louis, San Francisco, and Milwaukee, much still remains to be done. The 1991 Intermodal Surface Transportation Efficiency Act has been somewhat instrumental in stimulating community involvement in transportation decisions. The welfare reform model developed later offers a totally new perspective in terms of making jobs available to community residents, offsetting the need to develop high-cost transit systems.


**Harsh realities of employment in the service sector**

While the economy demands more highly educated workers, the need persists for more maids, sewing-machine operators, retail clerks, and maintenance personnel. Nearly 30 percent of all U.S. employees make $7.28 an hour or less, according to Economic Policy Institute, (Business Week, 1996, p. 109). Such low-paying jobs however bring a host of problems such as poor work habits, culture clashes, and employee theft. Moreover, workers who are unschooled in basic business etiquette tend not to call in when they are unable to make it to work, and many such workers lack telephones resulting in poor communication between employer and employee. An offshoot of such poor work habits is frequent job dislocation as employers fire and hire at higher rates of frequency. Corresponding to a high degree of job insecurity is a turbulence in personal lives resulting in domestic abuse.

As note in Figure 5.8 below, large numbers of low-wage workers have a high school degree or less, are female, and are under 30 years of age. In spite of the trials and tribulations associated with low-wage jobs, many companies still know relatively little about low-wage workers and their needs. In view of the myriad of problems employers face in hiring low-skilled service workers, many managers spend significant time doing the equivalent of social work such as counseling families about domestic problems, juggling work shifts to accommodate child care needs, and even lending money to pay pressing bills.

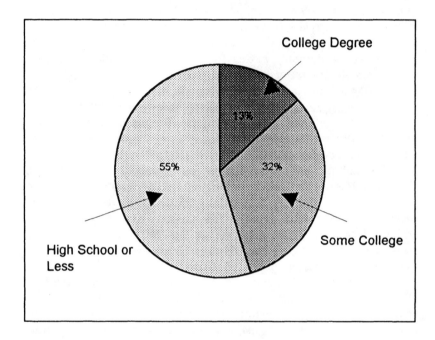

**Figure 5.8    Education of low wage workers**
Source:        Families & Work Institute, 1992

While there are job opportunities in the service sector for housekeepers laundry workers, dishwashers, and other hourly staffs in the hospitality industry, etc., the low-wages associated with such acerbate the problems of families on welfare. On a positive note, employers such as JC. Penney, Hyatt International, McDonald's, and Levi Strauss are attempting to work with the Families and Work Institute to create the first comprehensive demographic profiles of this workforce in an attempt to make suggestions for generating public polices that benefit low-wage workers. They also have begun to initial educational programs designed to enhance a worker's ability to speak English in addition to working with individuals from different cultures. Companies are developing programs to teach employees how to manage their money better and how to care for their children. The purpose of these educational programs is to help companies cut their operating costs by lifting productivity and therefore enhancing the bottom line.

One of the outcomes of the transformation of the economy into a global competitive marketplace is the trend towards stagnant wages, especially for those at the lower end of the socio-economic scale (Figure 5.9). For example, as the economy moved from that of a manufacturing-based market to a service sector orientation, the spread between higher and lower paying jobs has increased. For example, the average hourly rate for service jobs is approximately $15, replacing factory ones that customarily pay over $20 per hour, according to the Economic Policy Institute. (Bernstein, 1996). Further aggravating this trend towards lower-paying service jobs is approximately $15, replacing factory ones that customarily pay over $20 per hour, according to the Economic Policy Institute. (Bernstein, 1996). Further aggravating this trend towards lower-paying service jobs is the temporary help industry which has soared by 70 percent since 1990, (Bernstein, 1996). The impact upon wages has been downward as temp service jobs average just $8.79 an hour which is significantly below $11.44 for full-time employees, according to the Bureau of Labor Statistics of the U.S. Department of Labor.

The long-term trends holding down wages--the shift to services, a global economy, and weak unions--are all having impact upon the ability of heads of households of families in poverty to make their way up the economic ladder. Whereas many traditional service jobs held by heads of households with a high school diploma or less require lower skills, they also carry with them lower wages. The wage gap between the skilled and low-skilled and between the high school graduate and dropout continues to widen as new uses of technology enables businesses to substitute

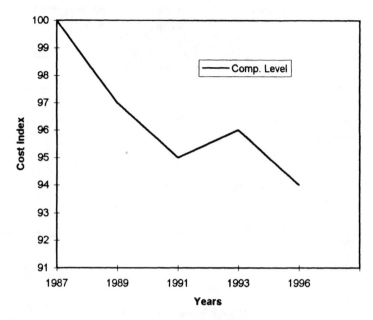

**Figure 5.9    Compensation levels 1987-1996**
Source:         Economic Policy Institute, 1996

machine power for manpower.   The heads of households of poverty may increase their earnings by working longer hours, but hourly wages are not expected to increase at sufficient rates to reduce the gap between those more fortunate.

However, for those who are educated and are computer literate, there are a good number of service jobs available that compare favorably in income generation to positions in the manufacturing sector.   Max Dupay and Mark Schweitzer (1994) argue that the service-producing industry offers wage opportunities very similar to those in construction and manufacturing, (Economic Commentary, 1994).   As illustrated in Table 5.2 on the following page, they report in that in 1992, the average weekly wage for full-time workers in the service sector was only 3.9 percent below the average in the goods-producing sector. Similarly, in 1992, the median service job pay was only $19 per week less than the median of goods-producing jobs.

## Table 5.2
### 1992 weekly wages of 8 major industries

|  | Mean | Median | |
|---|---|---|---|
|  |  |  | |
| **Goods Producing** *(Overall)* | $587 | $500 <-------- | |
| Construction | 565 | 485 | \| |
| Manufacturing | 693 | 500 | $19 |
|  |  |  | \| |
| **Service Producing** | $564 | $481 <------- | |
| Retail Trade | 425 | 340 | |
| Wholesale Trade | 611 | 500 | |
| FIRE | 636 | 498 | |
| Public Administration | 648 | 679 | |
| Transportation | 650 | 605 | |

Source: U.S. Depart. of Labor, Bureau of Labor Statistics, 1994

However, since many welfare recipients have only a high school diploma or less, their record of wage earnings in the service sector is significantly lower than the overall averages indicated in Table 5.3 on the next page. When examining the overall weekly median wages of workers with only a high school diploma, the difference in wages between those holding jobs in the goods-producing sector and those in the service-producing sector is $77 per week in 1992.

While there is a modest wage gap between goods-producing and service-producing jobs, there is a much larger weekly wage gap when a lack of education is introduced. The point to be noted, however, is that with sufficient training, the wages in the service sector can generate incomes comparable to those in the manufacturing sector. Therefore, there is a growing importance attached to advanced education if the service sector is expected to become a factor in hiring sufficient numbers of heads of households currently on welfare.

**Table 5.3**
**1992 weekly wages of workers**
**with only high school diploma**


**Median Wages**

| | | |
|---|---|---|
| **Goods-Producing (Overall)** | $462 <————————— | |
| Construction | 481 | \| |
| Manufacturing | 456 | $77 |
| | | \| |
| **Service-Producing (Overall)** | $385 <————————— | |
| Retail Trade | 313 | |
| Wholesale Trade | 459 | |
| FIRE | 386 | |
| Public Administration | 481 | |
| Transportation | 577 | |

Source:  U.S. Dept. of Labor, Bureau of Labor Statistics, 1994


**Enter the civilized job market**

The integration of the expectations of business executives and community residents into a common goal illustrates the need for one system to feed off the other.  The success of the family relies upon success at work and vice versa.  Personal agendas must give way to community goals similar to the way personal goals at work must give way to common goals for the benefit of the organization.  The way out of poverty, according to Gilder (1996), is the creation of a marriage between work, family, and faith. The way out of poverty is design public policies that motivate families to stay together in a monogamous marriage.  To Gilder, unrelated individuals in a family setting creates an undesirable tone for the entire community.  In addition, family anarchy results in impulsive youths rather than responsible young persons.   The result is what Guilder refers to as *disruptive aggression.  There*fore, Gilder argues that it is the bonds among people, whether the immediate family, relatives or fellow employees at work, that provides individuals with strength and focus.

   The notion that welfare recipients ought to be required to work is an easy sell, according to William Raspberry (1996) of the Washington Post Writers Group.  However, he goes on and asks the question where will all the jobs that are needed to place current welfare recipients in positions of employment come from? This question gains even more prominence today due to the fact that job requirements are increasing and the skills possessed by many citizens currently on welfare are decreasing. Jeremy Rifkin (1995) in *The End of Work* suggests that we look to the non-profit sector as a place of opportunity. Rifkin points out that with the trend toward smaller government budgets and with the decline in the labor-intensive industries, there is very little opportunity for either the business or public sector to produce a sufficient number of jobs. Therefore, Rifkin, suggests the creative use of a third sector, the non-profits, is in order.

In order to counteract the expanding requirement of possessing higher order thinking and reasoning skills in order to obtain employment, the nonprofit industry may provide an alternative, especially for those with less formal schooling and fewer abilities. Areas where possible employment may be found are in expanded daycare, caring for the elderly, mentoring children, recreation, and health care support. Nonprofit organizations such as churches, United Way, hospitals, and a variety of other voluntary organizations customarily found in many communities can be expanded, says Rifkin. By focusing more attention on what he refers to as the civilized market sector, the placement of large numbers of welfare recipients into productive jobs may become a reality.

What is suggested here is the creation of a new form of 'social capital' by letting people work in socially productive jobs. Rifkin writes that market capital works upon the theory that one can optimize personal well-being through hard work. In this regard, social capital emphasizes the theory that one can optimize the good of a community by serving others. The argument here is that the telecommunication's revolution and the digital economy where technical skills for employment are paramount may have also opened the door for the restoration of 'the civil sector', where such technical skills are not required   Where the funds should come from in order to support this movement remains up to debate, but one suggestion is the awarding of personal income tax breaks to individuals who serve others. Since those organizations in the profit sector get a tax break by donating to non-profit organizations, perhaps a similar policy could be adapted to the incomes of employees who are fulfilling careers in the non-profit sector.

The moment of truth is now upon us if members of families in the lower socio-economic levels cannot find employment in the profit sector. The related issue, of course, is finding employment with a living wage as well as with a likelihood that such employment will be continual. Frequent interruptions to employment are most difficult to endure especially for those who are basically living from paycheck to paycheck and have very little savings to fall back upon during periods of unemployment. If heads of households are unable to find consistent employment quickly and in jobs that carry respect, the likely result will be increasing numbers of both adults and youth committing more crimes out of desperation. The outcome of such a trend will no doubt be the placing of more individuals in prisons. With the average cost of imprisonment at the state level at about $30,000 per year, the increasing costs to society resulting from inaction in terms of implementing real welfare reform will become staggering as years progress. And one need not be reminded that inmates have no purchasing power, they pay no taxes, and they generally do not become better citizens.

**The harsh realities of poor education**

An area which is closely aligned to maintaining employment is that of educating the workforce of the future. The poor record of many public schools has been attributed to poor curriculum, lack of personal safety, and weak discipline of disruptive students that discourage children who want to learn. The irony of the public educational system is that the neighborhoods in which inner city schools are located consist of large numbers of families in poverty. However, in terms of financing public education, nationally, expenditures per student come to approximately $5,000. In many cities, it is between $9,000 to $11,000, (Becker, 1996). Whereas many inner city schools receive consider financial support above that of the national average, they also have the dubious distinction of graduating the least prepared for today's job market.

Given the deep and pervasive impact of poverty, a report in *Helping Families Work (1994)* indicated that students in low-poverty schools who received A's on their report cards scored in the 81st and 87th percentiles in reading and math. Meanwhile, students in high-poverty schools who received A's scored only at the 40th percentile, (Phi Delta Kappan, 1996). It is apparent that the expectations of classroom educators vary depending upon the makeup of the student body. This perception adds to the complexity of problems confronted by those families in poverty since their children are not graduating using the same standards as their peers in other schools. To overcome the effects of poor education, new kinds of strategies will be required, several of which are proposed in our model.

The basic assumption in our model is that parents must play the key role in educating their own children. Without continuous parental involvement, schools (especially those to which children in families close to poverty attend) cannot be reformed into effective learning institutions. The educational community is awash in many excellent ideas. However, what is required is a new mechanism for getting imaginative ideas into practice in the classroom. Our model shifts the power of a learning triad between school administrators, classroom teachers and state educational officials to parents. Rather than instituting reforms that empower a large educational bureaucracy, reduce teachers to paraprofessionals, and "marginalize" parents, our model integrates parents into a total learning consortium. The renewal community has local businesses, nonprofit organizations, and families commit to participating in the education of the next generation of workers.

### Privatizing employee training

In addition, private employment contractors are also expected to enter the training industry as they attempt to upgrade employees with the skills required to succeed in the global workplace. For example, Kelly Services Inc., has placed a recruitment center in a Detroit welfare office and offered free computer software training. The company hired and placed 288 welfare recipients in temporary jobs in one year. More than a third have worked 90 days or more. (Privatizing Welfare, 1996, p. 94). Another company known as Curtis & Associates in Casper, Wyoming, has put together a motivational program geared to chronic welfare recipients. With the counseling received by this company in conjunction with training obtained at the local community college, welfare recipients receive technical training leading to jobs in local hospitals and HMOs.

The private sector itself (business and industry) is another role player in the education of welfare recipients. Companies like Lockheed Information Services, IBM, and Electronic Data Systems are other examples of the private sector undertaking initiative to training welfare recipients for jobs of the future. This trend towards the privatization of employee training is similar to that associated with the U.S. postal system and public waste management systems whereby the private sector is permitted to compete with the public sector. As the need for new approaches for training future workers become evident, the entrance of the private sector in education provides families on welfare another alternative to consider as they plan strategies for enhancing the welfare of their households.

### Conclusion

Today's families in poverty face challenges that no other generation has been asked to face. With welfare reform on everyone's mind, the introduction of the element of technology adds to the complexity of the problem of raising the living conditions of those AFDC families whose heads are less educated and least prepared. The transformation from manual labor to technology calls for the creation of a whole new set of public policies to ensure work for all citizens of this nation. The need to revitalize neighborhoods and to find employment for thousands of welfare recipients requires the re-evaluation of the importance attached to personal responsibility. Our model city gives equal weight to the importance attached to working in the non-profit sector and that for profit. A new kind of personal responsibility becomes the core of community development.

In addition, the opportunity arises for creating a whole new set of role models for the next generation of workers. With children perceiving their parents in viable community roles, their expectations as to their future are likely to change. The spirit of sharing one's personal skills with others in time of need sets a powerful standard of performance for others to emulate. The *societal bonding* that integrates a variety of support systems for families in need will no doubt be reflected in regenerating those 'family bonds' that keep members of households together. The welfare reform model attempts to create a new kind of local community that brings together schools, hospitals, public safety, and other segments of a community with the objective of establishing commitment through a *rational choice model.* The premise upon which this new community is created is that both the marketplace and the workplace must be in balance if communities are to become united and prosperous. The non-profit sector plays an important part in this balance.

# Part Three

## LEARNING FROM THE PAST:

## GOOD INTENT GONE SOUR

# 6  America's attempt at compassion: a history of betrayal

Family and community involvement are two very essential components of a healthy society. Unfortunately, there are economic and social problems today that have prevented many families from living the type of life they expected. These problems include erratic employment, the rising costs of health care, and mediocre education. Each of these impact society, resulting in extraordinary costs to working citizens of this country. In order to address welfare reform with its idiosyncrasies, it is important to not to ignore past disappointments and failure. History supports the contention that the rate of growth in welfare costs over the past several decades has not resulted in a significant return on this investment for getting AFDC families in a position to become independent of public support. In other words, America's experiment with compassion has turned out to be an act of betrayal, where frustration and bewilderment remain a part of society's dream to eradicate poverty.

## Lingering poverty

Picture this scenario.  A single widowed mother has two small young children. They are living in an abandoned room in the darkness of the ghetto, where rats and cockroaches are common household pets. There is no heat or furniture, but hey, it's free and no one knows they live there. They can't afford anything more. The children's eyes are hollowed, and they have a constant look of hunger about them. The mother can't leave the children alone at 'home' to go to work for fear of their safety. Their Thanksgiving meal consists of left over scraps which they found in a nearby dumpsite. She prays everyday that her children will not be taken from her by social services, but she can't have them live like this or they will surely die.

A situation such as this has become rather commonplace. Poverty is a devastating state that no one expects will ever happen to them. Today, there are roughly 36 million people living *below* the poverty level in the United States. In fact, since 1973, the poverty rate has increased by 33 percent, standing at the highest rate since 1975. In addition to these 36 million, there are an estimated additional 40 million Americans who live on incomes estimated to be below a standard of adequacy as determined by the United States Department of Labor. For every seven people in the nation today, approximately one is living in poverty. Furthermore, one in four live in substandard housing. Other statistics have show that on the average, 20 million Americans go hungry each month, so the problem of poverty, homelessness, and starvation continues, (*New York Times*, July 15, 1994, p.D2).


## America's initial attempt at compassion

Public welfare subsidies initially appeared in response to the Great Depression of the 1930s. The system's mission was simply to address needs (e.g., economic, health, etc.) of the poor. The definition of the welfare system has fluctuated a great deal since it was created. This has occurred, in part, as a result of an expanded scope of services that have been created by government bodies. Another factor that has contributed to this constant state of flux in defining welfare's role in society is a lack of a consensus on the part of our two primary political parties as to an appropriate role for welfare assistance. Whereas one political party desires to expand child care services, job training, and family support services by means of centralized Federal mandates, the other desires to delegate such responsibilities to state governments. Another problem is that the American public has no interest in welfare reform unless the problem affects them directly.

We all know that poverty exists, but why? Does financial assistance do more harm than good for bringing those in poverty into mainstream America? Is poverty the result of people being just lazy, or is it a symptom of a larger problem? Are individuals in poverty beyond help? Is government alone capable of solving poverty in this country? These are difficult questions to answer as a society searches for new ways to implement a welfare policy for those in poverty. It is obvious that something is currently lacking in our system because we continue to witness considerable poverty among our citizens. American leadership in the 1930s created the welfare system in a response to a need, but no one ever thought they were creating a system that would leave people in continual despair.

# A continuing cycle of despair

While welfare is a system that was intended to be only a temporary resource, it has turned out to be a permanent for a significant number of families. More and more recipients are remaining on the program for much longer than was ever anticipated. One reason for such a result could be that welfare recipients are not being adequately trained for today's workplace, so it is very difficult to remove these individuals from public-support programs with welfare dependency a likely outcome. As technology enables the substitution of people with machines, competition for jobs become more fierce. Most welfare recipients do not have the necessary resources to achieve the required level of education to compete for these remaining jobs, thus becoming caught in the vicious web of unemployment, poverty, and hopelessness.

The cycle of despair continues. The children of parents on welfare are left with few chances of enjoying the economic and political freedom that American democracy offers many citizens. Almost 50 percent of children from the poorest homes endure with impaired learning abilities, while 5 percent are born with some kind of mental retardation due to lack of appropriate prenatal nutrition, (Barry, Vincent & Shaw, 1995). When one generation is 'struck' by poverty, many generations to follow are likely to face a similar battle. For instance, try to imagine a couple with very meager funds, who can barely afford life's bare essentials. They do not have the funds to purchase a residence in a school district that has excellent academic and vocational programs, and they are not trained for today's marketplace. Their children will have a high probability of growing up and repeating a similar lifestyle that their parents.

Poverty is not restricted to any one race, nationality, or culture. In Figure 6.1, data reported indicates that families classified as white far outnumber other races in terms of living below the poverty level as determined by the Federal government. As also noted in Figure 6.1, there has been no significant decrease in the number of white, black, and Hispanic families living in poverty between 1984 and 1992. The cycle of despair continues as past attempts to remedy poverty fail.

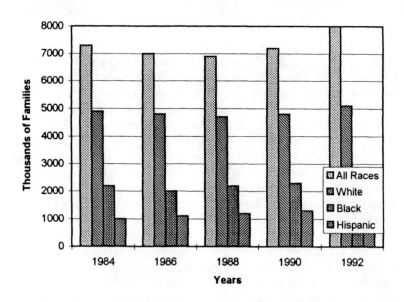

**Figure 6.1**    **Families below poverty level: 1984-1992**
Source:        U.S. Cong. Budget Office & Bureau of Census, 1994

**Welfare costs out of control**

There is no way one can deny that an exorbitant amount of funds have been allocated each year to support the income of the financially needy. For example, in Figure 6.2, the benefits related to Medicaid, a public program geared at helping those in poverty pay for medical care, have increased significantly between 1990 and 1992. With Medicaid costs almost doubling in a two-year period, it is no secret that supporting those with special financial needs can eventually bankrupt a nation if reforms are not put into place. Therefore, whereas society may feel that they have an obligation to help those in poverty, the reality of the costs involved results in a reexamination of how far the public can go in supporting more and more citizens each year.

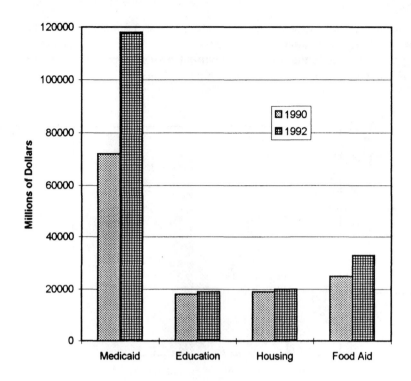

**Figure 6.2 Benefits to those with limited income: 1990-1992**
Source:     U.S. Cong. Research Service, Library of Congress &
            U.S. Bureau of Census, 1994

When examining total social welfare costs for state and federal governments between 1980 and 1991 in Figure 5.3 below, the data also indicates that public support has increased considerably. When comparing social welfare costs to state governments between 1980 and 1991, such costs have doubled over the 12-year period. Again, state governments are also perceiving welfare costs as out of control. Their need to bring these costs under control is apparent since many states are required by law to balance their yearly budgets. Uncontrollable costs are devastating as they affect a state's ability to provide for other services required of residents. The problem of caring for those in poverty continues to occupy the minds of governors and state legislatures as they attempt to manipulate limited resources to meet federal mandates.

State governments have been somewhat instrumental in the betrayal attributed to a misdirected compassion to help those in need. Whereas public support for assisting those in poverty has increased each year, the lack of accountability as to how effective the allocation of these funds were has resulted in a lingering poverty. Primarily relying upon public agencies through casework assignments, a loosely administered welfare policy has resulted in very little success reducing large numbers of heads of households in poverty. Therefore, the return on investment from state public funding has had a significant impact upon solving poverty in America.

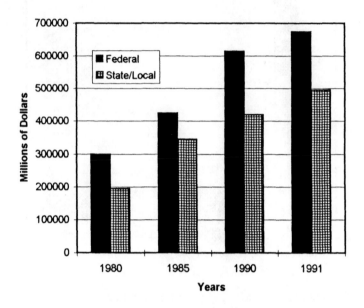

**Figure 6.3**   **Federal and state social welfare costs: 1980-1991**
Source:           U. S. Bureau of the Census, 1994

Since 1980, the federal government has also seen their social welfare expenses increased substantially. In Figure 6.3 above, the federal government portion of welfare expenditures increased from $300 billion in 1980 to $680 billion in 1991. Similar to social welfare costs at the state level, federal contributions have also doubled in the 11-year time span between 1980 and 1991. When we group state and federal welfare costs together and compare them between 1975 and 1991as in Figure 6.4 below, the data shows that there has been approximately 600 percent increase from $210 billion to $1.15 trillion. Welfare costs are indeed out of control and past strategies for eliminating poverty are not proving to be effective. Therefore, the federal government has also played an important role in a history of betrayal, not so much  in terms of available funding but in a similar lack of accountability for funds spent.

156

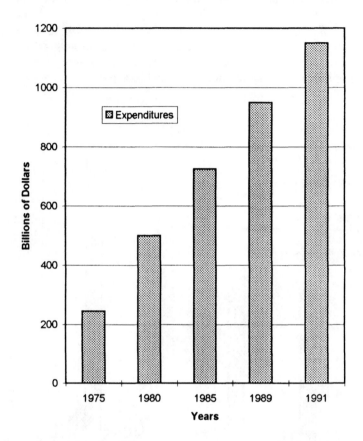

**Figure 6.4   Total state and federal social welfare costs combined**
Source:        U.S. Bureau of the Census, 1993


In addition, the private sector has also made considerable financial contributions to implementing programs to help those in poverty.  As noted in Figure 6.5 on the next page, businesses have targeted education as a primary factor for not only enhancing the lives of the everyday consumer but also those of their workers.  Attempting to increase the productivity of the workforce is in the best interest of business, and their effort to complement public spending in such an effort continues with each passing year.  In Figure 6.5, the amount business has contributed to education has almost doubled from $250 billion in 1985 to $440 billion in

1991. In terms of social welfare contributions, business has gradually increased its expenditures from $40 billion to $55 billion. The business community relies upon locating and hiring individuals who are capable of adding value to required work for producing products and services. In the future, many of those workers will come from a growing pool of immigrants and minorities. Although their compassion to help others may be selfish, motivated by the profit motive, their future role in eradicating poverty may be more important than in the past.

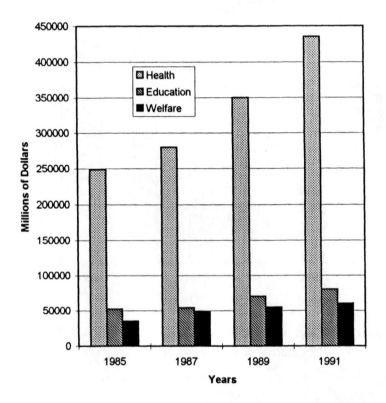

**Figure 6.5   Business expenditures for social and productive welfare**
Source:        U.S. Bureau of the Census, 1994

Since the 1930s, the federal government has taken on a major role in the public assistance. At the turn of the 20th Century, federal agencies and state/local governmental bodies had only a minor role in these matters. Today, the federal government continues to have considerable influence and authority.

One example in particular includes the authority to forbid state officials to advise or influence welfare recipients as to how they will spend their monthly benefits. Therefore, state governments have been under the direct authority of federal officials in terms of what they can do and cannot. State authorities have had to adhere to strict guidelines developed as a result of welfare legislation passed by Congress. One of the difficulties for states has been a gradual process by federal officials to transfer responsibility for implementing federal welfare programs to the states without providing the necessary funding to support such additional efforts. The result has been spiraling costs attached to welfare programs. Compounding the problem has been the effects of inflation upon benefits received by welfare recipients. Correspondingly, the Consumer Price Index (CPI) for each year between 1982 and 1992 clearly shows that prices continue to rise, making it even more difficult for the poor to purchase necessary goods. The CPI indexes 1982-1992 show that prices for food, transportation, medical care, and even fuel oil to keep homes warm have all increased substantially.

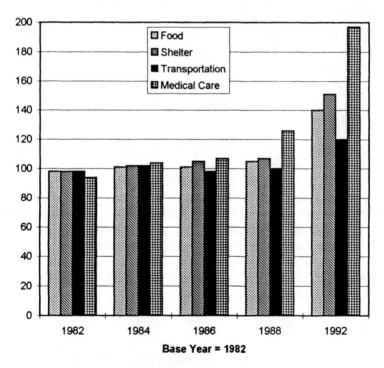

Base Year = 1982

**Figure 6.6    Consumer price indexes: 1982-1992**
Source:        Monthly Labor Review, 1994

**Complexities to administering welfare benefits add to woes**

When attempting to analyze the effectiveness of states in administering public welfare programs, recorded statistics have a tendency to become blurred. For example, the average case load of welfare recipients varies from state to state, and it changes each day. Since welfare covers so many different forms of aid (including social insurance, Medicare, housing, education, public aid, foods stamps, and much more), it is often difficult to obtain precise numbers as to the number of people who are on welfare at any specific time.

For example, let's take a brief look at attempts to evaluate welfare services of one of the smaller states in the union, Delaware. According to the Delaware Department of Health and Social Services (1995), there were approximately 11,000 average case loads of welfare recipients in October of 1994. This figure does not include any private cases of assistance (whose numbers also vary depending upon the source utilized). Out of that number, 39 cases required emergency housing in the same month.

In addition, there were 21,000 cases related to food stamp distribution in Delaware in November 1994. In order to be eligible for food stamps, there are certain financial requirements one must meet. According to the food stamp Hotline in Delaware, an individual is eligible to receive food stamps if he/she is part of a family of:

> 1 and earn less than $798 per month gross,
> 2 and earn less than $1,066 per month gross,
> 3 and earn less than $1,335 per month gross,
> 4 and earn less than $1,604 per month gross,

Keeping tract of all payments reflecting varying family makeup is a monstrous task--one that can easily be abused due to the complexity of the 'paper bureaucracy' required to process huge amounts of data from both private and public institutions. Therefore, with a myriad of welfare programs being offered by states in conjunction with the federal government, keeping track as to who is on what program becomes a problem. The outcome of such a complex welfare system is the likelihood of fraud, an issue that often results in a great deal of mental anguish on the part of society.

**Welfare fraud at its worse**

Unfortunately, there are those individuals who try to cheat the welfare system and use it to their own advantage. Chris Wallace, a reporter of NBC news, in the January 11, 1995, segment of the ten o'clock news from Capital Hill, highlighted examples of food stamp fraud. Apparently, a sizable number of both small and large food retailers make substantial profits gathering food stamps illegally from the government and redeeming them at face value. It

160

was also reported that food stamp fraud has almost virtually become a second currency to these business people. Chris Wallace stated that it has become so easy to get involved in this type of scam that numerous local businesses have begun to form illegal coalitions.

The saddest part of this problem is that the individuals and their families who are seeking assistance from the public to support their financial needs are sometimes found participating in welfare fraud themselves. According to the Wallace report, there are some recipients who obtain the food stamps, and then spend the majority of it on cigarettes, alcohol, and sometimes even marijuana. They often spend more of the food stamps on frivolous material goods rather than those basic to survival (food, clothing, etc.). Out of a $115 dollar food stamp, one man admitted that he only used $20 of it towards food, (Carper, 1995).

Republican Senator Rick Santorum (1996) of Pennsylvania has also commented upon the abuses in welfare suggesting that states must do a better job in making sure that welfare fraud is eliminated. In his opinion, the states are not being 'creative' enough in preventing fraud, especially since there is such an increase in fraud. In the end, deception and deceit of such services only results in a system where it is more difficult to distribute subsidies to those who are truly in need. For example, the New Jersey Port Authority Police discovered 324 cases of welfare fraud, a majority of which were of males who reside in New Jersey. They were not able to collect the $352 welfare checks from New York, so they resorted to forgery using through using 'fake' identification cards for collecting illegal welfare subsidies from both states.

Such welfare fraud results in making a mockery out of a well-intended program. Moreover, initiating preventive measures is rather difficult, especially for a program that operates under the protection of a Federal Constitution which requires due process of anyone accused of tampering with a government program. Therefore, the considerable time consumed in prosecuting incidents of welfare fraud prohibits sending appropriate signals to others that welfare fraud will not be permitted. Protecting the rights of perpetrators while being investigated by federal and state enforcement agencies frequently results in lengthy delays for bringing violators to justice. Our model includes a detail plan for how individuals can develop a justice system that is community based.

## States experiment with innovative strategies

Because of the difficulties in monitoring welfare practices decreed by federal officials as well as actions by recipients of welfare benefits, many states are electing to seek exemptions from the federal government for the purpose of getting better value from each dollar spent. One such an effort is that labeled

*The Better Chance* by Governor Carper in the State of Delaware. Governor Carper acknowledges that welfare should be transitional and not become a way of life. He proposes a system where two parents take responsibility for supporting their children, not just one. The Governor plans to abolish the current welfare system by 1999. In its place, he plans to establish support groups for families, child care, and improved access to health care, (Carper, 1995).

**Frightening health care reform contributes to betrayal**

A consequence to health care reform is Americans witnessing in the near future limited access to medical services as attempts to control costs continue. For those individuals on welfare or in low-income families just above the criteria for getting public assistance, these pending changes to health care access become more frightening. Since the establishment of the Department of Health and Human Services (DHHS) health care for the poor has been almost exclusively devised by the federal government, resulting in a diminishing role of the states. Many states have, in the past, often struggled to find moneys to support federal initiatives. Because of financial restraints upon state budgets and the concern for offering quality services to those in need, many of the grants-in-aid programs of the DHHS are used to fund part of state health responsibilities, leaving states to struggle to find other local funding sources to abide by federal mandates. As many of us are aware, health care costs have risen substantially over the past decade.

In Figure 6.7, data indicates that total national health expenditures in 1965 were approximately $45 billion. That amount has since soared to $450 billion in 1985. Although the rate of increase of health care costs has slowed somewhat between 1995 and 1997, it is anticipated that by the year 2000, health care costs may reach well over the $1 trillion mark. It is almost frightening to imagine how much will be spent on health care in the upcoming century. In addition, those in or just above the poverty level will be impacted upon greatly if we cannot generate a new approach to controlling health care costs.

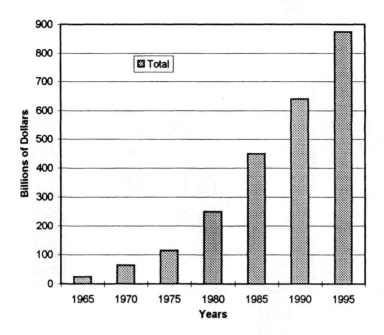

**Figure 6.7    National health care costs: 1965-1995**
Source:        U.S. Health Care Financing Administration, 1996

Although health care expenditures vary by state, each has been spending more on health care each year. The states that spent the most on health care between 1980 to 1991 were California, Texas, Florida, and Pennsylvania. California spent the most, totaling over $58 billion. This amount included expenses on hospitals, physician services and prescription drugs. Since 1980, health care expenditures in a majority of states throughout the nation has increased over 9 percent each year on the average, (U.S. Health Care Financing Administration, 1994, p. 111).

*An increasing reliance upon Medicaid*

In terms of assisting those at the lower end of the socio-economic scale, the costs of attending to health care problems has also continued to grow. From 1985 to 1992, the total number of Medicaid recipients indicated in Figure 6.8 below has increased from 21,814,000 to 31,150,000 people, (U.S. Health Care Financing Administration, 1994, p. 124). At the same time, Medicaid

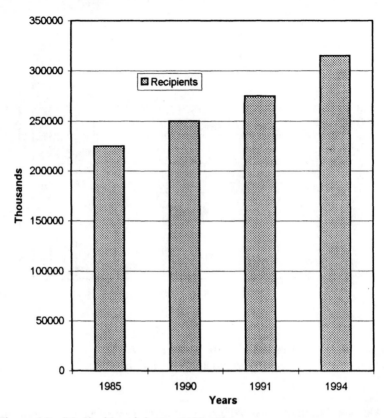

**Figure 6.8    Medicaid recipients: 1985-1994**
Source:        U.S. Health Care Financing Administration, 1994

payments have increased at even a faster rate, costing the government and taxpayers millions of dollars. Medicaid payments more than doubled between 1985 and 1994. In Figure 6.9, the data indicates that Medicaid payments rose from approximately $390 billion to approximately $1 trillion in 1994. Since Medicaid is paid partially by state contribution and partly from federal funds, the increase in costs between 1985 and 1994 have had substantial impact on both budgets. One factor influencing this increase is that the rate of increase in inflation rated to medical care in general. With over 14 percent of the population in America living with incomes below the poverty level, there are a lot of people who are not able to afford these increases in medical care. In this regard, Medicaid is a valuable program to them, (U.S. Bureau of Census, 1995).

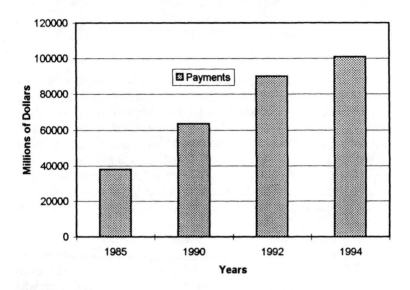

**Figure 6.9   Total Medicaid payments: 1985-1994**

Source:       U.S. Health Care Financing Administration,  1994

By the year 2000, the new millennium is expected to be greeted by Medicaid payments almost double of those of today, if nothing is done to control the rate of yearly increase.   These are astronomical numbers, and each year they continue to rise, costing government more and more to ensure that these needy Americans receive the adequate health care they deserve, (U.S. Health Administration, 1994).

**The history of betrayal results in poor housing**

The view during the 1950s concerning public housing subsidies was that they were an 'unnecessary evil', (Burno, 1948). Many spokespersons for welfare reform have pointed out the 'evils' of housing subsidies, one claiming that by placing individuals in overcrowded tenements, they were more prone to illness and disease, (Freeman, 1991). Even today, many recipients of housing subsidies are living in residences where urban and rural blight reflects abandoned buildings, where the crime rate is extremely high, and where overcrowding becomes commonplace. Although building codes have been established to eliminate many of the so called 'evils' of public housing, suitable shelter for many families remains difficult to locate.

*Public housing destroys the human spirit*

The 1994 Statistical Abstract shows that social welfare expenditures for housing in 1985 was $13 billion. In 1991, government spent $22 billion alone on housing. Henry Aaron, from the U.S. Department of Health and Human Services, once commented that 'subsidized housing is proving to be vastly more expensive than anyone anticipated,' (Freeman, 1981, p.303). For every new unit of public housing created, the federal/local government spends approximately $157,050. In 1981, there were 114,700 new units, totaling to well over $180,136,350. The majority of the costs of these housing units may be attributed to the rising costs of land, construction, financing, and maintenance, (Freeman, 1981, p. 301-2).

However, a major problem with our current system has to do with the upkeep of these dwellings. Many of the welfare recipients (not all) who receive public housing subsidies do not keep their residences in good repair, often resulting in the deterioration of buildings. After a period of time, those who have resided in the dwellings for longer periods of time end up with very poor living conditions, often resulting in an attitude of not caring for their property or the community in which they reside. At the same time, there are many recipients who do maintain their own homes or apartments, but they remain part of blighted communities. As a result, new housing units have a history of deteriorating at a record pace, accounting for a large part of the increases in housing expenditures, (Freeman, 1981, p.301).


**Community violence becomes an everyday reality**

For many on welfare, safety is utmost on the mind. Unfortunately, in the United States, the number of individuals victimized by violence has remained considerably high since 1984. As depicted in Figure 6.10 on the next page, the largest number of victims was in 1988. In that year alone, 19,966 acts of violence were committed against the general public, including women and small children. Murder, rape, theft, robbery, assault, and larceny are only a few of these hideous crimes. Over the next few years, that amount decreased slightly to 18,832 in 1992. These were crimes committed by whites, blacks, Hispanics, Asians, and other races, as well as those in varying age groups (all

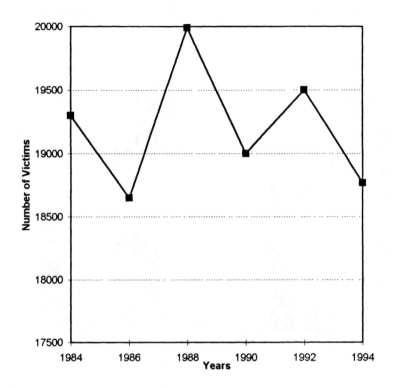

**Figure 6.10    Number of U.S. victims**

Source:        U.S. Bureau of Justice, 1995

12 years and older). The age group that most frequently committed these crimes were in the 20 to 24 year old range, (Bureau of Census, 1994).

Ironically, in comparison to other services, such as education, public welfare, and health care, crime prevention receive the least monetary support from government. In 1980, the state governments spent $2.2 billion on police protection, which increased to $5.5 billion in 1992, (U.S. Bureau of Census, 1994). In comparison to the other public funding for meeting the needs of society, funding for crime appears to be modest. These lack of sufficient funding for public safety may account for some of the increase in crime rate. America's attempt at compassion has resulted in many acts of crime are being committed by children. Over the past ten years, the number of juveniles (ages

167

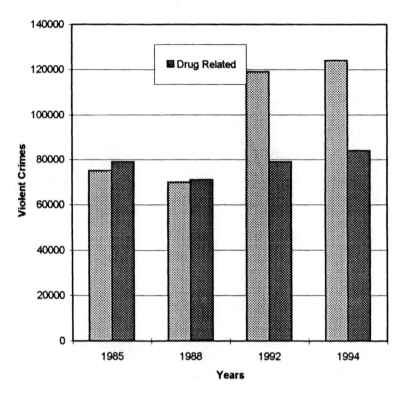

**Figure 6.11    Juvenile arrests for ages 10-17**
Source:           U.S. Federal Bureau of Investigation, 1995

10-17)who have been arrested range into the thousands. In Figure 6.11 above, the total number of juvenile arrests for violent crimes in 1985 were 75,077, soaring to 118,334 in 1992. Drug related arrests continue to be a serious aspect of juvenile arrests as they increased from approximately 80,000 in 1985 to 83,000 in 1994.

**Youth sabotage their neighborhoods**

In many areas of the United States, such as Little Rock, Arkansas, 'drive-by' shootings have disrupted neighborhoods and have resulted in the death of a considerable number of children. The catalyst for such destructive behavior is difficult to identify. However, an outbreak of 'drive-by' shooting occurred after a showing of Home Box Office (HBO) 1995 original movie entitled *Gang Wars: Bangin' in Little Rock.*   In some neighborhoods, these shootings occur every 20-30 minutes, many times resulting in a death or injury. The death rate for juveniles continues to escalate due to such acts of youth violence, and many of the victims know who their assailants are. Many of the perpetuators are residents of the same neighborhood where the acts of committed. The Reverend H. D. Stewart of the Gang Task Force feels that the primary reason why youth in poverty become so destructive is that many of them do not feel that they are cared about, so they will make people care by victimizing them. Many juveniles acknowledge that they do not want to continue to live a life of crime, but do not know how else to live. The result has been deteriorating neighborhoods and also the human spirit that generates life and compassion into a community. The deadly effects of the history of betrayal as America attempted to help those in need have put into place serious doubts as to the sincerity of public official in eradicating poverty.

## Mediocre education destroys any attempt at equal opportunity

Some Americans are very fortunate today to have access to good public schools. Each year the government spends millions and millions of dollars on such programs like Head Start to help steer youngsters towards a brighter future. However, federal funding for education has increased slowly over the past years. In Figure 6.12, the data reveals that the funding for education is primarily a state responsibility with local support ranking second. In terms of state funding, the amount of financial support for public education increased from $120 billion in 1980 to over $160 billion in 1994. In addition, local school district support increased from $78 billion in 1980 to $110 billion in 1994. In spite of such increases in the funding of public education, math and written test scores on national and international tests are average at best.

Moreover, public schools in poorer neighborhoods continue to be subjected to extraordinary problems that hinder the performance of students. Much has been said about schools in districts where there is a large number of households living in poverty. Such school districts are likely not to have the best teachers, the best equipment, or the best facilities. Student safety is more of a concern due to high rates of crime, drug usage, and simply bullying among students. When schools are not able to accomplish their goals of educating youth for eventual employment, two outcomes are likely. One is a high dropout rate and the other a higher rate of unemployment.

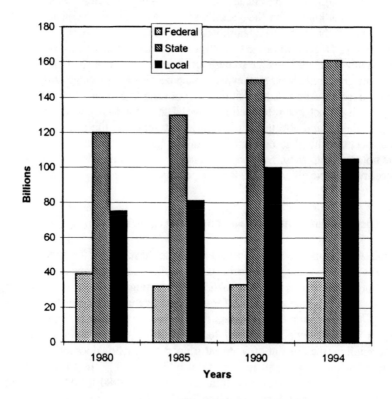

**Figure 6.12**    **School expenditures by source: 1980-1994**

Source:        U.S. Department of Education, 1995

While the rate of unemployment has generally varied between 4 and 9 percent over the past decade, in actuality it is 100 percent for those who are unemployed. Unfortunately, for those on welfare, higher rates of unemployment are felt during a down-cycle in the economy. However, even during relatively 'good times,' unemployment remains significant. For example, in Figure 6.13, the data reveals that there were 8,734,000 people out of work in the United States in 1994. It can be safely assumed that many of these unemployed are heads of households in poverty. In addition, many of those presently on welfare may be in part-time jobs which do not reflect in the unemployment figures but nevertheless may not be sufficient to result in getting such families to a standard of living above the poverty line.

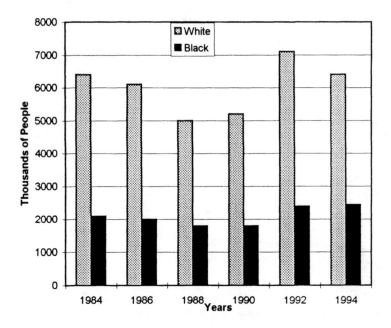

**Figure 6.13    Unemployment for ages 16 and up**
Source :         U.S. Department of Labor, 1995


It is difficult to determine if the education programs have failed to train these individuals or if the individuals failed to access the programs that were available to them. Also, one may question whether the poverty stricken are even aware of the programs that are provided in their community. There have been many instances where low income families are not able to attain the level of education they desire, thus resorting themselves to a lifetime of welfare support. Often, their children are left in the same predicament without a choice.

It has become evident over time that high school dropouts have a much lower chance of obtaining employment than if they had stayed in school. In Figure 6.14 below, the employment of high school dropouts has consistently decreased from 5.5 million to 3.6 million between 1975 and 1995. Moreover, children from families in poverty  are often located in inner city school districts. These schools are often characterized by having some of the worst teacher shortages and the most under qualified new hires. These factors alone may prevent these children from developing their skills to their potential, and

171

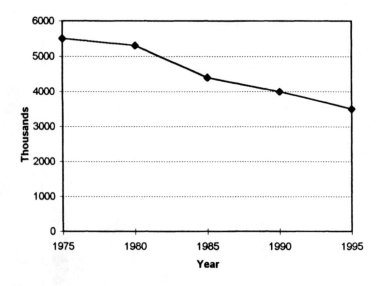

**Figure 6.14    Employment status of high school dropouts**
Source:            U.S. Bureau of Labor Statistics, 1995

thus preventing them from gaining access to jobs with a living wage.

There seems to be more and more schools with increased social needs but not enough funds to address these needs suitably. This Council received federal funding to establish innovative schools in urban centers where poverty persists. However, between 1980 and 1990, the percentage of GCS revenues from federal sources of income decreased from 11.9 percent to 9.1 percent. The inner city schools are the ones who have felt the greatest pinch of these dwindling resources. Four out of five GCS leaders have experienced a decline in local revenues in spite of increasing enrollments, making it more difficult to implement such programs. Many of these students consist of children from poor or immigrant families. Therefore, limited funding for special programs such as this is another example of the betrayal of welfare assistance. The number of years of schooling completed by segments of the population varies. Some students may opt to go on to a technical school after completing high school. On the other hand, there are great percentages of the population who have never even finished high school. In 1993, out of 162,826,000 people over the age 25, approximately 19 percent of them have not completed high school. There are more females (20 percent) without a

172

high school diploma than males (19.5 percent), and the majority of these dropouts were of Hispanic (46.9 percent) decent. A substantial number of students who do not complete high school are often left unemployed, (U.S. Bureau of Census, 1994).

**Conclusion:  The betrayal lingers on and on and on . . . . . .**

Welfare policy in the past has left many Americans asking the question, "where did we fail?" The federal, state, and local governments have spent billions of dollars each year to help needy Americans avoid a life of poverty, but the problem continues to worsen. A priority is to develop a new kind of system that enhances family unity and societal values reflecting the work ethic and the pride of ownership. It may be concluded that America's attempt at compassion has had good intent, but the continual presence of poverty is discouraging. Rebuilding the infrastructure (schools, transportation, and buildings? Of poor neighborhoods may help heads of households in poverty cope with some of their disappointments. However, rebuilding human spirit and faith in the free enterprise system must be addressed. Our welfare legacy is not a good one. Hopelessness still abounds for many of our less fortunate citizens. Our model focuses attention on a readily available source that could, if adapted, become the 'heart and soul' of a new welfare system, one that may provide thousands of individuals a desperately needed second chance. This resource can become an integral part of the healing of American that is very much needed if this country is to continue to progress under the banner of economic freedom and independence.

# 7 A welfare time bomb remains

Presently, those in leadership positions at the local, state, or federal level of government have been attempting to convince the public that welfare reform is a necessity, that government spending must be reduced significantly, and that state and local officials must come forth to solve local community problems. However, the strategies that are being debated appear to be somewhat inhumane and misdirected by putting additional hardship on most those in need assistance in order to survive in a democracy. As a degree of consensus is sought among individuals with good intent, the fear that is generated among present welfare recipients may generate in a whole new set of problems for families in poverty.

## A governmental assault on welfare recipients

A listing of programs to be eliminated in order to reduce the welfare expenses at the federal level appear overwhelming. The impact upon welfare families of America is unknown, but the perception is that significant adjustments in meeting formerly AFDC family financial obligations will be necessary. Listed below are programs that have been mentioned recently to be either eliminated or significantly reduced:

> low-income heating assistance
> upgrading public housing
> rental assistance to the poor
> summer jobs for youth
> building new public housing

anti-drug efforts (schools)
community service programs
community development grants
job training for youth
school-to-work programs
housing for AIDS patients
school improvement initiatives (Goals 2000)
special grants to local schools to assist
    low-income students
adoptions and foster care program
mass transit
school construction
Pell Grants
food and homemaking education programs
programs to prevent school dropouts
food programs for women, infants, and children
library construction
training counselors for children victimized by
    violence
and the list goes on and on . . . .


What appears to the thrust of the "new strategy for welfare reform" is the dismantling of the entire system based upon the argument that large sums of moneys are simply wasted by the recipients, that the outcome from existing approaches is welfare dependency, and that there are too many recipients who are doomed to demeaning unproductive jobs. Therefore, the approach to welfare reform is simply to dismantle it.

In addition, as programs targeting families in poverty are either reduced or eliminated at the federal level, there has been some movement to redirect welfare responsibilities to the states. One frequently suggested strategy for curing the welfare cycle is to have the federal government distribute 'block grants' to states for the purpose of providing child care assistance, nutrition programs, etc. One of the most frequently mentioned and perhaps one of the largest block grant programs to be revised is the Aid to Families with Dependent Children (AFDC).

The harshness of welfare reform is readily seen in the denying of cash benefits to mothers under the age of 18. There are some who suggest that welfare benefits should be reduced for those women who refuse to name the fathers of their children. There are others who suggest that existing mothers on welfare who keeping having children should not gain access to additional financial support. The theory here is that economic behavior will overcome sexual behavior in the moment of passion by giving females an economic incentive to say 'no'. Dictating morality has never been a strength of our government officials, and a continued desire to do can easily bring on the critics of the present direction of welfare reform.

As we continue to look for ways to reduce public expenditures at all levels of government, there is debate as to when to end cash benefits for welfare recipients once a parent has found a new job. A *politically correct* philosophy that continues to generate the most excitement is that welfare recipients must assume more responsibility for their own well being within a 3- to 5-year time limit. Of course, the momentum for reducing welfare benefits often stems from anecdotal data which often focuses upon welfare scams that make their way into our local and national newspapers, journals, Internet, and other forms of mass media.

One scam that comes to mind--whether it is true or not is another matter-- adds 'oil on a fire' by generating a public mood which assists our leaders in getting approval for reducing welfare budgets. For example, a secondary school student who is fairly bright comes to school with gum stuck in her hair. Her grades have gone 'sour' over a period of time. She is labeled 'learning- impaired'--and because she is categorized as poor, the family starts receiving federal welfare checks related to some kind of disability. The story goes on in that the family uses the welfare checks to pay for a van, a stereo, and a Florida vacation. There are perhaps many other stories that have appeared in the press reflecting other scams--too many to mention here. However, the reality is that these scams often receive much attention in the press and thus become part of the national debate as we attempt to build a consensus as to how to instill individual responsibility at the core of welfare reform.

### Blaming others becomes a national pastime

Blaming someone for welfare abuse often gains the attention of the public for generating a momentum towards reform. In this instance, much attention has been focused upon missing fathers who are often accused as one of the primary reasons for poverty among welfare mothers. In perpetuating the fatherless society theme, David Blankenhorn in *Fatherless American: Confronting Our Most Urgent Social Problem* (1995) discusses an increasing reality of children today not growing up with a father. In fact, he labels *fatherless families* as today's defining feature of children living in poverty. Astonishing facts are used to document the significance of this change to family structure. Blankenhorn reports statistics that depict 40 percent of U.S. children presently in homes in which their fathers do not live. He argues that *fatherless families* are the most harmful demographic trend of this generation. He goes on and suggests that it is a leading cause of poverty and the decline of the well-being of children.

Others attack the elderly for getting special treatment through welfare subsidies. Thus, reducing welfare benefits to the *elderly poor in our society* becomes part of the debate. Four programs--supplemental security insurance (SSI), food stamps, subsidized housing, and Medicaid--are means-tested (pegged to income) specially for low-income persons, young or old. In addition, two non means-tested programs, meals-on-wheels and congregate meals, are available to nearly all individuals age 60 and over. It is important to note that a significant number of elderly citizens who receive assistance from these programs are single, older women--many who are at or just above poverty level. The American Association of Retire People (AARP) has been most vocal in protecting the interests of those over 65, especially the poor receiving benefits from federal programs.

Compounding the problem of welfare reform has been the increasing numbers of illegal immigrants. These non-citizens have created a sense of panic among citizens in several areas of this country, most notably those in California. The argument focuses upon an unfair burden being placed upon families in the middle class who subsidize immigrants through public taxes. The argument goes that illegal immigrants often end up receiving both state and federal assistance for such programs as Medicaid, food stamps, disability aid, Aid to Families with Dependent Children, and social service programs known as Title XX.

In addition, a related local issue is the cost of constructing new schools and providing more diversity in present curricula and instructional methodology to accommodate the language differences among children with varying ethnic backgrounds. Robert Almanzan, director of communications for the Mexican American Legal Defense and Educational Fund, argues that it is unjust to eliminate support of immigrants from welfare policy in the United States. Immigrants form the backbone of our economic system, and their productivity enhances the profit for many small businesses in all regions of our nation.

### Federal mandates strain the system

Some argue that the federal government has heaped on more than 170 mandates upon states over the past three decades, resulting in billions of dollars being spent by state and local governments. Some of these mandates reflect state responsibilities for enhancing Medicaid requirements, job counseling/training, minimum wage, and other social services. Others argue that federal mandates have enabled the middle class to pay for care of elderly relatives without going broke as well as guarantee jobs to workers who take a leave of absence to care of a sick child or to give birth. Such Federal mandates are forcing local governments to increase taxes, placing additional burdens on many low-income consumers currently struggling to make ends meet. No matter what an individual's position is at the current time, the issue of federal mandates is very much part of the welfare reform debate.

Therefore, it appears under the banner of welfare reform that the federal government is reducing or eliminating programs which have been part of a societal *safety net*. However, reducing the Federal budget and corresponding deficit is a priority and a driving force behind the call for change. Moreover, the direction of welfare reform also appears to protect the welfare of the middle-class while at the same time targeting those in poverty to become independent. Considerable attention has been devoted to reducing the number of children out of wedlock. Whether it is eliminating program deficits, getting fathers back into the family, or reducing the number of children born out of wedlock, the attention of the public is upon motivating individuals to behave in their own best interests. Therefore, while protecting those public benefits assigned to the middle class, a resentment builds among those living in poverty. Our model addresses this important point.

**Welfare myths bias attempts at reform**

There are several divisive myths that continue to misdirect the welfare reform debate. These myths have a tendency to stigmatize non-traditional family styles, implying that there is a need to transform AFDC families into those nuclear families that dominated family life at the turn of the Twentieth Century. The premise is that the breakdown of the family is the primary cause of poverty, crime, and despair. Uninvolved parents are being accused as not providing appropriate role models for our children to imitate as they grow and mature. It is argued that these abuses by welfare recipients perpetuate a continual cycle of welfare dependency--and this must stop now!

The question here is what is reality and what is myth? Is the breakdown of the family the real core of the problem? Must the family first be restructured in order to eliminate the welfare cycle dependency? Is the fatherless home the primary reason why so many children are in poverty? Is the unwed mother the primary reason why welfare programs are abused? It is critical to delineate fact from fiction if an appropriate direction for welfare reform is going to take hold. Critics of welfare reform often refer to the following myths as a basis of how *not* to design welfare reform.

*Unwed mothers abuse the system (myth #1)*

This myth relies upon the premise that welfare reform must include incentives to prevent teenage pregnancies by eliminating subsidies going to unwed mothers (especially those who are not willing to identify the fathers of their children). Therefore, it is suggested that unwed mothers and welfare abuse are directly related. What is implied here is that AFDC payments give the welfare

179

mother the option of having a baby without working to support that child. However, sociologist Mike Rank reports in *Living on the Edge--The Realities of Welfare in America* that a typical woman on AFDC has only 1.9 children, which is fewer children than her counterpart who is not on welfare. In addition, Rank has concluded that the longer she stays on welfare, the *less* likely she is to have more children. Furthermore, he reports that illegitimacy rates are lowest in the states that have the highest benefits. (Columbia University Press, 1994).

The core of the problem of poverty and welfare abuse does not appear to be unwed mothers. While American politicians preach abstinence or how important it is to pass out condoms, dozens of research studies show that the most effective deterrent to early childbearing is a teen's access to other sources of satisfaction and hope for the future. Spencer Rich (1995) argues in the *Washington Post* that good schools and jobs are the best methods of birth control and escape from welfare, and no strategy exists that gets better results.

The myth targeting welfare mothers misdirects the attention of the public from the realities of living in poverty. The stereotyping of welfare mothers with children does nothing but harm the self-esteem and value associated with child-bearing. Those who criticize the harshness of welfare reform with its focus upon child-bearing abuse attack the sincerity of social reformers who justify their proposals for change based upon perpetuating this myth. Our model puts this myth to rest.

*Family lifestyle choices among those in poverty is the most significant contributor to poverty. (myth #2)*

This myth perpetuates the idea that lifestyle choice is the primary reason for such problems as poverty, racial inequities, urban blight, drug use, school failure and crime. The implied argument here is that single-parent families eliminate any hope of elevating a AFDC family from poverty. This myth puts forth a popular notion that a different set of rules must be put into place to avoid single-parent families from being formed in the first place. However, recent research suggests that changes in family lifestyles are less significant a contributor to poverty and crime than those factors related to changes in earnings and employment. The University of Michigan Panel Study of Income Dynamics, which has followed a representative sample of 5000 families since 1968, found that only one in seven of childhood transitions into long-term poverty were associated with loss of a parent, while more than one in two were linked to changes in labor market participation or pay.

A 1991 study of data from the U.S. Bureau of Census found that the typical family that falls into poverty after the father leaves was already in economic distress *before* his departure, typically because he had recently lost his job. Most poverty, in other words, comes from our changing earnings structure, not from our changing family structure. Donald Hernandez (1994), chief of the

Bureau of Marriage and Family Statistics at the U.S. Census Bureau, reports that even if we could reunite every child in America with his or her biological father, two-third's of those children who are poor today would still be poor. In addition, Frank Furstenberg (1995) points out that most indicators of declining well-being for children--low test scores, drug use, teen pregnancy, and growing crime rates--began to rise before a divorce or breakup of a family. Furstenberg further points out that the educational and work status of a child's mother has more impact on that child's welfare than marital status (or family style). Our model focuses upon employment and not family structure as to way to end poverty.

*The nuclear family serves as the best role model for those in poverty. (myth #3)*

This myth perpetuates the fantasy that the nuclear family is the best family style for welfare recipients, while any other simply results in a continual decay. Therefore, welfare reform implies that there is primarily one answer to the problem of poverty. Simply, incentives must be put into place to generate two-parent nuclear family role models. Other family models put children at risk. The argument suggests that in order to change family structure among those who are presently on welfare, it is necessary to change the values of AFDC heads of households. The argument continues that it is critical to adopt a social policy that stigmatizes family structures that do not reflect the two-parent, one major breadwinner style. Our model suggests that there is no one kind of family or one approach to solve the complexities surrounding living in poverty. Our model provides a framework where diversity is accepted as a valuable aspect of welfare reform.

Attaching a stigma to single parents on welfare may deter some couples from divorce or prevent some women from having babies out of wedlock, but it is unlikely to reverse the larger trend toward declining centrality of life-long marriage. In the real world of 1994, only 50.8 percent of all youths live with both biological parents; 24 percent live in one-parent families; 21.1 percent live in stepfamilies. The real world indicates that there are many different kinds of families which do not reflect the traditional two-parent biological family structure, and all such families are not necessarily on welfare. Therefore, it appears inappropriate to assign higher expectations to those individuals on welfare than what is occurring to all families in general.

There must be something else to serve as a role model for those on welfare rather using the nuclear family. It is argued here that the rhetoric of family lifestyle does not assist us in attacking the core of the problem. The argument that nuclear families are the bedrock of stable communities may be misleading at best. What is argued here is that stable communities with a solid employment base are the bedrock of stable families. It makes more sense to build new kinds of communities where jobs and local community pride are imbedded rather than attempt to convince AFDC families that it in their best interest to become a nuclear family.

*Jobs will break cycle of despair. (myth #4)*

In the past, the focus has been upon providing welfare recipients with job training that will result in job entry. Employment therefore would instill pride in the parent, leading to the breaking  welfare dependency.  The myth perpetuated here is that to break the cycle of despair simply requires employment of some kind. However, many of the low-skilled jobs are disappearing as many of the larger corporations are downsizing their workforce.  Moreover, the kinds of jobs available require an individual who is flexible as well as capable of fulfilling a variety of roles while on the job, and one who has an excellent work ethic.  What is expected today for job entry and especially career advancement is an individual who will show up at work on time, be capable of working with others who may be from different cultures with different expectations, and one who can read, write, and perform basic logic routines for making decisions.

The myth that one must primarily be skilled in a specific trade or craft to gain employment may be misleading to welfare recipients. The fear is that we may be generating a whole new underclass by perpetuating the idea that well-paying jobs may be only accessible by having specialized technical skills.  It is argued here that a totally new training format must be initiated by the private sector that differentiates between what is required for initial job entry and what is required for career advancement.  It is argued here that job entry may not be the key to ending welfare subsidies for families in need but success in advancing in that job.  In our model, the focus is upon developing careers and not preparing an individual for job entry.

The significance to welfare reform is the building of a 'cyberworker' where dependability, commitment, and cooperation become part of the work ethic. Since adding value to work is the basic premise for hiring new workers, the retraining of welfare mothers and fathers must be accomplished in a completely different structure than that relied upon  in the past.  The expectation that placing heads of AFDC families in quick-response training programs for a duration of  three to six months will result in an employable individual is more of a fantasy than reality.  What may be accomplished in such a short duration is perhaps the development of a few trade skills at a marginal level of competency.  Such a program at best may help get some one employed in a low-level job entry position, but the wage earned will likely not raise a family out of poverty.

One only has to look to the recent past to determine that real wages of those in poverty have decreased. The kinds of jobs in which those on welfare have customarily entered have resulted in real disappointed. For example, the real wages have been falling for those in poverty. This has been particularly true for younger workers below age 18. Since the mid-1970s, both absolute and relative poverty have grown steadily, with inequality reaching every new heights. Even after taxes, the top 20 percent of American families now earn 44 percent of total incomes; the bottom 20 percent must get by on only 3.9 percent. In fact, the top 1 percent of the working population has as much income as the entire bottom 40 percent.

Therefore, placing individuals in job entry positions where one skill may be the prerequisite for employment and expecting real wages to increase automatically over a period of a decade may not be realistic. The cure is not job entry but job advancement. The best kind of training for today's jobs is 'on-the-job training'. In this regard, the business sector is in need of reevaluating how it is going to fill job vacancies using former welfare recipients since the 'baby bust' generation with fewer eligible workers will not meet demand. Our model addresses job preparation by supporting the contention that on-the-job training is the most cost-efficient strategy for upgrading employment skills. In this regard, where downsizing and job layoffs are an accepted part of business life, individuals must continually be in a 'training mode' whereby acquiring new skills is an everyday expectation. Quick one- or two-day seminars and workshops will not suffice.

*Individuals on welfare have different aspirations (myth #5)*

There is a perception held by many that heads of households of families in poverty have reduced aspirations because of their financial hardship. Realizing that they are mired in communities somewhat isolated from mainstream America, the reasoning goes that they willing to accept less in terms of the outcomes of their work. Their low income status results in setting lower standards of expectations, separating them from others in society who are more fortunate.

In reality, families in poverty generally have the same goals, aspirations and abilities of all Americans--whether upper, middle, or lower income status. However, there are market imperfections that have prevented them from 'enjoying' the success that a vast majority of Americans have experienced over the past several decades. These market imperfections include access to poor education, abrupt changes in employment due to a roller coaster economy, lack of information, and/or the absence of family role models.

In spite of being considered an 'economic and social outcast' by mainstream American, welfare recipients do seek to purchase a home, to send their children to good schools, and to live in safe communities. Earning wages at or near minimum wage in uninspiring jobs will not result in advancing the interests of families in need of a second change. Getting that initial job is not the solution to welfare reform. Our model demonstrates how one can gain access to the American dream--a well-paying job, a home in a safe neighborhood, and career advancement. Our model for welfare reform focuses upon raising the human spirit, resulting in a work ethic that has a positive effect on both home and work life.

*Heads of AFDC families are uneducable (Myth #6)*

Many Americans perceive heads of households in poverty as individuals who are shortsighted, who are filled with self-pity, and who care for no one but themselves. To some, welfare recipients are simply individuals who cannot read, write, or do math. They are incapable of doing anything productive or meaningful for society. Their role is at best to fulfill menial jobs that no one else wants to do. They are basically part of a 'nightmare' that depicts life as perpetually drifting from one public agency to another. There is no chance for changing their lives since they are basically uneducable.

In reality, this nation was based upon the principle that each child should have an equal opportunity to learn and obtain a job. The assumption was that public schools were structured to care to the learning needs of all students. However, Hirsh (1995) in *The Schools We Need* argues that our public schools are archaic, out of touch with students, and are dinosaurs. He argues that those who are most in need of personalized attention for developing important job skills and maturity are at a significant disadvantage in public institutions that are 'outrageously highly chaotic'. He goes on an argues that attempts to put together national standards and tests to measure progress towards these standards as proposed in the Goals 2000 Project are unlikely to succeed considering the realities of American education today.

Therefore, the real myth here is that American education is delivering the promise of enabling all citizens to learn how to read, write, and do math at a reasonable standard of performance. It is not that heads of AFDC are uneducable, it is the reality that our public schools are incapable of teaching all students with varying abilities and needs. A school that is situated in a thriving community with good parental involvement is likely to be one that teaches critical thinking, values clarification, and commitment. Public schools without a cohesive community behind it will likely teach bad learning habits, inappropriate workplace behavior, and out of date job skills, resulting in a poor work ethic.

By focusing upon the individual as being uneducable distracts society from the fact that many of their public schools are doing a disservice to many Americans. It is not that heads of AFDC households are uneducable, it is that public schools are incapable of educating many American youth. Hirsch (1995) uses the example that the average performance of American students in international competition in science, math, and language skills has been declining over the past decade. Test scores of poorer students labeled by some as the "underclass" have shown substantial declines. The conclusion is that the public educational model, especially those in urban centers, is failing

American youth. An entirely new kind of public education as proposed in our model city is required to meet the needs of children presently living in poverty.

*We don't subsidize middle-class families. (Myth #7)*

Much of the welfare debate has centered around the idea of placing financial limits on the amount of assistance that a family on welfare can receive. One popular financial cap is the denying of additional benefits to women who give birth to additional children while currently on welfare. The argument here is that if a citizen is working and receiving a wage in the private sector, that person does *not* receive a raise for having a child. Therefore, anyone who receives income, whether from public welfare program or through work, should all be treated identically.

However, it should also be noted that parents in middle class families do receive additional support from their government for helping to support additional children. In this regard, both men and women receive a premium for additional children in the form of a 'tax allowance/deduction' for each year when filing their income tax returns to the Internal Revenue Service. There are also tax credits given to families in the middle and upper class to partially cover child care expenses, up to a maximum of $2,400 per child. Therefore, the myth that only families on welfare receive additional aid for additional children is a myth that deserves some attention as welfare reform is planned. In our model, all families are treated equally and have access to the same opportunities.

*The public is fed up with spending money on the poor. (myth #8)*

According to a December 1994 poll conducted by the Center for the Study of Policy Attitudes, 80 percent of the respondents agreed that the federal government has an obligation to do away with poverty in this country. Therefore, Americans still remain committed to helping those who cannot reap the benefits of a free enterprise system. In addition, it was reported in the same study that 29 percent of those responding indicated that financial support for unemployed poor single mothers with children should be increased, whereas only 21 percent indicated a desire to reduce such benefits. Therefore, having families in poverty remains on the conscience of the American citizenry. There remains a commitment to find a strategy to rectify an unfortunate circumstance which could happen to any family at any time, (Center for the Study of Public Policy Attitudes, 1994).

What is more truthful is that many American citizens are fed up with sloppy unconscionable welfare policies that do more harm than good to those to whom they are directed. In this regard, the general public gets annoyed at programs that direct funds in ways that result in wasting their tax dollars. For example, according to the Children's Defense League (1997), it costs approximately $1600 to care for the medical needs of a child from prenatal care to age 12. Conversely, to tend to the medical needs of the child after age 12, especially one that requires admission to a hospital, one day's stay in a medical institution will likely result in a medical bill of $1100 per day, (State of America's Children, 1997).

In addition, such young children whose family has no medical insurance, are unlikely to seek a doctor regularly. It is a likely event that such children may develop vision problems, may become ill more frequently, and may be subjected to serious illnesses that could have been cured at the early stages of infection. The consequence is that students who cannot see the blackboard will have difficulty learning. Students who are continually absent from class will have difficult keeping up in their studies. Children who develop serious illnesses may have their lives shorten due to lack of treatment. All these children may opt to drop out of school since they are unable to keep up with their peers. The alternative to being in school is being in the streets, where children may turn to crime, drugs, or other kinds of violent behavior. What the public is fed up with are public policies that continue to ignore common sense and simply perpetuate past failures. Our model suggests a strong commitment to healthcare as the centerpiece of community building.

*We have spent over $5 trillion on public welfare over the past three decades and nothing seems to work. (myth #8)*

The perception here reflects the experience of a society spending huge amounts of money to bring families out of poverty, and past strategies have not worked. Such 'lavish' spending is perceived as wasteful since we still have a considerable number of families in poverty. However, in truth, $5 trillion has not been targeted totally to those families on welfare. In fact, the largest component of what is generally considered welfare support goes to the elderly and the disabled. Only about 16 percent of Medicaid goes to families on welfare requiring medical treatment for family members.

If we target just AFDC aid to families in poverty, only approximately $500 billion was spent on the entire program between 1964 and 1994, which is less that 1.5 percent of all federal outlays for this same period. Therefore, the myth that huge sums of the federal budget ends up in the hands of families in poverty is just not so. At best, it could be said that for the $500 billion spent in welfare programs over the past 30 years, the return on investment has not been impressive. Although we see signs of progress as shown in Figure 7.1, there are about 4.5 million families on the public welfare role in this nation. This figure computes to approximately 16 million individuals of which one-half are children between the ages of 1 and 12, (DHHS, 1997). Our model illustrates a better way to get value from tax dollars.

**Lack of consensus for direction of welfare reform**

Based upon a 1996 survey of academic economists by the Wall Street Journal (1997), the poll found little consensus as to how the federal government might

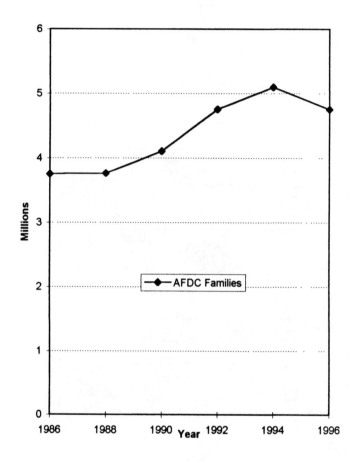

**Figure 7.1  Number of families receiving AFDC payments**
Source:      U.S. Dept. of Health & Human Services, 1987

enhance the lives of poor families in the United States. As shown in Figure 7.2 on the next page, approximately one in three suggest that boosting the nation's economic growth rate by one-quarter percentage point would do a lot for the poor. However, about the same number of economists polled predicted that spending more money on education and training would also be a big help in reducing poverty in this country. It should also be noted that while 15 percent indicated that increasing cash welfare benefits would have a positive impact upon families in poor financial circumstances, only 5 percent had a similar opinion related to increasing the minimum wage. Finally, only

## How to Help the Poor the Most

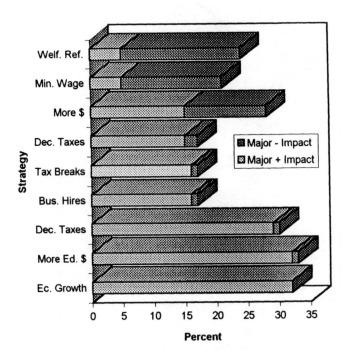

**Figure 7.2    Impact upon increasing income of the poor**
Source:        Wall Street Journal, 1997

5 percent of the economists agreed that pursuing welfare reform as enacted in 1996 would have a major positive impact upon the poor in this country. However, 19 percent felt it would have a major negative impact. A small percentage of the economists polled, between 15 and 16 percent, predicted that providing businesses with incentives to hire families on welfare would have a major impact upon their incomes. Only a very small percentage of the economists thought such a strategy would have a major negative impact

One of the few things that the economists surveyed agreed upon was that economic growth is very important to enhancing the lives of a majority of consumers. The economists consider education the number one priority in terms of enabling workers to achieve the productivity levels necessary to reap the benefits from global competition. In Figure 7.3 on the next page reporting data from the same Wall Street Journal survey, increased spending on education was indicated by 43 percent of the economists as the one policy that would have the most impact upon long-term economic growth rates in this country. These economists also reported that by expanding the economy by an extra one-half percent, in ten years Americans would generate approximately $375 billion more in earnings. The key to welfare reform as viewed by academic economists is getting individuals into jobs that have a living wage. Without an appropriate rate of growth, welfare reform is bound to fizzle. In this regard, the centerpiece is education and research and development. By combining these two pieces, a coherent growth policy would also reach those in need of jobs, presently families on welfare.

In examining Figure 7.3 on the next page, it should be noted that generating a balance budget does not result in much enthusiasm by academic economists surveyed. In this regard, only 5 percent indicated that such an achievement would have a most positive impact as the centerpiece of policy to generate sufficient economic growth to enhance consumer welfare. Such a position is consistent with our model of welfare reform that suggests that the centerpiece must be an integrated system of education and work, with the two complementing each other through a community that holds schools and business accountable. The remaining economic policy alternatives did not generate much of a consensus as to the impact upon spurring economic growth.

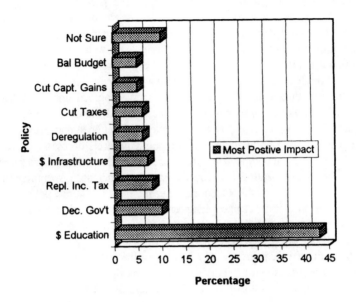

**Figure 7.3    One economic policy with most impact**
Source:        Wall Street Journal, 1997

### A contradiction between political promises and delivery

Politicians like to tell people what they want to hear. However, what the public is likely to hear during the election process will probably not happen. What the frequent promise is that all entitlements—whether it be social security, Medicare, Medicaid, AFDC payments, etc.—will somewhat be continued  even if there is to be a shortfall of some kind in the public funds that are required to keep a program running. It is evident that when a political figure is under fire during a campaign for election, proposals made generally reflect everything that might make people feel good.  Opposing anything usually results in a disaster of some kind as the mass media capitalizes on any proposal suggesting a need to sacrifice. The contradiction that often entices citizens to vote for their favorite candidate is the promising of a balance budget while denouncing cuts in popular programs such as food stamps, Medicaid, and social security.

What results is a continuing dialogue of contradictions which places a wedge between promises and expectations. Sooner or later, something has to give, and it is usually the promises first followed by disappointment in expectations on the part of the voter. The cover up usually includes a political figure generating a 'feel good' attitude suggesting that things are not as bad as we think they are. The assumption here is that when Americans are generally employed and earning livable wages, then maybe a little more patience may be in order. Any inequities in employment, heath care, or education for varying segments of the American society will simply be tolerated until the critics become so vocal that they demand reform.

The result of this inability to deliver on promise of political leaders is the pulling apart of America. The vast differences among Americans as delineated by   religion, ethnic background, and race place a strain upon developing unity of purpose. Paul Samuelson (1996) suggests that citizens who are deprived of basic rights and treatment perceive themselves as being victims of an uncaring public, and they search for scapegoats to explain their plight.   The result is a breakdown in civility and our sense of  national cohesion. Samuelson points out that a likely consequence of not being able to deliver on promises to help families in their time of need is an increase in household violence and despair.

Based upon a study completed by the Anne E. Casey Foundation in 1997, it was found that large numbers of children in poor neighborhoods are basically isolated from the mainstream, closed off from opportunity, and are sentenced to endless poverty and failure. Cities such as Baltimore, Washington, and Detroit, among many others, remain divided in that the poor and the affluent live in different neighborhoods, their children go to different schools, and their outlook on life is completely different.

The political right during the Reagan presidency has resulted in a gradual separation of the rich and poor in this nation. With the political left incapable of clearly delineating their strategy for welfare reform, those citizens presently on welfare have basically been required to make their way through a 'jungle' of public agencies, each with a particular mission. With the political right relying more upon the power of the free enterprise system to provide the way for welfare reform, there is great uncertainty as to what is going to work and what may not.

The Age of Entitlement between 1945 and 1997 was suppose to result in a new society where all Americans would reap the benefits of the free enterprise system. A compassionate government would protect the poor and the unlucky. However, a flawed society still exists, and there remain significant inequities among the American citizenry which appear to be even more entrenched today. Equal opportunity for all citizens is more of a dream rather than a reality. Just ask the 16 million Americans who remain in poverty today how they feel about the promises that have been broken over the past decades.

### States remain edgy about welfare reform

Even though governors of states have been very vocal about being permitted to assume more control over entitlement programs, they do remain edgy as to how the wholesale restructuring of welfare will affect their budgets. The challenge before the governors is how to cope with the projected $56 billion in reduced federal funding that is projected to be a reality over the next 5 to 10 years. What effect this has upon a state's ability to compete to attract consumers, workers, and visitors into commercial centers is a matter of concern.

The state of Florida expects to be in need of over $500 million to meet the financial needs of a growing immigrant population. New York expects to have to come up with an extra $300 million just to cope with the child care needs of former welfare recipients who must now obtain a job within 6 months to a year. Most states must decide what to do after the easy-to-place jobs are filled and there are still large numbers of immigrants unemployed. Other states where large numbers of unemployed immigrants must find jobs include Texas, California, Arizona and New Mexico. Governors fear that larger welfare burdens may have a substantial impact upon their fiscal policies, especially since many must adhere to a balance budget by law.

The fear is that the federal block grants to states under welfare reform will not be sufficient to pay for the increasing responsibilities assigned to the states. The unknown is if there will be a new set of incentives put into place for governors to simply cut people off welfare. Another fear is that governors may be pressured to reduce funds in other social service programs such as education, public libraries, and mass transit. A third fear is that states may have to reduce spending for social services already being provided to heads of households working in low-paying jobs. A spin off of this event is a need to take funds currently allocated for job training and use them to fund other welfare programs now required by the states. In such an event, by helping some new workers, others who need retraining may be harmed. Our model relieves states of much of these monetary pressures. Existing governmental programs can be adopted for providing the necessary 'seed funds' for creating caring communities within the confines of many of the military bases planned to be closed.

States that have a high percentage of immigrants, a high unemployment rate, and have a low percentage of employed welfare recipients are expected to face the more difficult challenge related to new mandates coming from the federal government. Other states with a low percentage of immigrants and a low unemployment rate will be less at risk for adhering to the requirement of finding employment for state welfare recipients over the next 5 year period. Table 7.1 below indicates those states considered in the high risk category and those in the low risk category. While the list may be subject to debate, those states that form the southern boundary of the nation are expected to have the greatest difficulty of putting federal mandates into action. However, those states in the Midwest and northern tier of the country are predicted to have the least difficulty.

The states missing from Table 7.1 are those which have been identified as states with moderate to low risk. In spite of additional pressures being placed

### Table 7.1
### Welfare risk state by state, 1996

| High Risk States | Low Risk States |
|---|---|
| Washington | Montana |
| California | Utah |
| Nevada | North Dakota |
| New Mexico | South Dakota |
| Arizona | Iowa |
| Texas | Nebraska |
| Louisiana | Kansas |
| Alabama | Mississippi |
| Florida | South Carolina |
| West Virginia | North Carolina |
| Maryland | Virginia |
| New Jersey | Kentucky |
| New York | Connecticut |
| Massachusetts | New Hampshire |
| Rhode Island | Wisconsin |
| Arkansas | Indiana |

Source: Center for the Study of the States, 1997

upon governors to assume a more active role in managing the affairs of local residents in dire need of financial aid, the scenario is in place that workfare is the solution. Although governors may feel they are on the edge in regard to solving an historic problem of accelerating costs associated with subsidizing families in extreme poverty, there is a 'light of hope at the end of the tunnel'. Our model is based upon raising the hopes of not individuals where few have been part of their lives, but of governmental officials who are facing a serious problem in cities and towns all over this country.

**Learning from adversity**

Sometimes failure is a good thing! Even though the Age of Entitlement may not have resulted in the eradication of poverty, it did give a nation a chance to explore different strategies in an effort to find a solution to poverty. The intriguing aspect to welfare reform is that those interested in welfare policy have had time to test their theories and eliminate what does not work. However, the freedom to innovative and try new ideas is the reward for living in a democracy. Designing new ways to solve a nagging problem can result in dramatic results, and that is exactly what happened to Governor Thompson of Wisconsin.

The number of AFDC families in Wisconsin have decreased substantially since 1986. In Figure 7.4 below, the data shows that the number of welfare families decreased from 9.5 to 4.5 thousand between 1986 and 1997. Wisconsin's innovative program, which has received national recognition, entails three strands or targets. Governor Thompson's assumption was that the easiest way to break debilitating welfare dependency is to prevent it from

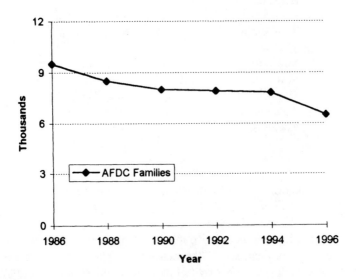

**Figure 7.4 AFDC families in Wisconsin, 1986-1996**
Source:        U.S. Dept. of Health & Human Services, 1997

forming in the first place. By putting forth the image of *self-sufficiency*, the state of Wisconsin focused upon reducing the number of entrants into welfare. The initial thrust of welfare reform in Wisconsin was to quickly counsel applicants on the negative effects of welfare dependence in an attempt to persuade individuals to avoid enrolling into the program. The program offered assistance to applicants in an attempt to get them a job in the private-sector or a community-service position. In other words, getting the applicant a job immediately upon entering the AFDC program or equivalent geared the recipient into a direction for self-dependency, as soon as possible.

The second strand of the welfare strategy was to assure that a work ethic was adopted for a long period of time. Each recipient of financial assistance who either failed to find a private-sector job within a few weeks of entering AFDC program or whose job was discontinued after a short term at work was directed to perform community service as a condition for continuing receiving welfare payments. Welfare recipients are required to work in order to receive benefits. Individuals who do not commit to community service see their welfare checks slashed significantly. No work means no AFDC payments or food stamps. The key to its success is rigorous enforcement of this aspect of the program.

The third stand of welfare reform in Wisconsin was to motivate employees in social agencies to reduce caseloads by setting target goals. The alternative was to replace government agencies by outside private groups if such goals could not be met. The reward for the government employees was a larger budget, higher salaries, and more control over their jobs.

The introduction of 'privatization' spurred government workers to participate in the welfare experiment in the state. Their enthusiasm for change is a very important aspect to the welfare reform effort in Wisconsin. Based upon examining the failures attributed to welfare reform in the past, Governor Thompson developed a program of inclusion in which three aspects were integrated into a policy, clearly identifying the purpose and role for each. In the plan, the focus was upon *the welfare applicant*, the private-sector and community-service sector for offering opportunities to work, and the social agencies for stimulating the entire system through an energetic program of counseling. With the three components *'feeding off'* each another, the applicant receives consistent signals as to what is expected and what the penalties are for not abiding by the rules. The renewal community suggested as part of our model for welfare reform relies more on the private sector than local government for providing to the needs of residents.


## Conclusion

The current national movement towards putting welfare recipients to work as soon as possible has placed many public officials on the edge. Anticipating the best is all we can currently ask for in terms of eradicating poverty in this country. However, the critics of the policy of delegating responsibility from the federal government to that of the state feel that what we may have in actuality is the basis for a welfare time bomb. The key to this welfare strategy is job placement, whether in the private sector or the community-service sector. Therefore, the frightening aspect of such welfare reform is what happens after all the easy-to-place AFDC heads of households have jobs but many others do not. What happens to those who remain unemployed and yet are required to have a job within designated time periods.

In addition, the other critical element here is the current strategy of the Federal Reserve System which affects employment. For example, in the past, the U.S. Federal Reserve Board has had a policy of raising interest rates whenever unemployment falls below a certain point. In raising interest rates, the end goal is to curtail inflation. However, a consequence of such a policy is that unemployment will likely increase. Therefore, too much employment is considered detrimental to the marketplace, a philosophy that may need to be reexamined if welfare reform in its present format is to be successful.

If the Federal Reserve Board continues to focus upon reducing inflationary pressures by adjusting interest rates upward, such a policy may undermine the key component of welfare reform. Having a low unemployment rate in critical if states are going to be in a position to place welfare recipients into work. Therefore, there may indeed by a welfare time bomb surfacing if the Federal Reserve Board makes a slight error in judgment which results in increasing unemployment. The conclusion here is that the welfare time bomb may be a reality if an unexpected recession strikes the marketplace.

It would be a most unfortunate situation if the private sector was unable to employ additional workers due to a down turn in the economy. Another alternative could be state governors pressuring business to eliminate individuals currently in their employ for the purpose of hiring heads of AFDC households who require a job in meeting a federal mandate. When the economy is expanding, meeting federal mandates as to employing AFDC heads of households may be relatively easy. However, what this nation requires is long-term uninterrupted employment for its AFDC heads of households, and interruptions to wage earning must be kept to a minimum. With state budgets already tight, very few governors are in a position to ask citizens to place more funds into welfare by redirecting funds from other much needed social services.

The complexities of welfare reform become evident, especially when state governments and the Federal Reserve Board have different objectives. The opportunity for a new dilemma to emerge is at hand; and unless both segments are in sync, great uncertainty will prevail. With so much at stake in terms of turning welfare policy around, having a continual welfare time bomb ticking in the background (in this case, the Federal Reserve Board) does not ease the tension among the 'players' of welfare reform. The need to have a long-term program in place for bringing stability to the lives of former AFDC families, state officials, and federal legislators is paramount if poverty is going to be erased from the conscience of America. Our model city illustrates a strategy for ensuring a long-term commitment to enhancing the quality of life for those presently struggling to survive.

# Part Four

## THE TURNING POINT:

## ENTERING THE FAST LANE

## OF THE CYBER ECONOMY

# 8 The family at warp speed in the digital economy

The new *digital economy* is gaining momentum. The convergence of computer, the entertainment, and telephony industries has propelled change geometrically. Personal computers, multimedia CD-ROM software, high-capacity cable television networks, wire and wireless telephone networks, and the Internet are all part of our future, writes Bill Gates in *The Road Ahead* (1995). He goes on and suggests that the Internet is the most single new development in the world since the invention of the television. The Internet is simply a group of computers linked together to exchange information.

Much of the technologies to advance the Internet rely on telephone networks. As bandwidth increases, modems become faster, and ISDN (integrated services digital network) advances, high quality two-way audio and video will become commonplace to residents across the country. Online households are expected to become a reality for large numbers of citizens, not only in the United States but worldwide. The challenge, though, is how to bring heads of households of AFDC families into the digital economy quickly in order not to develop a new class 'have nots' who are technically illiterate.

Fiber optics technology is redefining how residents of communities will interact within their own families, in the workplace, and with their neighbors. With the telecommunication's industry rewiring the infrastructure of many parts of the United States--and that of the world, the marketplace is now global. As companies and consumers redefine their role in the marketplace, a need to continually upgrade one's knowledge and skills presents another challenge, especially for heads of households of families who may have dropped out of school.

**Online households increasing**

Fiber optics technology enables the transmission of text, photographs, video, sound, and live images to distant points around the world. The Web (World Wide Web or WWW) revolution, a term associated with the use of the Internet, is expected to become more of a part of the American way of life over the next several years. For example, in 1995, only 9.6 million households actually gained access to the Internet, whereas in the year 2000, the number is expected to quadruple to over 38 millions. (See Table 8.1.)

**Table 8.1**
**Projected growth of online households in North America**

| Year | Population (Millions) |
|------|----------------------|
| 1995 | 9.6 |
| 1996 | 15.4 |
| 1997 | 22.3 |
| 1998 | 28.7 |
| 1999 | 34.6 |
| 2000 | 38.2 |

Source: Jupiter Communications: World Online Markets, 1995

The digital economy may still have a long way to go, but its direction is firmly in place. Online households will eventually be able to do their banking, shopping, investing, communicating, and a myriad of other activities from their homes. However, a whole new vocabulary will become part of everyday dialogue for the online family. Terms such as cyberspace, infonauts, browsers, and hyperlinks will become an integral part of the lifestyle. Using computer technology in some form to send mail, access information from virtual libraries, and communicate both through oral and video formats will become commonplace. Community gatherings will become interactive over two-way audio/video arrangements that connect households to public meetings. Educational strategies used by family members will include distant learning whereby online courses can be delivered directly to the home at the convenience of the resident.

In the past, paper has been the primary means of communicating information from once source to another. Paper traditionally consisted of print with at best tables, charts, or graphs interwoven among the content. Paper has been used as the medium of generating books, magazines, and a variety of publications (pamphlets, brochures, advertisements, etc.) However, information is taking on a whole new dimension. The availability of *e-books, e-journals,* and *e-documents* (e = electronics) through CD-ROM technology, among others, has changed how information may be 'wrapped and published.' In addition to print, we are readily able to find high-resolution text, graphics, and even video. Using hyperlinks, text from a variety of sources can be connected, enabling the reader to synthesize information quickly and accurately.

With the paper document becoming a digital document, its content reflects a 'living experience' in which the senses of hearing, touching, feeling, and seeing become an integral part of the process of communicating. Encyclopedias become living instruments of knowledge whereby users can gain a physical presence by witnessing important times in history through two-dimensional interactive opportunities. Whereas it is almost impossible to locate the best information on a specific topic in paper format without consuming an extraordinary amount of time, the opposite is true in the electronic age. Using the World Wide Web (WWW), the information on a specific topic may be easily located utilizing user friendly browsing software. The outcome of multimedia searching strategies is that content can be shaped different ways through the eyes of an historian, an economist, or a preacher.

Desktop publishing software along with laser printers and facsimile technology enables individuals to generate new forms of information within the confines of their own homes. In addition, information can be created and passed along over the Internet at warp speed. Commercial on-line services such as Prodigy, America Online, and Microsoft Net provide user friendly paths for both residents and businesses to access data. In essence, everyone in society becomes an information provider, if and only when they become part of the online community. For example, motion pictures, shopping catalogs, museum tours, textbooks, and music can be delivered by means of multimedia CD-ROM technology. Content takes on so many different forms that it is basically up to the creativity and imagination of the user that sets the boundaries of possibilities.

Today, the personal computer, as the name suggests, is a tool of the individual. The personal computer or some form of it assumes the role of the telephone, the television, and the radio in the household In the past, there has been almost universal access to these three modes of entertainment, bringing into the mainstream of society all families of varying socio-economic levels. Families in poverty were able to have access to the same technology as those of greater means. In the same vein, the personal computer is simply the combination of these three tools, but adds the element of 'interactivity'. As these three forms of technology continually merge, adults and children will gradually become more comfortable with the idea of generating and sharing information across distances. However, it is a societal responsibility to assure that economics (price) does not become the dividing line between those who participate in the telecommunication's revolution and those who do not. The likely outcome of online content is consumers having more choices available to them in that they will be able to live anywhere, work anywhere, and interact with anyone throughout the world.

It is critical that a fully developed information superhighway is be affordable to all residents. The reason for this expectation is that the Internet can not attract sufficient online content is only the most affluent can avail themselves to it. The information superhighway involves high fixed costs to initiate it, so a large number of participants is required. The information highway is a mass phenomenon, and without mass involvement, it simply will not work. According to Bill Gates (1996), the costs of home technology and access to the Internet will become quite low with much of the content available being free. In this regard, much of current moneys spent in paying the telephone and television service will likely to reallocated by residents for spending on the information superhighway. It is likely to level the playing field somewhat not only for the family living in a poor neighborhood, but for their public schools and libraries who now will have access to the same world that others in more wealthy neighborhoods do. Part of the beauty of the information superhighway is that it provides a mechanism for equalizing opportunity.

*Women at warp speed*

The high tech household may be a force bringing family members together, argues Luanne Flikkema (1996), a psychologist and research director for Gateway 2000. Based up surveys administered to more than 30,000 customers, Flikkema concludes that attitudes and beliefs held by many about the impacts computer technology may have on family stability *may be changing.* Technology watchers are now suggesting that the father in the household is not the controlling factor. In reality, mothers and children are joining in at warp speed on using personal computers to complete money management, entertainment, and educational tasks. In fact, there is a revolution going on in the household.

204

- Women are now becoming what Flikkema labels as 'gatekeepers' of personal computers in the household by determining what technology comes into the home and how children use technology to better educate themselves.

- Women have passed over men in 1996 to become the primary users of personal computers in the home, although men tend to spend more time individually 'surfing' the net.

- Children play a decisive role in family decisions to purchase new pc features and upgrades with 57 percent directly influencing purchasing decisions for acquiring of CD-ROM drives.

- Women and children are not loyal to any particular brand of pc— they know what functions they want, but are less technologically confident than men.

Flikkema further concludes from his research of computer customers that the personal computer and other technology making their way into the homes of residents are bringing families together. For example, women in particular seek technology as a tool to improve education for their children, to keep scores during athletic events, manage family records, or create a home-based job for additional income.

These observations are confirmed by Josh Hawkins, project coordinator for Mighty Media, a Minneapolis-based developer of educational software and Web sites. His research similarly concludes that shifting user demographics in today's households is resulting in a new rallying point for family cohesion similar to when television was making its original appearance in households during the 1950s. Acting as a catalyst for his interest in personal computers in the home is the growing availability of technology in public schools, public libraries, YMCAs, retailers, museums, exhibits, and athletic events, etc. Adults and their children are viewing different aspects of technology daily as they make their way the maze of everyday tasks. The availability of Web TV is the continuation of this fascination towards using technology to enhance the quality of family life. Web TV is simply *technology in a box* that enables members of households to browse the World Wide Web on a big TV screen in the home, rather than on a monitor attached to a personal computer.

Another important dimension to this change in user demographics is the finding of Flikkema that the gap between those who have grasped and are using Web technologies and those who have not is rapidly closing. In this regard, there is a growing second-hand market for computing equipment and other technology (such as fax machines, etc.), suggesting that while men still may desire the most latest technology, women and children gravitate toward bargains now available is used computers. In addition, the emergence of a *technology leasing service* also adds to the availability of personal computers and other technology in the homes of households of varying socioeconomic levels.

Still the significant costs associated with purchasing personal computers and other forms of technology is out of the reach of most of these families. Relying upon local public schools to have children learn about the benefits of personal computers in job preparation will only come about if educational institutions are *remodeled*. One of the continuing problems associated with public education, especially for those in poorer neighborhoods, is the likelihood that mediocrity prevails in many inner city schools. Based upon findings gathered from the National Assessment of Educational Progress (1996), equal educational opportunities for all students do not exist. For example, the study findings indicate that in 1990, predominantly white schools with low poverty levels spent an average of $6,565 per student while those with higher poverty levels spent an average of $5,173. In addition, poor students were found to be more frequently taught by teachers not qualified in their field For example, while 86 percent of science teachers in wealthier schools districts were state certified, only 54 percent in schools closely aligned to poorer neighborhoods. In addition, in schools with fewer poor students, more than 80 percent of English classes were taught by classroom faculty with at least a minor in English. However, in poor schools about 67 percent of the English teachers had at least a minor in English.

There appears to be a continuing lack of support for public education in both inner-city and rural communities where large pockets of families in poverty reside. The tragedy is that the continuation of inequality in public education will likely result in large numbers of our youth becoming 'have nots' in terms of being outside the mainstream of society (not being both computer literate). However, computer technology is generally simple to learn and easy to use. Using the Word Wide Web is becoming easier with each passing moment as user friendly software packages become the order of the day. However, the basic requirements for its effective use is the ability to read, write (compose), and use logic. In addition, becoming exposed to computer and other technology is a big step in making members of households aware of its simplicity. Since there is evidence that technology can unite families into cohesive units, there appears to be a mechanism on the horizon that may be able to turn things around for many families, especially those in poverty. Our model addresses this issue in great detail.

Larry Lannon (1996) argues that the emergence of the digital economy will make a significant contribution in assisting families presently on welfare to advance to an independent status. His focus is upon a likelihood that these families who are currently isolated in either inner cities or rural neighborhoods may now be connected to a whole set of new alternatives. To Lannon, the telecommunication's era conquers two of the primary obstacles faced by families of poverty; those being, *time and distance*. He argues that the using of public libraries and other social agencies, heads of households of families in poverty may be easily trained to learn how to pull up information about local employment opportunities, thus reducing the time being unemployed. In addition, these individuals may be able to advance in their wage generating capacity by applying for better jobs as they come along.

Many of the better paying jobs in the future will require workers to be knowledgeable of the World-Wide-Web and its varied uses within a business operation. Learning how to use email, to access information from a world wide network of data sources, and to serve customers online will be expected of future employees of an increasing number of employers. Lannon claims that the private sector will be better capable of assisting those families on welfare by creating, updating, and distributing information to offset the personal weaknesses of such newly employed individuals.

It terms of remedying the problem of distance, more efficient delivery systems will likely be devised that enable families in poverty better access to education, health care, and banking services. To Lannon, the telecommunication's revolution possesses tremendous power in that in can connect individuals to services at the time of need. In terms of health care, medical advice can readily become available. Money can be transmitted to and from banks by electronic networks, assisting families in bypassing traditionally more expensive strategies related to check cashing and credit management. Online courses can be delivered at times of convenience as those who need to upgrade their skills seek retraining.

Lannon sees welfare reform and advances in the digital economy as proceeding simultaneously. However, since connecting households to the information superhighway does not come cheap, there will be a need for public-private partnerships that enable low-wage heads of households in poverty to access the Internet, etc., and keep up with the rapid pace of changes in technology. With the current emphasis of removing families from welfare within short time periods, the need to assist adults in locating suitable employment becomes more paramount. By harnessing the power of fiber optics technology, a tremendous *social power* can be gained by those in poverty. The opportunity arises to bring these families out of isolation, with the first step distributing information to them about employment opportunities. Similarly, Beer and Barringer (1996) indicate a similar point of view as to the potential of the telecommunication's revolution to help solve the problems of many families currently on welfare. They suggest *five positive impacts* upon what they refer to as consumers living in poverty.

Initially, they argue that the information superhighway (or the World Wide Web) creates a whole new *form of transportation* that carries similar significance as did the development of the current interstate highway system begun in the 1960s. They suggest that individuals may now need not worry about how to get to work. They write about the probability of low-skilled service workers being retrained to perform functions out of their homes. They see a dramatic increase in telecommuting whereby clerical jobs can be performed at distant sites, rather than only at a company's headquarters. Physical transportation to places of work may be replaced with electronic transportation with information and communication moving at warp speed. Therefore, jobs traditionally out of reach of many service workers will become viable alternatives by the networking of households throughout the nation. In this regard, businesses may open satellite offices in local communities that are more readily accessible by residents (within walking distance of homes) as they expand operations for becoming part of a world-wide competitor. With small businesses having the capability of establishing an international presence through online marketing schemes, the opportunities for employment are likely to increase.

A second positive outcome from online households is the ability to gain access to mainstream society. Gaining access to newsgroups, bulletin boards, online chats, and listserves enables families in poverty to become part of a network where information flows freely and quickly. A third outcome afforded by the information superhighway is that purchasing of goods and services over the Internet. By participating in newsgroups, etc., many families will be able to transmit such information into purchases directly from producers, thus bypassing both the wholesaler and retailer. In the past, many families in inner cities or in rural areas have been isolated from the mainstream marketplace, having to rely upon local stores for access to goods and services. However, in view of being connected to the world-wide marketplace, families can easily have access to many more stores and services, thus enabling them to get better value for their money. Again, the Internet narrows distance between sellers and purchases, a phenomenon that will likely enrich the lives of many Americans. A side benefit to being able shop in the same stores as everyone else is AFDC families not having to be as concerned with purchasing high-priced housing in order to reach better shopping outlets.

Now, many retailers traditionally out of physical reach of families on welfare can be accessed with the depressing of a button.

Another positive outcome of the telecommunication's revolution is the ability of families in poverty to expand their leisure activities. By connecting to the Internet, families will be capable of previewing a new movie, playing chess with another person in another state, or enjoying a Broadway show in their homes. The emergence of digital technology reduces the cost of expanding one's horizons in terms of enjoying the theater and the arts. Visiting art museums from all over the world, interacting with a national news service, or communicating with your favorite actor or athlete will all become commonplace. The exposure of children to events outside of their local neighborhoods will enable the youth of our country to identify with a variety of new role models, resulting in enhancing their aspirations.

A fifth benefit to online households will be the opportunity to become self-employed without having to generate huge sums of money to establish a retail site. Not having to commute by automobile to work enables individuals to market goods and services over the Internet. In addition, households will have the opportunity to market and sell their skills to companies over the Internet. This should benefit those wage earners with small children at home who may be relieved of pressures of obtaining expensive daycare in order to work. In the same vein, members of households may be able to obtained direct employment from their home with companies that may be based overseas. Therefore, the finding of employment need not be restricted to companies and businesses in the local community.

There is considerable speculation as to how the current digital economy can root out the causes of poverty and corresponding economic misery. There is a growing consensus that if proper policies are put in place by government officials and that partnerships between the private and public sector are generated, families who have been customarily out of the main stream of society can be brought back into the excitement of the marketplace. Key to this success is how we address the issue of economics--the cost associated with connecting to the information superhighway. However, with creative thinking and with a proper set of incentives put into place through national policy, business and industry can tap into varying sources of expertise. The competition for qualified employees is expected to increase as the baby boomers age and the baby bust generation arrives. The digital economy has put into place many alternatives--some of which should help families on welfare to move from public support to independence.

It is hardly news that college graduates continue to enjoy a higher standard of living than their counterparts with a high school diploma. Moreover, what is important to note is that there continues to be a widening income gap between the more and less educated citizens on this nation. Jackie Calmes of the Wall Street Journal (1996) reports that between 1980 and 1995, the average weekly earnings of a male high-school graduate fell to just under 60 percent of a male college graduates ,down from 77 percent a decade ago. Similarly, women high-school graduates earned only 55 percent of college graduates, down from yearly 70 percent in 1980. Economist Frank Levy of the Massachusetts Institute of Technology (1996) states in a new study for the Competitiveness Policy Council, a federal advisory committee, that one of the most important developments of recent year is the growth in the earnings gap between high school and college graduates.

The implications of this gap can be seen if we examine the distribution of the present U.S. population in terms of their educational attainment. In Table 8.2 below, over 50 percent of the U.S. population has a high school diploma or less. Related is the fact that many heads of households of AFDC families are high school dropouts or at best have earned a high

**Table 8.2**
**Educational attainment of population 18 and over**

| Degree | Percent |
| --- | --- |
| Less Than High School | 19 |
| High School Diploma | 34 |
| Some College | 26 |
| Bachelor Degree or Higher | 21 |

Source: 1995 Census Data

school diploma. The implications are that in a workplace where the possession of technical skills is a general advantage to those seeking employment, the need to upgrade job skills of a large percentage of families on welfare is very much evident. In this regard, the telecommunication's revolution may be providing such heads of households viable alternatives for maneuvering themselves into a better position for employment through the capability of online education.

The most elementary form of online education is that of videotape, whereby classes are mailed to the resident. Therefore, the obstacles of time and distance are overcome since students can preview the videotaped classes anytime during the day, and at any site--including one's home. The target audience for such videotapes is the working adult or the adult who has children at home and my be currently unemployed. The source for such videotaped classes are local community colleges and continuing education divisions of colleges and universities with 4-year undergraduate programs. All one needs in the household is a VCR and a television screen. Some educational institutions will also permit adults to 'check out' a VCR in order to preview the videotapes, if one is not readily available. Others have remote sites where residents can view such videotapes at their own leisure.

Another more advanced strategy for delivering education to *non-traditional* students is direct online. In this instance, residents through their television screens and a special two-way audio electronic box can participate in a 'live class' from their homes. Being online enables students to converse with other classmates and their instructor. Another version of online classes is online courses. What is required by the resident is a modem connected to a personal computer. Then, courses can be downloaded to a resident's home, and the resident interacts with the instructor by means of the personal computer. What is a likely event is that public libraries may lend out the necessary equipment to community residents who do not have funds to access online education. Another likely scenario is that a business seeking qualified employees may provide the necessary online equipment under the condition that he or she will accept employment with that company upon the conclusion of specified courses. Again, if incentives are put into place that encourage private and public partnerships through national public policy, the cost of delivering such online education can be addressed.

The likely outcome of ignoring the potential of online education is that large numbers of residents, especially those with low-incomes, will become the 'have nots' of society, resulting in a continuation of income support in the years ahead. Of course, associated with greater numbers of individuals on welfare will be higher taxes to the more affluent to provide food and health care for the less fortunate. For those who can use the time and convenience afforded by the telecommunication's revolution to upgrade job skills relevant to the information age, the rewards to society is a group of workers who pay taxes themselves, purchased goods and services in the marketplace, and raise the living standards of not only their own household but that of the community in which they live.

The telecommunication's industry has been responsible for wiring the business, educational, and residential communities with the fiber optic technology necessary to network business administrators, educators, and home residents. While business has generally been paying their own way onto the network, the K-12 public educational community has received both technical expertise and financial support from companies expected to reap large profits from the conversion from analog to digital technology. Currently, companies are volunteering to 'wire' public schools to statewide networks in an effort to bring educational institutions up to par with the rapid changes in technology. Large sums of money have been set aside to subsidize public education to have future generations of children benefit from connecting to *the world bank of information*.

A whole new industry of access providers has enabled both small and large businesses to connect to the Internet. Such strategies include the marketing of goods and services by generating a new dimension of convenience to today's shopper. The remaining part of the puzzle is wiring the millions of households among the many communities throughout the entire nation. The challenge before us is the establishment of a universal system whereby everyone in society becomes part of the new era where they can converse, trade information, and receive job training at the 'flick' of a button. Families on welfare must not be left out of this transformation of the economy from that of a physical movement of goods and services to the electronic movement of information. The answer to welfare reform is not to ignore the plight of others through apathy and withdrawal, but to demonstrate a caring attitude and an national commitment.

The digital infused community reflects an emerging synergy whereby the family is immersed in an interactive marketplace consisting of librarians, teachers, reporters, businesspersons, government officials, bankers, athletes, and other consumers. In reality, the *brains* of each family member is basically wired to a vast number of community resources. What results are linkages to schools, newspapers, libraries, publishers of magazines, banks, stores, and physicians. Whereas many consider Ben Franklin as the first *media mogul* in this country, all of us may view ourselves in a similar manner. Basically, the digital infused community encourages personal responsibility for knowing what we need, using available tools to accomplish what we want to achieve, and caring not only about ourselves but other members in our family.

The digital infused community is the result of tremendous advances in technology since the creation of communications satellites in 1958. In accepting the Russian challenge related to Sputnik, the American economy and ingenuity of its workers has resulted in the development of interactive cable TV, computers of many sizes and capabilities, wireless telephony, and two-way audio/video conferencing. Today, the computer is now integrated into tele-work, tele-learning, tele-entertainment, tele-marketing, and tele-medicine. Of course, all these technologies have implications in terms of how families are expected to conduct their everyday activities. For heads of AFDC households, a whole new set of opportunities are now available, but how to take advantage of these technologies is another matter. Again, this dimension is an integral part of our model for welfare reform.


## Adding value to the workplace and home life

Whereas future workers are now required to add value to their jobs by devising new and better ways to work, families in communities are similarly required to devise better ways to advance their living conditions. The transformation to the digital economy calls for the infusing of nonprofit service oriented community organizations with business networks. As families search for their independence and destinies, the intertwining of the needs of the workplace with those of the family is inevitable. To survive in a technological environment where change becomes part of the norm, business must continue to find innovative ways to reduce costs while at the same time preserving what has made this country so great where a spirit of pride and independence prevails.

Similarly, families will be identifying new ways to take advantage of advancing technology for making home life less hectic and more productive. For example, personal technology is expected to change how family members plan and organize their activities. In this regard, the element of cost becomes an item of great importance. However, such firms as Packard Bell, Compaq, and even Apple are marketing personal computers for use in homes at prices below $999. These models will enable families to handle most of the basic tasks such as word processing, general recordkeeping and browsing the Internet. The cost of user friendly personal computer is becoming more in line with the everyday consumer who is looking to become part of the cyberspace generation.

Web-TV is another inexpensive alternative for enabling consumers to become part of the information superhighway. For approximately $350, a consumer can utilize the television set as a way to gain access to the Internet. A more sophisticated version of Web-TV is Webcasting whereby the consumer downloads special software to a personal computer (and eventually a television set) for the purpose of establishing a profile as to user preferences. The profile simply indicates the desires of each member of a family and sends this information to a Webcasting service. Therefore, the heads of households and other family members can determine what kinds of entertainment should be delivered to their residences based upon personal choices. Companies such as Microsoft, Netscape, and AOL are all attempting to offer such services to home users.

With *Netmania* currently the rage of American society, the opportunities for families of all socioeconomic classes to become part of cyberspace are likely to increase substantially in the coming years. For example, weather reports, sporting events, and news broadcasting are very conducive to Webcasting. In terms of assisting heads of households to locate housing,, there are services who provide updated apartment-rental listings for up to a 1,000 cities. Similar online services are available for finding employment. As Webcasting transforms the way consumers gather information, families will be better able to plan and organize their activities. Instead of being swamped by information, Webcasting technology delivers only that information that is requested.

This new era of personalize service brings with it a great deal of excitement. With the costs of connecting to the Internet coming down, the economic barrier associated with purchasing personal computers is gradually being eliminated. Today, a booming industry offers products and services that will allow families to take a giant leap into cyberspace. Currently, the biggest trend to watch is the emergence of *Web commerce*. The expectation is that during the coming decade, cash will flow in earnest over telephone lines between consumers and businesses all over the world. It is happening because Microsoft, IBM, Netscape, AT&T, Visa, MasterCard and many banks and telecommunication companies now have the technology to initiate electronic payment methods that are secure. A good example of such a system is SET (secure electronic transactions) which is designed to protect both buyer and seller from credit card fraud.

Adding value to both the home and workplace is required if advancing technology is going to have a significant impact upon our quality of life. The creation of a low-cost universal consumer-oriented system is at hand and is an integral part of our model city. The new cybergroups representing neighbors from all over the world results in new kinds of opportunities for enhancing home, work, and shopping. The changing roles of banks, retailers, schools, and entrepreneurs in the American economy will result is a new social structure where honesty, loyalty, and ethical conduct become the norm. The reason for this renewed emphasis on those traits that are held in high esteem in society is the need for individuals to rely upon one another for accomplishing tasks that cannot now be accomplished alone. This is true in the workplace and also true at home.

With life becoming more open, competitive, fast-paced, and complex, collective responsibility becomes more attractive as a strategy for coping with everyday challenges. The pressure to add value to both the workplace and household forces society to look at welfare reform in a new dimension, one that organizes community residents based upon incentives that bring out the best in all its residents. That is what welfare reform is all about, and our model attempts to redefine liberty, responsibility, and work through the reemergence of an informal contract that binds families together for a common good.

## The rational choice model

The infused community impacts upon parenting to such a degree that many of past traditions no longer can survive. Relationships between parents and their children will continue to change. New sets of choices will emerge as families adopt a new *rational choice model*. A technological infused community suggests that families are likely to make decisions based upon having a great number of options, evaluating them in terms of their value system and preferences, and then selecting the option that brings them the greatest utility or satisfaction. Moreover, the long-term welfare of a family is based upon 'free choices' that are consistent with the values held by members in a household. The infused community results in an entirely different decision-making process based on personal accountability. Historically, policy makers have attempted through paternalism and elitism to 'steer' families into the right direction. However, an infused community opens families to many new avenues for accomplishing goals and choices appropriate for one family but perhaps inappropriate for another.

For example, parenting, health care, education, work, and shopping can be accomplished through differing strategies depending upon the composition of the family. Time and distance are no longer inhibitors. Personal preferences dominate outside intrusion by public agencies. What is suggested here that the telecommunication's era places a whole new set of incentives in existence, and these incentives are likely to result in better solutions to welfare reform. However, the solutions will be basically outside the control of government.

The most widespread personal anxiety is how will my family fit into this infused digital community. Heads of AFDC families are worried that jobs for which they are now qualified will become obsolete, that they will not be able to adapt to new ways of working, and that they will only find jobs in low paying industries. Therefore, there is a risk that some heads of AFDC households will become so disenchanted that they will dropout of the labor market and become invisible to the rest of the world. Their children will then become the next in line of the disenchanted and the cycle continues.

Bane and Ellwood (1996) sum up the influence of the infused technological community by suggesting that most important way to resolve problems associated with families on welfare is through experimentation. It is the ability to experiment that reflects the greatness of the free enterprise system. Yes, there is some risk to experimentation, but history has continual proven that the best results come from freedom to make choices. The key here is that all citizens of this country have the basic tools with which to make decisions. Our model for welfare reform takes on the risk associated with such experimentation by tapping into the technology that is at the 'heart' of the telecommunication's revolution.

## Conclusion: Online world hits adolescence

Big changes occurred in the online world during the early stages of the present decade. We saw Apple Computer's version of the Internet and AT&T Interchange services disappear. While an online service called CompuServe suffered, Genie and Delphi enter into obscurity. Once enemies, CompuServe and AOL join Microsoft in a partnership to attract new sets of customers to the Internet. Finally, all of a sudden, families are being offered unlimited monthly access to the Internet for fees as modest as $19.95—or even a one-time yearly fee of $169. The online world is growing up quickly, but the future remains in doubt as to where service provides will take us.

The traits that differentiate Americans from other societies is our respect for individualism, freedom, and utilitarianism, according to economist Robert Samuelson (1996). The reason the United States citizenry are so curious about computers and all the technology that surrounds them is our love to create and experiment. We have a passion for progress, writes Samuelson   This is what the telecommunication's revolution is all about, a passion for leadership and greatness. It is this passion that must be instilled in heads of households of families in poverty.

As Bill Gates (1995) suggests in *The Road Ahead*, new alliances will be formed between families, communities, and business. A whole new set of parameters will be put in place as families socialize, shop, and work. To the heads of AFDC families, such change can be disastrous or they can be the beginning of a new way of life. What is now required is a forward looking vision as to how all families can reap the benefits of one of the most significant revolutions in the history of this nation. Instilling a vision that anything is possible is the challenge. To accomplish this rekindling of attitudes and beliefs that democracy does work for all Americans, the 'playing field' must be leveled. It now appears that the development of the world-wide information superhighway is providing more families with a new mechanism for overcoming obstacles of the past: those being, time, distance, and know-how. The simplicity associated with new technology for the home enables all families to participate. Finding the financial means to incorporate all families into the mix is the challenge of the modern day marketplace. Our model accepts this challenge.

# 9 Healing family and societal guilt: the turning point

Families attempting to improve upon their position in society are often faced with decisions that also bring upon them a sense of guilt. For example, if a head of a household of a AFDC family seeks and obtains employment, a corresponding decision is how to provide for the children during long periods of absence. If such a new job results in less health care coverage, the guilt is what happens to family members if they become seriously ill emerges. Guilt feelings are often difficult to cope with as additional job opportunities often result in agonizing decisions as to the consequences of personal actions.

Compounding these guilt feelings is a desperate need to pay accumulating bills and to generate earnings that enable individuals to seek their own destiny. Living in a world without hope does not make one feel good about himself or herself. Parents want their children to be happy, but being in poverty is not a good role model. To David Elwood (1996), heads of households of AFDC families often perceive themselves as living in isolation and being subjected to discrimination. As a result, desperation often leads to drastic measures as heads of households seek to meet family basic needs of food, clothing, and housing. When accomplishing the American dream becomes unachievable, the spirit and pride connected to a family is undermined. Attempting to keep a family together that has no vision or dreams is a formidable challenge. Rekindling a new kind of family spirit, one where a dream can become reality, is an integral part of the renewal community.

## Responsibility and guilt

What welfare reform is all about is assisting heads of households to take on the responsibility of caring for not only themselves but for others in a family. Those in favor of advocating financial subsidies as part of a welfare policy did not foresee the demise of the family structure resulting from such generous acts of assistance. But over the past several decades, poverty has not been eliminated, and the guilt of society as to how to remedy this failure of the past remains. Therefore, the conscience of society and the guilt surrounding failure adds to the frustration of finding new strategies for ending welfare.

Attempts to overcome societal guilt often leads to transferring similar guilt to heads of households. Past welfare strategy has attempted to guide families into a feeling of security by reducing the risk of being without health care, food, clothing, or housing. Public funds were utilized to transfer responsibility for one's own future to that of society. Individual initiative gave way to a new kind of morality, one that reflects a permissive tolerance of moral irresponsibility. As years past by, heads of households of AFDC simply demanded more financial assistance as the need for work became less important.

However, with society searching for a new approach to a welfare policy, heads of AFDC households are now required to take some initiative, find work, and generate sufficient earnings to tend to the needs of one's family. Taking on responsibility is the 'new kid on the block' The consensus appears to be that societal guilt relating to past failures can be eliminated by putting into place incentives for individuals to work on their own behalf. However, with the reducing of societal guilt is the emergence of personal guilt as heads of households assume new pressures contrary to bringing families together. Leaving children in day care centers often leads to guilt about being a 'good parent.' Not being available to their children during after school hours to tend to their educational and other personal needs may result in a sense of guilt. The key issue here is whether taking on more personal responsibility for one's own future can eliminate parental feelings of guilt of neglecting their children—or, in other words, or we really at a turning point in welfare reform?

*The turning point*

According to Strauss and Howe in *Fourth Turning (1996)*, America can still be classified as a great country in the year 2020 if appropriate decisions are made to assure its wealth is shared by large numbers of its citizens. The rich traditions associated with democracy and the corresponding free enterprise system must be re-examined and repackaged in a way that helps society as a whole address the critical issue of poverty.

Maintaining equity among all citizens in terms of reaping the benefits of technological advances is at the core of the fourth turning.

If we are expected to be a caring, sharing, and connecting society, then fundamental changes must occur. There have been many suggestions for how to rid America of unrelenting individualism, social fragmentation, and weakening government. With the economy becoming more global, the bringing together of families and consumers throughout the world will very likely create new kind of 'world socialism'. The current obsession with individualism should give way to a new form of collectivism with an expanded vision for community involvement. The influence of government upon residents of communities should become less of a factor as new relationships are formed. However, in such a vision, the possibility of the rich getting richer and the poor getting poorer must be addressed to avoid the new form of segregation of neighborhoods. To avoid the likelihood of these two socio-economic extremes, the issue of equity becomes the over-riding factor when designing public policy to eradicate poverty (not only in this nation but that of the world).

On fundamental aspect of the workplace that requires a reevaluation is career advancement. This segment of life is crucial if guilt feelings among heads of households are going to be reduced. Working is critical to generating sufficient funds to provide for family members, but at the same time it can undermine family bonds by destroying relationships between children and parents. Being unable to tend to the perceived needs of children can result in destructive behavior by those children who are likely to become frustrated when parents are not available to participate in important times in their lives.

*Easing the pain of pressures to work*

Anne Roiphe in *Fruitful: On Motherhood and Feminism* (1996) suggests the time has come to slow down career pressures to let families form and grow in the early years. Roiphe concludes that the feminist movement has resulted in many females feeling guilty about both working and raising a family. She argues that females--and males--are caught between a rock and a hard place in terms of being pressured to increase their hours at work in order to advance careers. At the same time, she points to societal repercussions when females are also labeled as failing to raise their children by neglecting important traditions and customs. The need to sacrifice one's family in order to be successful at work is filled with anxiety, guilt, and stress.

While business has generally attempted to ease the pain of work by providing for day care support, flexible work schedules, and maternity leave, a counter movement has been its downsizing with the expectation that remaining workers increase their productivity. With business now competing in a global marketplace, additional pressures are being placed upon today' parents to work longer hours. If family stability is to be considered a top priority of society, then a re-evaluation of work responsibilities and career advancement is in order. Such an examination challenges the roots of the modern American workplace, but it also symbolizes a major turning point that must occur if disruptions to family cohesiveness are to be avoided.

*Entering a decisive era*

In a similar regard, Strauss and Howe (1996) see the need for the replacement of the old industrial order for a new civic one. In modern times, the first turning point was from 1946-64 which was considered an upbeat era where societal institutions (e.g., education, government, etc.) were strengthened. The second turning point was a national awakening during 1964-84 when riots and protests among our youth questioned societal values, especially those associated with protecting the environment and advancing the rights of females. The third turning point between 1984-2000 is labeled the unraveling whereby a cultural war breaks out between the 'haves and have nots.' Under attack are family values, high-tech individualism, and basic morality. The fourth turning point after the year 2000 will be the decisive era in which society must resolve past conflict and come to a consensus as to how to proceed into the future.

One of the crises to be resolved is the role of work in the American culture. Are future children to be sacrificed as parents are increasingly pressured to work longer hours in their search of career advancement? Are the roles of mothers and fathers going to significantly change to permit equity in parenting? Are we in society going to help parents teach civic habits and group skills to the children who will become the next generation of workers and leaders? Are we in society seriously going to address the needs of families in poverty by creating a caring, sharing, and connecting network of support? How can work be redesigned to effectuate a change in employer expectations, especially during the early years of career development?

Answers to these questions are critical. We appear to be at a turning point where we as individuals must change how we feel about ourselves, our culture and our future. To resolve crime in society, we have to rehabilitate local communities. To revitalize neighborhoods, we must re-energize the family. To enhance family stability, we must assure access to a decent living wage for everyone. To afford access to a decent job, we must fix our schools. We do appear to be a turning point, and our model addresses each of these aspects of the American marketplace.

## Shifting from individualism to collectivism

At the essence of any reform is instilling an attitude of caring about others. In an era where knowledge is power, the ability to connect with sources of power is central to success in the technical revolution. Knowledge is the new wealth in the world, the basic economic resource of the marketplace. As information and new technologies emerge at warp speed, a creation of a new alliance is now in order. The alliance requires a shifting of human roles in three sectors of the marketplace. In the *business sector*, employees will be expected to form work teams with the expectation that they can produce more in groups than acting alone. In the *consumer sector*, individuals will be expected to seek information in many different forms from all parts of the world as they make decisions as to the purchasing of goods and services. In the *government sector*, the diversity of relationships will likely result in less intrusion on the part of third parties (e.g., public social agencies) to solve problems related to work and the family. Changing daily routines, whether at home or at work, will put into place a whole new set of parameters which redefine what a family is, what a neighborhood is, and what is a nation.

In order for information to be powerful, it must be generated and delivered to those who make decisions. In this regard, decision making is likely to move from that based upon an individualistic viewpoint to that of collectivism whereby a broader perspective is a basis for action. In reference to a crucial aspect of the turning point described earlier, caring about others by sharing thoughts and ideas comes about through networking. It is the ability to network that connects persons as new social and business relationships are formed. Collective wisdom suggests that more can be accomplished with group involvement than when acting in isolation. Therefore, collectivism becomes the new 'power move' in the coming decades.

The important element in the tech revolution is not to have families get lost in cyberspace. When problems arise, solutions must come quickly. As with any form of technology, when things go right, the system is fantastic. When things go wrong, agony and despair run rapid. Why the Internet is so popular is that is enables a person to communicate quickly and easily with people all over the world. It is a basic collective tool that relies upon a person's willingness to care about others by sharing solutions to problems presented. Although the Internet connects people to people, it is a likelihood that these consumers of technology will never physically meet. However, with the Internet becoming user friendly, this may encourage family members to reach out from the confines of their homes to that of the world.

The World Wide Web is simply a multimedia version of the Internet, where families cannot only obtain text but also pictures, sounds, and video on topics of interest. Again, it is the sharing of these items with others that makes the system work. Therefore, in reality, newly created documents become shared documents. The entire document is the summation of input from others, resulting in a team effort. Collective wisdom becomes the integral part of creating new information as an outgrowth of existing information. The world becomes a collective data base of information. Therefore, the *language of information* is universal, coming from many different parts of the world.

By becoming exposed to others to such a degree, heads of AFDC households will also be capable of seeing similarities among other families in terms of needs and feelings. Being able to interact with additional families will enable an informal support system to emerge, a system where individuals can exchange their feelings with others in an effort to reduce guilt feelings. Since guilt can be the result of not having sufficient information to deal with a problem, the collectivism that is expected to result through a new kind of 'world order' can eliminate the existence of 'information void'. The turning point here is an international society playing an expanded role in local community development and family stability. Even though future neighbors may be 'faceless' in this expanded community at first, our model address the importance of such an outcome.

### It all comes down to parenting

Unemployment, unwed mothers, and absentee fathers are just a few problems that contribute to a difficult life for children. In addition, many children in poverty only sense what a family actually is through relationships with nearby relatives such as grandparents, uncles, aunts, or cousins. Without parents playing a major role in their upbringing, children have only a limited view of what a family actually means to them. A family can be described as individuals bonded together by love and a sense of unity of purpose. A family is where individuals can gain pride in one's culture, heritage, and personal being. The values learned in a family setting enable individuals to venture out into the world with the interpersonal skills required to work with others. The healing of the American family can only come about by reducing guilt feelings about not being a good parent. Having attentive parents is critical to children in their growth and development toward becoming responsible citizens.

*The battle for the child's brain*

What this is all about is children. Moving children into a whole new frame of reference whereby collective arrangements, teamwork, and societal needs take precedence over personal needs and wants. The framework moves from that of relying upon outside sources that generally intrude into the most sensitive areas of family relationships to solve problems to depending upon a self-initiated support system that includes a 'global neighborhood'. The essence of this new framework is a stream of new role models. With children being able to expand their friendships beyond those in the local public school or in their neighborhood, the opportunity to witness a global society in action brings new energy and vision.

By becoming part of the information superhighway, children get an opportunity to read every day, to write by composing their thoughts into clear, concise statements, and to perform problem-solving routines as challenges are readily accepted on a voluntary basis. Nothing is required of anyone on the Internet. No one dictates to anybody what must or must not be taken on as a challenge. Children are therefore in a constant state of volunteerism in that they perceive themselves as benefiting from the efforts of others while at other times making personal contributions to enhance the welfare of others. The child's brain becomes intuitive in that the creative as well as logical side merge into a productive unit.

The child has total control over what he or she does as part of the information superhighway. Therefore, a great deal of independence emerges, suggesting that one can handle personal problems without having to rely upon an outside force to intrude upon ones feelings and desires. Independence generates a spirit of pride in what one does, and pride sets a positive mind frame from which decisions are made. Moreover, children have other sources of information besides that of their own parents, thus being able to supplement or even verify what they have obtained from their own family members. Sensing a new kind of confidence coming from being independent, the dependency trap associated with welfare can be negated.

The importance for children to respect their mothers and fathers, to trust their neighbors and local community leaders, and to admire the President and other national figures is at the heart for the drive towards public civility. The admiration of role models provides American youth with examples of the 'worthiness of assisting others'. Successful role models attach children to that 'thread of morality' that internalizes those values and beliefs that enhances one's ability to contribute to the benefit of society. Following in the footsteps of another whose impact upon society is substantial enables our youth to gain a perspective as to what it means to live and work in a democracy and how one's choices can impact upon others. It reintroduces the notion of caring, sharing, and connecting, ideals that also enhance family stability.

Through the World Wide Web, children may also interact with their idols such as a famous artist or a star athlete. They can ask questions, seek advice, and benefits from the experiences of others simply by connecting electronically. Getting children into the pattern of connecting to others throughout the world can become as commonplace as connecting to friends and relatives in a particular neighborhood. Moreover, the interacting with a role model is likely to be an experience that one does not forget easily. In this regard, realizing that role models are extremely goal oriented as well as disciplined in their effort to achieve greatness, children will be able to see how they can synthesize their energies into goals for making their dreams become reality. Therefore, having goals and setting a strategy to achieve those goals are two important accomplishments for our youth. Once dreams are set, they can guide American youth into positive behavior rather than destructive outcomes, which is our next topic.


## The return to patriotism

According to a 1996 poll of over 1000 adults conducted by Bozell Worldwide in US News & World Report (1996), the lack of civility is a serious problem in society. Ninety-one percent said that incivility contributes to increased violence, and 80 percent said the problem has worsened since 1985. Two of the behaviors people associate with declining civility are rudeness and selfishness. The primary culprits pointed out by the respondents in the poll were television, rock music, and talk radio. On the other hand, what access to the information superhighway does is reintroduce the importance of civility through the notion that caring about others is the basis for its successful use. Whatever is shared over the World Wide Web becomes documented knowledge, and the creator of that information is generally accountable. Therefore, the important element of accountability is introduced into a child's realm of experience early in life. Being respectful of the ideas of others and being held accountable for one's actions over the Internet counteract the notion that rudeness and selfishness are acceptable behavior.

The focus of attention upon civility reintroduces the goal of renewing a spirit of patriotism among citizens of this nation. However, with so much diversity in the American culture, the tendency is for residents to debate issues that 'tear us apart'. For example, local issues such as land development, police harassment, zoning restrictions, and school busing pressure residents to take sides. The assumption of a position aligns persons into adversarial groups which divides society into 'power clusters', each attempting to get their way in a political arena.

At the national level, issues such as abortion, equality of the justice system, public safety, and welfare reform grab the attention of the political right, left, and center. The political left has seen a significant change since the late 1980s when the Russian Empire crumbled before our eyes. The credibility of this group has been subjected to repeated attacks by the political right, where conservatism reigns as the cornerstone of its philosophy. The emphasis upon personal freedom, individualism and undeniable  trust in decisions made within a free enterprise system dominates the political right's agenda. The moderates approach societal problems by focusing upon 'glitter issues' which attract the attention of society in general, but whose solutions at best reflect a compromise of the two other political extremes. However, the political rhetoric associated with those who dominate the media results in the public being more confused about issues that affect their lives.

The tech revolution enables families to enter into cordial dialogue rather than argue feverishly  about issues of personal significance. For example, access to the World Wide Web permits adults and children to obtain information from a variety of sources besides the local newspapers, the national press, and political leaders.  In order to counteract possible distortion of the facts, family members are able to seek out the truth and make their own judgments as to what is fact and what has no basis or foundation.  Through interactive technology, accountability is a critical element in the dialogue whereby participants on the Internet are subjected to a self-imposed code of ethics that suggests a respect for others and a responsibility for what is written.  The ability of families to connect to other families enables both children and adults to maintain continual dialogue outside the political arena that often confuses Americans more than puts them at ease.  Enhanced dialogue among residents may result in the reemergence of a new form of patriotism, one that brings citizens of all races, creeds, and socioeconomic levels together through consensus building.

*Guiding youth away from crime*

Being situated in a crime-ridden neighborhood with decrepit schools, crowded streets with no playgrounds for children, and vacant buildings, families on welfare have many obstacles to overcome.  The attractiveness of crime among our youth is not astonishing since there is a feeling that hard work will not lead one out of such misery and despair.  It is rather easy to turn to criminal behavior since it has its immediate financial rewards.  The violence that emerges from criminal behavior has impact upon the spirit and energies of those who live in that neighborhood. However, the violence in the streets often reappears in a similar fashion between children and their parents.  Moving out of a violent climate is not a likely alternative for most AFDC families, since the costs associated with purchasing or renting a new residence is out of the reach of most in poverty.

The violence that stalks the cities today eats at the soul of teenage boys and girls who are fatherless and lost, so much so that guns and gangs are the only solace. As Aristotle stated, 'poverty is the parent of revolution and crime'. Many children from families of poverty end up incarcerated. During the 1980s, the fastest growing category of housing was prisons. One out of every 250 Americans in this decade ended up housed in a correctional facility--the highest incarceration rate in the world, (New War on Poverty, 1995, p. 105). In 1980, the U.S. Bureaus of Census reported 315,974 inmates in correctional institutions where in 1990, that number had increased to 1.1 million, (Census Bureau, 1996).

Drug related violence has also escalated over the past decade. The number of deaths from drug overdoses indicated in Table 9.1 below increased by 60 percent between 1980 and 1988. Male deaths almost doubled during that same time period. Drugs are now part of everyday life for many children as well as adults.

**Table 9.1**
**Death by drug overdoses**

| Year | No. of Deaths |
|------|---------------|
| 1980 | 6,900 |
| 1982 | 7,310 |
| 1984 | 7,892 |
| 1986 | 9,876 |
| 1988 | 10,917 |

Source: The American Enterprise (1991)

Children attending schools are subjected to ever constant pressures generated from others seeking out to make a 'fast buck.' Since there is minimal respect for the welfare of others, and since hate and fear permeate every aspect of life for some youth and adults in both rural and urban areas. The high level of violence resulting is not surprising. If one learns at an early age not to trust anyone and there are no role models to offset such a belief, the outcome for many families in poverty is their dissolution.

Family abuse, violence, and breakup affects all races, cultures, and nationalities. As of 1990, two-parent families were almost twice as likely to break up if they were living in poverty. As shown in Table 9.2 below, the rate of family breakup for poor African-American families was 21 percent, compare to 12 percent for white and 11 percent for Hispanic. In addition, the marriage rate among African-Americans dropped 20 percentage points between 1970 and 1991 (64 percent to 44 percent), a decrease twice as marked as that of whites (from 73 percent to 64 percent).

**Table 9.2**
**Poverty and family breakup**
**(Percentage of Families That Breakup)**

| Race | Poor Families % | Non-Poor Families % |
|------|------|------|
| Hispanic | 11 | 9 |
| African-American | 21 | 11 |
| White | 12 | 7 |

Source: Census Bureau (1993)

Since 1970, the marriage rate for Hispanics remained stable at 61 percent. Not that all these poor families lived in crime ridden cities. However, the fact remains that crime is a part of many of these families lifestyle, and the impact is likely to have influence on family stability.

W. Kip Viscusi (1986) estimates that after adjusting for under reporting of crime in this country, roughly one-quarter of all income reported by youths (age 16-24) comes from criminal sources. His research findings indicate that more than half of all youth may have engaged in crime at one time or another. Crime is both a source of danger and insecurity and an alternative to employment for many youth. This demonstration of 'socially deviant behavior' is no doubt a reflection of a lack of trust, respect, and social responsibility that permeates some families in the American social structure.

The basis for criminal behavior is inevitably tied to family values and expectations. Once such values and expectations are firmly in place, it is difficult to change them without a 'major overhaul' of family perceptions. Of course, not all families in poverty are living in 'ghetto poverty' in our inner cities. Many of those in poverty are located in rural and suburban areas where pockets of poverty exist. Residence, however, is a critical factor in criminal incidents. The rate of violent crime for center city residents is more than twice that for residents in non-metropolitan areas, reports Susan Estrich in *Crime and the Poor* (1984). The larger the metropolitan area, the higher the crime rate.

As to who commits crime, the evidence is clear that they are mostly young men and women who grow up in center cities, drop out of school, and have trouble holding jobs. However, it must be noted that by their mid-twenties, violent young persons generally leave criminal behavior behind them. The reason is that they tend to find jobs during this age frame that results in a steady source of income and the influence of teen gangs decreases. It is also important to note that some who grow up in middle- and upper-class neighborhoods and are employed also commit crimes. However, there still remains a strong correlation between poverty, poor education, and poor employment records. Economists often focus on the opportunity costs of crime noting that the poor have less to lose by crime and that there are few other avenues to satisfy widely shared desires for affluence.

However, no matter where one lives, the point here is that criminal behavior is increasingly nasty, and its impact upon children and their outlook on life is significant. Crime touches everyone, but the poor are extremely sensitive toward the impact of crime since they are least able to purchase protection against crime, to insure themselves against losses, or to avoid areas where crime strikes them the most often. Disproportionately the poor are both the victims and the offenders of crimes of violence. As a group, they are among the most afraid in our society.

The intriguing element here is that those families in poorer neighborhoods generally rely upon linking with neighbors, kin, and friends through informal reciprocal agreements reflecting spontaneous acts of generosity to combat crime in their communities. These linkages are often the target of criminals who use intimidation as a way to destroy the unity and spirit of a neighborhood. In addition, these important linkages are also strained by urban development which often results in dispersing neighbors to distant suburban communities, thus destroying any bond that had previously existed.

Therefore, finding new ways to mobilize families in our urban centers in order to combat crime is extremely important. The spending of additional public funds for placing greater numbers of police in urban neighbors may prove to be somewhat successful. However, a general distrust of families in poorer neighborhoods of those in charge of enforcing local laws brings another factor into play.    A lack of respect for a local police force adds to the dilemma of how to provide for the personal safety of residents.

The global economy brings with it a national community with vast amount of resources.    Families in need can now mobilize new and expanded sets of networks by connecting with individuals who can provide services, support, and ideas.  With children spending more time at public libraries, at school, or in the home using the personal computer to interact with new sets of  acquaintances, less time will be spent on the streets or joining gangs.    Through the Internet, instead of focusing upon crime, drugs, and assaults, children can reap the benefits of legitimate societal behavior which encourages caring, sharing, and connecting.

As noted earlier, most violent youth eventually do take a stake in their communities in their mid-twenties, leaving the life of crime, and settling down with their own newly formed families.    Therefore, the window of opportunity for changing this cycle of expectations appears to be between age 10 and 18.    The constant exposure to opportunity as a benefit as gaining access to the Internet creates a whole new community, one where 'free time' becomes productive time  rather than wasted time.    The Internet can easily connect individuals within a local neighborhood.  It is a well established fact that community participation can make people feel safer.  The Internet can easily connect residents for the purpose of creating a dialogue  about community issues and needs.  Community news groups are just one avenue.  The use of basic email technology is another.

The result is that families in poverty are no longer isolated from each other and are capable of devising innovative strategies as a collective force to protect their neighborhoods from crime.    The guilt feeling associated with not being able to confront crime in a neighborhood can be reduced through a new form of reciprocity—a combination of  electronic and human intervention in which communication becomes the key mechanism for keeping neighbors 'in touch with one another'. Our model for welfare reform addresses this community need in great detail.


## A new camaraderie in America

Even since the Civil War, there remains a harsh reality that discrimination among many citizens continues to exist and nags at the soul of a nation.  What the Civil War was all about was the treating of all Americans equally, without regard to culture, nationality, or race,  Even though this war was fought over 125 years ago, society still agonizes over issues of race not only in the workplace but in zoning for residential housing, voting within politically drawn boundaries, and access to health care. According to a Newsweek Report (1995), Americans claimed membership in nearly 300 races or ethnic groups.    Hispanics alone considered themselves to be 70 different groups. The U.S. Census Bureau projects that by the year 2010, Hispanics will become the largest minority in this country. In terms of ethnic discrimination, the issues of affirmative action, quotas, and goals and timetables for hiring women and minorities command the attention of the media.

There remains resentment among large segments of the population towards any kind of affirmative-action preference when hiring, contracting for services, or in admission to educational institutions at any level of education. As depicted in Table 9.3 below, an argument for affirmative action programs is that whites far outnumber other ethnic groups in the higher paying U.S. white-collar careers.

**Table 9.3**
**U.S. white collar workers by race**

| Race | 1975 % | 1994 % |
|------|--------|--------|
| White | 92.3 | 89.7 |
| Non-White* | 7.7 | 10.3 |

Source:   U.S. Department of Labor
Bureau of Labor Statistics, 1995

*Note: Non-white include blacks, Hispanics, Asians and other minorities

However, the setting of quotas for hiring based upon race, gender, ethnicity, or national origin has become a rallying point for discontent. There continues to be sense of guilt on the part of the general public as to what is fair and what is not in terms of the process of recruiting individuals for possible employment. The struggle continues between the philosophies of *equal outcome* and *equal opportunity* and how equity can be achieved for all races. There continue to be a need for the mainstream American society to make amends for the injustices perpetuated upon segments of its citizens over past decades. Not being able to come to consensus as to how to eliminate discrimination is embedded in the conscience of America, and addressing economic inequities remains an obsession.

In terms of race relations, there also appears to be a continuation of a concern among citizens as to how to get along better in the future. Solidarity on this issue is hard to find. According to a Newsweek poll in February 1995, over 70 percent of whites and 80 percent of blacks rate race relations in this country as only fair to poor. In Table 9.4 below, it is interesting to note that only 2 percent of blacks and 1 percent of whites perceive race relations as excellent.

**Table 9.4**
**Race relations in the U.S.**

|  | Blacks % | Whites % |
|---|---|---|
| Excellent | 2 | 1 |
| Good | 10 | 22 |
| Fair | 45 | 44 |
| Poor | 41 | 31 |

Source: Newsweek Poll, February 1-3, 1995

A related issue is the anti-immigration sentiment also held among many citizens of this country. Anti-immigration actions continue to polarize society, especially at times of elections of representatives at the local, state, and national level. The argument focuses upon the issue of 'fairness' as related to people who work hard, pay their taxes, and play by the rules. It is estimated that in 1996, over 1 million immigrants made their way into this country. It is predicted that one in four citizens of this country will be immigrants by the year 2050. Whereas Asian residents in 1996 made up approximately 3 percent of the population, by the year 2050, it will likely increase to 8 percent. Because of the divisiveness of the issue, instead of finding solutions, the debate results in confusion, distortion of the facts, and a desertion of American principles and ideals, (Race & Rage, 1995, pp. 23-34).

An increasing number of interracial marriages have added to the complexity of the issue. As shown in Figure 9.1, approximately 310,000 interracial married couples existed in this country in 1970 with that number increasing to over one million by 1973. According to the 1990 U.S. Census Bureau, the rate of increase is expected to continue as

American becomes more integrated. The diversity among its citizens creates vast opportunities for new kinds of families to be formed, resulting in parents coming from diverse cultures, nationalities, and races.

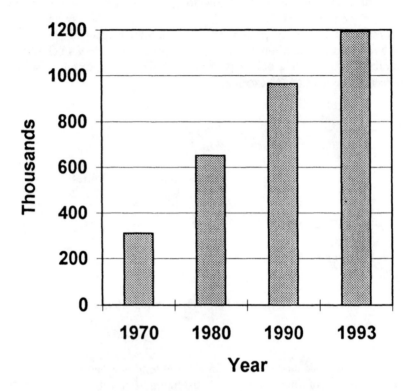

**Figure 9.1** **Interracial married couples**
Source:        U.S. Census Statistics, 1990

In terms of the kinds of interracial marriages depicted in Figure 9.2 on the following page, 20 percent involve black/white marriages while over 70 percent white and another race. The movement to categorize households by the 'color of the skin' continues to be hotly debated in the U.S. Bureau of Census. The fascination with ethnicity in this country constantly reinforces our differences. With interracial marriages becoming more commonplace, gaining a different kind of perspective as to the similarities of families becomes more important with each passing day. With neighborhoods becoming more diverse, finding commonalties that make communities stronger poses a great challenge.

The bringing together of families into a communal bond is important to creating a perception of trust. Depending upon others in time of need is systematic to the concept of a neighborhood. Since a strong neighborhood is conducive for building strong families, the ability to reconcile differences enhances the likelihood that support systems may be put into place that permit children and parents to bond. While schooling is important to the youth of this country, children do spend more time in their community than in school. Much can be learned from participating in one's neighborhood in terms of how to work with others for a common purpose. Therefore, the frequency of interacting with families of different races, etc., can become a learning experience as neighborhoods form with different characteristics from those of the past.

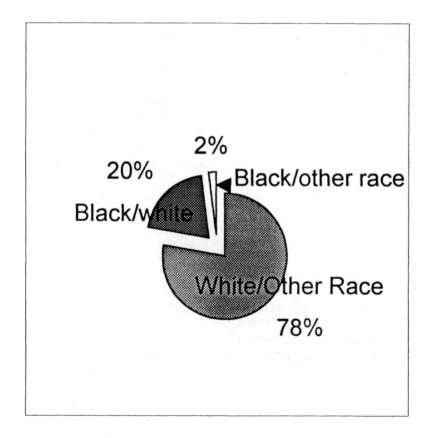

**Figure 9.2   Interracial marriages, 1993**
Source:        U.S. Census Bureau, 1995

235

However, what is intriguing about information superhighway is that it is color-blind, age-blind, and sex-blind. When one interacts with another, the mysterious nature of the communication is that the other party cannot be seen. What is provided is as level playing ground which gives parties an opportunity to interact with one another by evaluating the merits of the communication without being distracted by ethnicity, nationality, or color of skin. What is created for families is an atmosphere of equality. Although curiosity becomes part of the scheme of things in the world of the Internet, getting to know the other person becomes a goal rather than attempting to avoid that person upon first glance. Getting to know others from different cultures, etc., brings the world together. It also creates a positive climate for perceiving how much we have in common rather than how different we are.

What is created is a new sense of understanding. Treating others as equals is the first step towards understanding the significance of human dignity. The dismantling of personal and family biases reduces the impact of sex, age, and race discrimination upon social relationships. Gaining a better understanding as to how others think and comparing such ideas to one's own beliefs enables children and adults to test their commitment to societal expectations. By networking through neighborhoods, families are able to neutralize distracting elements such as vandalism, graffiti, and hate language. Also, political rhetoric becomes less dominating in one's life and as the distortion of facts becomes more recognizable. The dialogue conducted within the openness of the Internet spurs freedom of thought where behavior among participants is controlled by informally established guidelines as to what is acceptable and what is not accepted.

Although there will always be a few who attempt to destroy the greatness of an open system of communication, the fact that each is accountable for his or her own actions, bringing civility to the system. Since most documents and communications created through the Internet can be traced to the owner, there is a natural accountability already in place. Of course, what permeates the whole system is a camaraderie based upon respect and trust. Such civility encourages a new spirit of patriotism. The social bonding enables the positive attributes of caring, sharing, and connecting to becomes the core of new relationships with the outcome a different set of expectations for each other, the press, and our political leaders. In our model, public civility and patriotism work 'hand in hand' as a new spirit of congeniality replaces rudeness, selfishness, and self-pity.

**Replacing guilt with information**

Broadening our own perspectives of how individuals in other cultures act and think can only lead to better understanding as we learn to live and work together. The emphasis upon civility emphasizes the need to respect not only each other but those of other cultures and ethnicity. The intriguing attribute of the telecommunication's revolution and the emergence of the World Wide Web is that it makes it not only easier but more likely for both residents and workers to become informed about the attributes of others. Becoming more informed should result in greater respect for differing options and ideas suggested for solving today's societal problems. Thus, the opportunity to enable the inclusion of all into the mainstream of society will eventually bring varying groups of Americans together as we note the similarities to our own heritage.

Ethnic groups generally desire the same things; those being, to be treated fairly both at home and at work; to achieve the American dream; to control one's destiny; and to make lives better for their children. What civility means in this context is 'leveling the playing field' where citizens can rid themselves of prejudice and biases. In other words, civility brings into our model for welfare reform the crucial element of loyalty. Civility suggests that individuals as workers must be loyal to others in society in that actions and thoughts must result in everyone being treated with the same degree of respect. Civility similar suggests that being loyal to one's neighborhood and to one's country also generates a patriotic spirit that focuses upon the positive aspects of a democracy.

In the democracy, the ideas of the average citizen direct political leaders in their charge to devise policies that reflect important American principles. For example, the goal in the early 1930s was to end the depression and in the later 1940s, to win World War II as well as to rebuild war-torn Europe. In the 1950s, the national objective was to lead both developed and undeveloped nations against the 'evil Russian Empire'. In the 1960s, the goal of society was to end poverty while assuring the civil rights of all individuals. In the 1970s, a national effort focused upon cleaning up the environment whereas the 1980s saw the triumphant of conservatism and the retrenchment of government. A new life to laissez-faire capitalism dominated the workplace. Lowering taxes, deregulating major industries, and cutting back in 'liberal' social programs were viewed as appropriate strategies for curtailing inflation while at the same time stimulating an economic boom which meant jobs, jobs, and jobs.

In the 1990s, the telecommunication's revolution has resulted in enhanced capabilities of business to become highly sought after global competitors. Improving product quality by producing products using fewer production hours, less materials, and fewer people has been the objective of research and development efforts. The newly created wealth generated by business was expected by society to be used to solve some of the pressing problems still plaguing our cities and many households in the U.S. However, a consensus has not developed as to how to bring society together in an attempt to take America to the next level.

David Barry (1996) describes the 1990s as an 'interactive salad bar' in that Americans are dabbling with solutions to health care, government deficits, welfare reform, public education, affirmative-action, and censorship of the Internet. Society appears to be becoming polarized as to how to solve the persistent problems related to poverty. However, the number of choices available for solving problems of society are increasing. With the explosion of fiber-optic technology in the digital economy enhancing our ability to communicate with one another, and with more citizens being hooked up to an international computer network, there will likely be attempts to restructure the American political and economic system. Traditional values and beliefs will no doubt give way to new ones as society attempts to evaluate what changes are beneficial to advancing society and which ones are not. The restructuring of the American way of life will likely impact upon how we relate to one another in an environment where a contemporary national purpose is yet clearly identified. How we reorganize ourselves and reallocate our resources are two challenges for the coming decade. Our model offers one suggestion.


## Success, failure, and guilt

An important observation not to be overlooked is an importance attached to studying past failures to eliminate poverty as a basis for generating new and better ideas. By primarily focusing upon societal guilt as the motivating factor for mobilizing the citizenry to end poverty, it is easy to become frustrated when things do not turn out as expected. This is fundamental to the general discouragement that arises when 'quick fixes' are unattainable. However, failure also brings experience, and such experience should help us to design new and better alternatives for ending public welfare. History informs us that Thomas Edison failed in each of 90 experiments on how to design a light bulb. When asked how he felt about being a failure, he indicated that it was a great experience on his part. His reason was that he learned 90 ways of how not to make a light bulb. He is inferring that he learned much from failure, and having guilt was not part of his mindset.

Similarly, in terms of welfare reform, being stymied by guilt misdirects our attention and energy. What we have learned through past failures is that having failed can lead the American society to better ways for achieving important goals. This may also be a good message to the next generation of leaders, our children, in that failing is not bad. Failing should not make one feel guilty. Failing should not result in society retreating into isolation and turn its back on families in need of a second chance. Failing is a 'fact of life', and overcoming failure can be a wonderful accomplishment.

Therefore, the healing of a society and its families involves erasing the 'presence of guilt' and in its place instituting a new set of ideas about how to resolve nagging problems. The telecommunication's revolution is here for all of us. It must include families of all socioeconomic levels. Living in poverty should not be the defining line between being accepted or rejected as a valuable member of society. As with most issues, the resolution of a problem usually comes down to economics or cost. In this regard, does society have sufficient resources to put a new plan into operation for resolving poverty? Our model for welfare reform suggests that the answer is 'yes'. If this country is to maintain its greatness and be a symbol of fairness and justice to citizens around the world, then solving the problem of poverty must remain as a top priority. Being both the wealthiest nation in the world while having a huge population of its own in poverty is not an appropriate legacy from the this generation to the next.

## Conclusion: turning poverty around

What this chapter is all about is the reemergence of the community, citizenship, and responsibility. The community is no longer consists of neighbors in close proximity. It is now a global community. Friends are no longer physical friends that are seen everyday. Relationships are no longer based upon predetermined biases. Individualism no longer is the only measure of success of one's efforts. The element of civility introduces a new basis for action, a new sensitivity towards what is important, and a new vision for families. In order for crime, unemployment, despair, and family breakup to become a thing of the past, a new world order is indeed being put into place. However, the new world order is not only related to how political leaders relate or how companies compete with one another. The new world order is the emerging importance of collectivism and the corresponding attention to civility and patriotism as the basis of future growth.

Families on welfare can now be provided with new sets of alternatives. Instead of becoming welfare dependent, they must become independent units seeking solutions to their own problems by connecting to others. Instead of depending upon third parties (e.g., public social agencies) for securing their future, heads of AFDC families must be released from an 'elitist' mentality by relying upon their own imagination, ingenuity, and drive to enhance their own welfare. Instead of the immediate family having the sole responsibility for instilling the values and beliefs that are transported from one generation to the next, a whole new set of players enter into this scheme. Instead of being 'pigeon holed' into a rigid welfare system where third parties make the rules, AFDC families have new opportunities before them which if adopted could redefine how welfare policy is implemented. We are indeed at a turning point, and relieving society and its families of guilt feelings for past failures is critical to welfare reform becoming a reality.

# Part Five

## THE CONCLUSION:

## GAINING STABILITY

## WITHIN CONTINUAL CHANGE

# 10 Healing America: welfare reform from anxiety to hope

The inner city is the land of the forgotten, high on crime and low on hope. The inner city is considered by many as equal to 'the drug capital of the state'. In addition, those residents in the poorer neighborhoods are the last to get hired and the first to get fired. The work that comes their way is work no other could want. Such work is often part time and at minimum wage with no upward mobility. Raising children based upon the minimum wage is most difficult, even though the minimum wage has gradually increased over the past decades. The minimum wage, many argue, may be counter productive as it reduces the number of jobs available. The inner city is the place of the least educated and the most prolific unemployment. Finding work that requires low-level skills is getting more difficult as we move into the telecommunication's revolution where technical skills are at a premium.

The fact that the welfare system has long been abused has elicited harsh rhetoric and a demand for reform. At either end of the welfare reform spectrum are two opposing philosophies that are based upon two distinguishable premises. The first and simplest strategy for reforming the present welfare system is to get the federal government out of the welfare business. Ideally this allows local people familiar with local problems to deal with poverty within their communities. At the other end of the spectrum is the suggestion that the federal government take the leadership in welfare reform by eliminating welfare payments and instituting a mandate that pressures individuals into job training programs.

The strategy proposed here takes another point of view. It is about the healing of America by focusing upon the building of trust among those who are most suspicious of governmental efforts to enhance their lives. Trust is something on which hopes are centered. What the healing of America is all about is hope. Its premise is that having hope creates the desire to do something about one's problems and position in life. Hope provides the energy and drive to accomplish those things that provide substance to our lives. Therefore, without building the feeling of trust among former welfare recipients, any strategy is subject to 'doom'.

Related to trust are the values individuals possess. It is the promoting of commonly accepted values within a community that enable individuals to become believers of themselves. Believing that we each have value and can make important contributions to our community results in confidence. The end result is a feeling of power in that one can gain some degree of control over his or her future. In order to reach this level of confidence, a complete welfare package is proposed. The model city described in the previous chapters suggests that unless individuals take on the responsibility of helping themselves, a long-term solution to the problems associated with current welfare efforts is not likely.

**There is a marketplace revolution going on out there**

Welfare reform requires a significant and comprehensive change in public policy. The summary here reiterates the major points which remain vital to the justification of the proposed implementation of the model city. Consumers are in the midst of witnessing significant changes in their lives as related to the workplace, home life, and leisure activities. In review, there are three basic forces driving a revolution bigger than any other which has faced society in the current century.

The most immediate is that of *technology*. Much of the routine work customarily assigned to low-skill service workers is quickly being eliminated. With technology and robotics, it is expected that significant numbers of jobs traditionally available in both the manufacturing and service sectors will be eliminated. If not eliminated, the wages associated with any manual jobs remaining will certainly be adjusted downward to reflect the pressures of international competition. However, as business and industry continues to find ways to automate their operations, the opportunity for those on welfare to locate needed jobs will likely be reduced.

*Global competition* is a second factor that is requiring businesses to look at employees as cost items rather than an investment through a lifelong commitment. In order to complete globally, business requires much flexibility in the way it operates in order to change its direction quickly as competition requires. The need to hire and replace employees is now a necessity. The time of the permanent employee has been replaced with the expendable employee. Employees must also be flexible for moving from position to position within a company when the needs of a business change. The strategy of using 'cheap' labor through legal immigrants or importing low-wage labor from other countries  is now accepted alternative for reducing labor costs. Exploiting labor capital by seeking out an employee in every part of the world is a strategy of survival for many in the business community.  An example of how fierce global competition is the witnessing of  South Korea moving from not being a player in the international marketplace to a major supplier of consumer electronics with a 30-year period.

A third driving force is the *knowledge explosion* where new products being designed and produced consist of 80 percent  knowledge and 20 percent actual materials.  Business now succeeds by applying knowledge to enhance the design of products and in this process uses less materials and time in its actual production.  With the knowledge explosion, the key to success is not finding information, but learning how to sort it out.  Any one using the World Wide Web quickly realizes that there is a huge amount of information readily available, and it is growing by leaps and bounds every day.

However, information is not knowledge.  Using knowledge to achieve something new and different, and to do it quickly, is the essence of the turnaround now required from concept to production.  Again, families in poverty have had little experience in working in such an environment. With their education relatively weak in the area of problem-solving,  use of logic, and teamwork, new obstacles are now in place for preventing families in poverty to enter into meaningful work where a livable  wage is likely. The question is how do we educate individuals in large numbers who are currently heads of households living in poverty and without the skills necessary to access today's competitive job?  That is what our model of hope is all about.


**Old habits die hard**

The justification for the need for a more comprehensive approach to welfare reform is also based upon the premise that today's workplace no longer reflects the rich tradition of the past.  It has been argued here that a primary change has occurred in the workplace in that business leaders have reneged on the traditional economic contract with labor that basically guaranteed most employees  higher wages that were generated from the prosperous company they help create. Workers customarily received a wage that did not reflect the forces of supply and demand.

They simply were rewarded for their efforts by receiving wage increases each year. Therefore, the relationship between management and the worker has significantly changed with a set of old realities being replaced with new ones. Some of the 'old habits' of business that have 'died' remain important and should be remembered since some are to be resurrected by the model neighborhood proposed.

1.  Job security whereby employees could expect full-time employment year after year has been *replaced* with the reality of impermanence in which part-time working arrangements become more commonplace. Evidence of such a reality is the increase in temp agencies which have grown over 300 percent since 1985.

2.  Employees customarily in the past designed work strategies to please their supervisors. Conformity led to success as long as the goals of the employee were identical to the goals of the supervisors. The need to conform to the desires of their supervisors has been *replaced* with knowing how to do things better. Therefore, helping supervisors to do their jobs better through innovative strategies is now expected if one is to survive in the workplace.

3.  Employees in the past generally knew what to expect everyday when they went to work. There was great predictability in that every day resembled the day before. However, such work routines have been *replaced* with a working environment of organized chaos in which changes come quickly, challenges occur every moment, and uncertainty reigns.

4.  Individuality in the workplace has been *replaced* with teamwork collaboration. Many of tasks assigned employees are beyond their individual abilities to complete by working alone. The pressures of time and limited resources put a premium of getting tasks done quicker and with greater ease.

5.  Yearly salary increases which have been routine have been *replaced* with rewarding work in terms of measurable accomplishments related to the 'bottom line.' In a more current workplace, employees are expected to *add value* to their work which will result in increase profits to the company.

What has emerged in the current workplace is the realization that every worker must become self-directed and responsible for career advancement. Therefore, it is concluded that personal ambition drives effort not only to get employment but to keep up it. Correspondingly, it is also concluded that significant welfare reform will not occur unless individuals take personal responsibility to enhance their own lives.

Taking initiative to learn new sets of skills while working on a present jobs is now a requirement. As businesses move to decentralize operations in a knowledge-based economy, workers will likely find themselves in differing working environments depending upon the needs of employers. This may result in workers moving from company to company, from position to position in a company, or perhaps moving from one job to another. Based upon this revolution in the workplace, it is concluded that heads of households of families in poverty are completely out of this kind of employment cycle. In its place a new kind of employment sector must be established if there is any chance for families on welfare to be lifted out of poverty. Reliance upon low-wage jobs associated with limited skills as a way to lead former welfare recipients out of poverty is not a viable alternative. It is thus concluded that the retraining of heads of AFDC families requires much more of a comprehensive effort than what is now available. Welfare reform is much more than job entry.

## Reacting to the cyber-revolution with narrow logic

The cyber-revolution reflects an era where expectations are high, job instability is the norm, and cost measures dominate corporate decision making. Government intrusion into the marketplace through laws will not likely have a significant impact upon the entrenchment of existing welfare policy. For example, in order to better prepare individuals for job placement opportunities, Congress passed Public Law 97-300 in 1982 ,known as the *Job Partnership Act*, to establish programs to prepare youth and unskilled adults for entry into the labor force and to afford job training to those economically disadvantaged individuals and other individuals facing serious barriers to employment, (U.S.C. SS 1501). Section 1505 of the Act entitled *Employment and Training Assistance for Dislocated Workers* empowers the Secretary of Labor to allocate special funds to the United States Employment Service for development and implementation of a job bank system for each State to identify job openings and refer job seekers to such openings. Areas of the United States are designated as service delivery areas to receive financial assistance under the act. The chief elected official in each designated service delivery area is to appoint members to private industry council. The council consists of entrepreneurs, chief operating officers of corporations, educational administrators and faculty as well as representatives from organized labor, rehabilitation agencies, community-based economic development agencies and public employment service.

247

Over 50 percent of the members of the industry council must be from the private sector.

The purpose and function of the private industry council is to prepare a job training plan to be submitted to a governor of a state and the legislature for approval. While the intent is a good one, the ability to deliver appropriate training to large numbers of welfare recipients remains a serious question. It is concluded that job training is only one part of the package required to turn the lives of welfare recipients around. It is concluded that the best training to be received is that of actually being on the job. In reality, job training must be continually re-enforced by applying job skills everyday in one's neighborhood. The narrow scope of welfare reform is challenged in the model city proposed. The logic behind piecemeal attempts to assist those in need leaves little left to be desired. In our model, we propose an expanded plan combining the resources of small and larger businesses, vocational schools and training centers, colleges and universities, government, the non-profit sector, and most importantly a personal commitment of community residents for taking on a great deal of responsibility for enhancing their own lives. Does the 1982 Job Training Partnership Act miss the point? We think it does. In our view, the result has been new levels of unwanted and unneeded anxiety.


**Anxiety leads to frustration**

Increasing the anxiety levels among welfare recipients will likely result as welfare roles are reduced in the short run. Unfortunately, such anxiety may have a long-term negative effect as well. The frustrations of the past are bound to come back to 'haunt America again' instead of healing America. For example, in the Washington Post (January 5, 1997), a series of articles by staff reporters Barbara Vobejda and Judith Havemann on welfare reform illustrate the frustration associated with attempting to reduce public subsidies. They cite the case of a teenage mother and her two year-old son who are ineligible to receive welfare payments because she is unable to live with her mother. She is not on the welfare roll but her job at the local McDonald's only brings home $100 per week, hardly a living wage. The article points out that while the welfare rolls have diminished since 1992, the cause for that decline is not apparent. Many people may simply believe they are not eligible for welfare under the new regulations and don't apply. Others have been denied benefits for the wrong reason such as failure to provide information about the father of a child on welfare even if that father's whereabouts is completely unknown. Being unable to work on a job that has a living wage results in anxiety that is likely to place more pressure of families to breakup rather than act as an incentive to keep them together.

Our political leaders continually publicize the decrease in welfare rolls since welfare reform became a salient issue. However, the problem with welfare reform is that those targeted for help are not getting jobs in which they can have a great deal of economic success, or not receiving the appropriate education they need to remain employed. The Washington Post article cites the Massachusetts experience. Only about half the adults who left welfare have found jobs. Only 13 percent of the 2,000 job set-asides in private industry for former welfare recipients have been filled. Companies which are participating in the Massachusetts experiment are not attracting welfare recipients in expected numbers. Ironically, since the experiment began, there has been no increase over the last year in the use of the State's program for transitional child day care.

Under new federal mandates, Massachusetts like other states, has reduced its welfare caseload by changing the means test to qualify for financial assistance, thereby reducing the number of people in the welfare program. They limit the time persons can remain on welfare by pressuring them to get any job. It is concluded here that such pressure ultimately increases the anxiety level of individuals perceiving a public support system disintegrating right before their eyes. Welfare reform is not easy, and unless a complete package is offered, making significant progress will be likely hard to achieve.

Welfare reform has been characterized in this rendition as a 'political football' whereby one strategist attempts to outdo another in terms of indicating how the number on welfare has decreased while another notes that the reduced numbers hide the fact that people are not better off. It has been argued here that impressive economic growth over the past decade may have much more to do with reducing the welfare roles than the implementation of any real welfare reform. Therefore, the credit attributed to the implementation of true welfare reform may not be accurate. On the other hand, even though many new jobs emerged as a part of the high growth experienced in the U.S. economy, this occurrence does not resolve the problem of decaying neighborhoods, high community crime, and a continuation of poverty.

It is concluded that job growth may have been substantial in recent years, but the low-wage jobs which welfare recipients can fulfill do not change their lives much. Despair and uncertainty still reign as dominating forces in the home life of many of these new workers. The reality of work for many is that available jobs are located in the suburbs and public transportation to get to them is inadequate, unreliable and expensive. In this regard, one anecdote reported in the Washington Post article related to a worker having to take a bus for four hours to get to and from work. An anxiety persists as those on welfare weigh alternatives for surviving in the future without a public safety net to fall back on if they are unsuccessful obtaining employment. What is hidden behind the reduction in welfare rolls must not be downplayed as human lives and dreams are at stake.

*A nation of loners emerges*

The current welfare reform movement appears to have focused upon employment as the key to becoming independent and gives very little consideration to the mental health and dignity of the worker. As a code of behavior, we are becoming a nation of loners. Our routine is to get up go to work, assuming we have a job, and return home. Wanda Urbanska (1996) in *Circle of Friends* explains the loneliness phenomenon stating that we are a nation of watchers hidden behind closed doors watching television. Hillary Clinton (1996) in *It Takes a Village* states that in many communities, crime and fear keep us behind closed doors. Divorce, family violence, a decline in those who practice religion, and greater mobility have made us a nation of loners. For many, the computer with its Internet and video games has captured the attention of youth and act as our national baby sitter to the detriment of our national health and welfare.

An increasing number of those accepting isolation as a fact of life has resulted in a growing cluster of the depressed. In this regard, individuals may opt to relieve their anxieties by turning their backs on their responsibilities, thus becoming more self-focused and at the same time irresponsible. Becoming a loner may be considered an easy way out of a constant stream of negatives in one's life. It is concluded therefore that regaining a 'spirit of enthusiasm' for life in general, not only for each individual but for an entire community, is essential if any long-term benefit to welfare reform will occur. Community building must be an integral part of welfare reform, and initiating a new movement for regenerating readily available land and sites may now be at hand.

Although our focus here is upon utilizing soon to be abandoned military sites, the model cities proposed are not limited to such sites. The concept may be implemented by any innovative public planner or private entrepreneur with a profit motive. The concept may be overpowering in its design, but the reality is that there are large numbers of potential consumers eager to work if they have the opportunity to do so. Establishing a 'second chance alternative' within the framework of welfare reform has merit in a free enterprise system where imagination combined with the creative talents of American ingenuity can result in dynamic solutions. Our model provides a second chance.

## Avoiding a new invisible poor

The danger with the current welfare reform movement is that it may create a new class of 'invisible poor' who are uncounted in official statistics. However, they may be quite visible on our town and city streets as their numbers grow. The centerpiece of welfare reform that pressures individuals to find jobs quickly poses significant problems for those living in urban areas. Unemployment rates in urban areas are typically higher than those in surrounding suburban communities. Unemployment rates for major urban centers such as New York, Detroit, Los Angeles, and Chicago often are found between 8 and 10 percent. It has been estimated that if all those presently unemployed and on AFDC were to look for jobs, there would be six workers for every entry-level job in these major cities. The barriers to seeking job opportunities in suburban areas that surround these cities are often insurmountable with transportation being one. Problems associated with transportation systems in urban centers have been daunting to say the least. Moving out to suburban areas is also unlikely since there has been limited housing available for low-income workers.

Compounding the problem of welfare reform is that city governments often operate on budgets that have few resources to assume greater responsibility for attending to the needs of an increasing number of poor. There remain concerns on the part of many that social programs in cities will not be able to be maintained as they are required by federal mandates. Being able to shoulder the new burdens associated with welfare reform is of great interest to union leaders, consumer advocates, and the religious community. There is also a probable new danger that federal mandates to states and cities will result in the shifting of responsibilities from one level of government to the next until the welfare system itself is totally destroyed. The result in the 'invisible poor' emerging whereby the public safety net disappears leaving those in poverty drifting hopelessly as new sets of barriers make lives worse.

Reducing welfare benefits may also have a 'rippling effect' upon entire neighborhoods. As cuts in welfare checks endanger the ability of residents to pay their rents and to patronize local retailers, neighborhoods were bear the brunt of the reduce wealth among its residents. The likely result will be residents force to abandon their homes. In addition, stores will become empty. The return to another form of urban plight will likely result. Empty houses and stores is a welcome signal to crime and drugs. The spirit of a neighborhood dies as does the social fabric of a community.

Ultimately, true welfare reform will cost money, a fact that federal, state, and local governmental units prefer not to admit. The current emphasis on becoming employed obscures the fact that families with low-wage jobs will continue to need income support as well as social services related to health care, dental care, and rental assistance. However, the delegating of responsibility of welfare reform from federal to local governments has as its target the pushing down of costs. The problem of cost can be easily acerbated anytime there is a recession. In such an instance, states and cities will be hard press as to what to do about welfare reform. One solution that has been proposed to help employ heads of AFDC households, especially during times of a recession, is for governmental agencies to hire those residents unable to find employment for the purpose of providing the necessary training. After a brief amount of service by means of the public sector, those individuals will be prepared to enter the private sector. However, again, such a plan will likely result in significant opposition, one of note being public service labor unions. In this regard, undermining the significance of unions in protecting the rights of workers is not the answer to welfare reform.

The 1996 Personal Responsibility and Work Opportunity Act is a decisive break from the past. It removes the guarantee of public money (in the form of cash) to families and their children who are in need of support just to survive. Cash assistance appears to be a thing of the past. The current feeling is that all able-bodied adults should earn their own way in the marketplace. But this strategy has serious shortcomings. By abolishing cash assistance programs to the poor, it places a considerable number of families at risk. Particularly at risk are children. Sensible reform can correct the defects of the current emphasis toward work requirements. Since states and local governmental units are likely to fail in such welfare reform efforts during 'hard economic times', welfare policy should be reinvented, especially before the next recession when a whole new group of the 'invisible poor' will likely emerge.

**Turning around lives**

Moving toward a *self-directed community* whereby residents are empowered to design their own futures through expanded opportunities is necessitated by a need to turn lives around for many Americans who have not been able to reap the benefits of a free enterprise system. With the 'downsizing' of management in many of the conglomerates, a dependency upon a company for continual employment has virtually disappeared. This is particularly important to families on welfare since their lives are also being changed significantly as welfare reform pressures the heads of such households to find employment.

However, welfare reform has to be more than 'go out and fine a job'. Relying upon the service sector as the primary mechanism to locate long-term employment may not be in the best interests of families on welfare.

Employment in the service sector, where skill levels required are rather low when compared to other sectors, may serve short-term objectives of getting individuals off welfare. However, in the long-term, such a strategy may simply result in the inevitable consequence of perpetuating a whole new generation of poverty. What drives the global economy is very relevant here in that it sets the stage for a dialogue as to what significant changes must occur in welfare reform if families in poverty will have any chance to enhancing their living conditions. To turn the lives of those in poverty around, a more balanced approach may be required. What is suggested in the welfare reform model proposed here is a need to balance *community rights with individual rights.*

The challenge is how to create an important moral foundation on which both a community and family can grow while respecting the rich traditions of a democracy and the corresponding freedom. Our model calls for a new kind of leadership go heal America. The moral foundation of the model city proposed is based upon welfare recipients being provided a second chance to make a commitment, demonstrate a desire to serve, exhibit integrity, create a personal vision, and utilize a work ethic that reinforces a new kind of loyalty between business and employee. On the other hand, there must also be a willingness to take risk and embrace change in order to achieve a new vision for one's family and community.

Finally, to turn lives around, such a plan for welfare reform must have 'inclusivity'. People are the 'heart and soul' of the model city, and they must be instilled with a sense of responsibility, not only for themselves but for others with whom they live. It is concluded that providing the opportunity to restart lives, the moral foundation required to support the model city can be developed if all the pieces are put into place from the beginning of this new movement for change. Whirlwind changes that are part of the telecommunication's revolution are also expected to impact upon the reality of welfare reform. Our model relies upon teamwork, technology, and commitment to make true welfare reform a reality.

**Balancing individual and community rights**

The need for stable neighborhoods while at the same time preserving individual rights with a minimum of government intrusion is at the centerpiece of the model for welfare reform proposed here. Building ties among residents at the same time of creating a new kind of loyalty with business and industry introduces a two dimensional strategy that expands welfare reform. In this regard, the struggle for equal rights among all residents is extremely important. The premise here is that when an individual exhibits integrity, accountability, and perseverance, that person becomes stronger and more self-reliant. However, being accountable to only oneself may not in the best interests the community in which he or she lives. Participating in the freedom afforded in a democracy with a 'careless' attitude and flaunting one's lack of concern for others results in an atmosphere where a feeling of trust is likely inhibited. The renewal community proposed here is based upon the ability of neighbors to join together to help each other in time of need. Community support systems are critical to assuring that the model city proposed is successful. Therefore, community obligations are taken seriously with everyone, from adult to children, being expected to make a contribution for enhancing both the spirits of neighbors and vitality of the business and retail sectors.

Transforming clusters of the poor into middle-class is extraordinarily difficult to achieved. The difficulty is not with welfare recipients who often find themselves living in conditions less desirable, but the 'disinvestment' that has been characteristic of their neighborhoods. With community apathy replacing community pride, the results have been high rates of drug usage and crime. However, in the model city proposed, there is an effort to disperse poverty into new neighborhoods for accomplishing two objectives. By generating an entirely new kind of public education designed specifically with the objective of preparing and training individuals for jobs within their local community, the dispersing of poverty relieves a community of some of the strain typical of large concentrations of the poor; those being, overstressed schools, underfunded infrastructure, and overcrowded housing. Secondly, for the community, the breaking down of poverty allows for the ability to instill changes by having to motivate smaller groups of individuals. Therefore, it enhances the ability to reverse community decline by creating stability in the lives of residents. It is concluded that the basic premise of the welfare reform must be the 'deconcentration of poverty,' and the model city proposed provides a way to revitalize not only individuals but the community as a whole.

Therefore, the issue of rights is an important one in the renewal community. While participating in the renewal community is voluntary, the assumption remains that those residents who decide to join in must abide by the rules and regulations set by the town designers, and subsequently by the town councils. Even though there are specific obligations expected to be assumed by every resident, and although these expectations may hinder the absolute freedom that individuals have in a democracy, their acceptance is vital to developing the climate for change. Residents still have many freedoms as is in any community, but it is the obligations that differentiate its design from those of the past.

## From dependency to self-determination

It is concluded that the whirlwind changes presently occurring in the workplace will likely result in a need for the formation of new kinds of partnerships between the private and public sector. The bottom line is that government cannot solve the problems related to welfare reform alone. It is concluded that a triad between business, government, and the non-profit sector must be formalized in order to react to all the ramifications of welfare reform. Addressing problems of AFDC families in isolation is not the way to continue. A new partnership within the confines of the model city calls for a coordinated strategy whereby residents can seek assistance for getting their lives back in order.

In terms of local government involvement, the model city suggests zoning laws related to housing must be altered to allow for more flexibility in residential construction. In addition, the cost of constructing such a model city will rely upon utilizing a community development corporation that is capable of designing creative ways to generate required funds. Financial incentives will be required to attract businesses to become part of this new venture. A region-wide property tax-base plan may be required to get a model city erected.. It is concluded that an economic development fund of some kind would have to be created in order to get the model city to become a reality.

Since wealthier neighborhoods, usually suburban in nature, have reaped the success of past public policy through tax-deductible mortgages, new roads supported by state money, and a modern infrastructure, a new kind of property-tax base may be in order. Reverting to a consumption tax plan in place of local real estate or income taxes may now be in order. Outside sources of funding will no doubt be required to underwrite the renewal community. It is also being implied in this proposal that the current income tax structure be revisited for the purpose of changing the focus of this country. In this regard, the telecommunication's revolution may be an invitation to not only significantly change welfare policy in this country but also tax policy.

The private sector an extremely important part of the core of the renewal community. However, because of the changing nature of work, the need to get residents trained in order that they qualify for jobs requiring higher level skills is paramount. It is concluded that the businesses that anchor the renewal community must play an active role in bringing community resources together for effective use. Business initiatives for engaging both public and privates schools in the process of generating closely aligned job related educational programs is a necessity. In support of such efforts, a new form of financing of such ventures through 'liberty bonds' can be adopted in which funds may be sought from investors at reduced, tax-free basis. In this regard, private charter schools sponsored

255

by businesses which anchor the commercial sector of the model city could be created for initiating innovative educational programs.

In addition, while working for someone else has its merits, enterpreneurship should not be overlooked as a possibility, especially in retail trade. It is concluded that retail trade offers an excellent path to economic success. In reality, it is the second largest industry group within the nation's small business sector, employing approximately 14 percent of all entrepreneurs. For such an occurrence to become a reality, an innovative strategy would have to be put into place to assist residents to begin such business ventures. The educational system would have to be geared for preparing residents for small business management. However, new entrepreneurs would need assistance in organizing, financing, and implementing a small business in a different kind of support system than that of the past. In order for local community retailers to succeed, they must have a competitive or price advantage over stores in other nearby communities and especially those in large shopping malls. Therefore, retailers would have to be permitted to join together into a purchasing group to get preferred lines of products at reduced wholesale prices.

A team of small business experts would be required to help new entrepreneurs keep up with market trends, locate products, promote those products, and maintain financial records. It is concluded that some kind of voluntary retail-wholesale arrangement would have to be initiated for giving these retailers extra attention. Relying upon seminars and stop-gap training programs offered by local government and/or colleges and universities will not suffice. An added dimension to retailing is franchising whereby the franchiser provides the training and expertise to initiate a new business. The disadvantage to relying upon a franchise is that the cost involved is significant. The purchasing of a franchise is likely to be out of reach of most residents in the renewal community. Therefore, a unique plan of action would have to be initiated for motivating the franchise industry to assist residents of the renewal community to overcome economic barriers.

It is also concluded that the non-profit sector must play a vital role in the renewal community. It is concluded that to heal America, a concentrated effort to organize citizen groups, churches, and foundations to serve as volunteers for assisting community residents with their needs. Volunteers may be used to care for an sick child or parent at home. The purpose is to generate a catalyst for getting residents 'off the sidelines and onto the playing field' in regards to helping others. In a similar regard, corporations could initiate public service programs with their own employees. Again, great ingenuity would be required here. One suggestion already in practice by Americorps is having students who volunteer their services to their community earn college tuition credits for their service. Such a policy could be implemented as part of the model city.  Other areas for volunteerism could be the development of mentoring relationships between students and the elderly, the structuring of recreational programs in place of day care for children, and the adopting of a neighbor-to-neighbor program by which neighbors earn 'time credits' by helping others.  Again, whatever the need, citizen service can prove to be a very valuable part of the fabric of the renewal community.

The result of a reinvigorated alliance between the for profit, government, and non-profit sectors of the community is a feeling of self-reliance on the part of residents.  The dimension to self-reliance is somewhat different from the usual interpretation of the term.  The subtle but significant difference is that residents make the offer for help based upon their own interpretation of their needs and not an impersonal social worker that jumps into and out of their lives, as is customarily the case today.  Therefore, by generating a spirit of camaraderie, the focus is upon helping others and not intruding in the lives of others.  The healing of America refers to the emergence of a new spirit where one resident heals the spirit of another.  It is the healing of ones wounds, whether physical or psychological,  that brings satisfaction and a corresponding self-worth.  It is knowing that your efforts are appreciated by others that results in the emergence of self-dignity.  It is the healing process that generates the momentum required to change attitudes and beliefs about ones future.  The ultimate outcome is self-determination.  It is concluded that AFDC families must go through a healing process themselves in order for the feeling of self-determination to become a reality.


**Enter mind fitness**

What the healing of America is all about is the instituting the dimension of mind fitness into the welfare reform equation.  Mind fitness is the process of equipping residents with the psychological and physical 'toughness' to develop their own visions through self-determination.  It reflects the development of operating styles that raise awareness as to how one can adapt to changes occurring around them.  With AFDC families in the midst of a cyber-revolution, they will have to learn quickly how to deal with change.

The mindset that is fundamental to the renewal community is one that accepts creativity and ingenuity as ways to solve every day problems.  Dealing with the unexpected and the unanticipated has always been part of the lives of AFDC families.  However, in the renewal community, these two elements are perceived as opportunities for enhancing ones life, rather than obstacles to endure.  The other aspect of the mindset in the model city is the acceptance of teamwork rather than individuality as the primary strategy for solving problems. The reality of the cyber-revolution is that tasks may at times seem overwhelming for one individual; but if a group gets together and draws on the strengths of each member, anything can be accomplished.

Therefore, moving from an individualistic mindset to one that is group-minded is a major change that some may find more difficult to accept. However, in the model city, it is concluded that leaving families alone to fend for themselves is 'fatalistic' in that tasks to be accomplished are likely to be perceived as overwhelming and unattainable. Broadening community networks (beyond the immediate family and relatives who are nearby) results in a perception that anything can be accomplished. The model city improves the likelihood that better information will get to the resident so more informed decisions can be made.

### Bulldoze anxiety and bolster confidence

The opportunity is now at hand to bulldoze the anxieties associated with welfare reform and to initiate a new era in confidence building. With AFDC families becoming cynical and disconnected from their government in the past, there is a need to rebuild these families into units of trust. It is concluded in the model city that there is a need to restore power to the local level. Reconstituting the community is just the first step. Promoting new relationships between residents is another. Having neighborhoods consisting of all kinds of people is important so everyone can see that they are just like everyone else. It is the sharing of ideas and oneself that places emphasis upon how common we all are. It is concluded that to bolster confidence, it is necessary to create an intimacy among neighbors without violating individual rights. It is a fine line between helping and intruding, but the renewal community attempts to 'blur' this relationship by balancing the needs of society with those of the individual.

The lesson learned here is the need to move from dependency--whether it is public welfare dependence or corporate dependency--to that of self-direction where a new degree of risk must be assumed by heads of families in poverty. When formerly self-worth was determined by the company to which one was employed, self-worth currently is more likely to be determined by the results of one's own actions. It may be concluded that the key to advancing one's welfare is to 'actively participate in life'. The intriguing aspect of the model city is that is attempts to make the every day experience of a resident 'a training ground' for reinforcing those skills to be required when they assume roles as an employee. What family members commit to every day is the assumption of responsibilities and obligations that are inter-related as one performs as a parent, a neighbor, and an employee. It is argued here that a planned community must foster those skills required for future employment.

In order to bulldoze anxiety, the *educational system,* whether public or private, must instill in the next generation of leaders a new attitude about change and self-determination. In this regard, business is not looking for individuals that get other people to make things happen, they are looking for individuals themselves to make things happen. There is a subtle difference in the meaning of these two perspectives of good employees. One puts the onus on the individual and the other on the backs of other people. Delegating work has its role, but participating in work and accomplishing something of value as part of a team member lifts ones spirit. In this regard, technology must be used to liberate our students from their teachers, to instill a sense of freedom to experiment according to ones ambition, and to take risk if the benefits are likely to outweigh the costs.

Building confidence comes more easily through the process of interdependency. The *community* must instill in residents, both adults and children, a new attitude that reflects the importance of giving and receiving. It is only by donating one's skills to others is it likely for that person to appreciate individual self-worth as well as the value of living in a neighborhood.. Reciprocity is the central focus of survival. Similarly in the workplace, when an employee shares skills with others, then that employee will receive help in time of need. It is the development of the mutual respect of the skills of others that results in a caring environment which replaces the safety net that was put into place by traditional government intervention. The issue of caring is critical to the success of an independent family, and the need to perceive others caring about them creates a comfort level that replaces anxiety with a feeling of confidence. In our model, the strategy for accomplishing this reciprocity is through a voluntary service attached to the *health and fitness center.* With such a strategy, each resident--both adult and children--will have vast opportunities to give of themselves as community needs change.


**The reinstitution of the economic contract**

The closing of U.S. military installations may be considered by some as a threat to local economies which depend on that base for its vitality. However, others feel that defense downturn may be a golden opportunity to redesign not only local areas but an entire region. However, a number of downsized air bases, navy facilities and army posts have already been converted into world-class business ventures. For example, the Lockbourne Air Force Base in Columbus, Ohio, has already been converted into a transportation-business support center known as the

Rickenbacker International Airport. Rockwell International has plans to convert the Newark, Ohio, Air Force Base into a high-tech business complex. In Charleston, South Carolina, the Charleston Naval Base and Shipyard has been leased providing over six million square feet of industrial warehousing to a variety of businesses. In California, 29 bases have been closed, significantly impacting upon both local and regional economies. A Local Area Military Base Recovery area program is being put into place for attracting tenants to these bases.

The time may be 'ripe' for expanding the scope of such military base conversion from that of a pure business purpose to that of a residential community. While the movement toward attracting a variety of businesses is a valiant one, a complementary step is that of creating new kinds of partnerships which create new alliances between neighborhoods, government, and business and industry. Expanding the scope of military base transformation to that of a renewal community as suggested here may result in a significant innovative strategy for solving two problems are once. Enhancing the lives of the less fortunate while at the same time instituting an economic recovery strategy in areas heavily dependent upon the military for economic growth and vitality provides for a win-win situation. It is very likely that many households can win if a detailed plan incorporating those characteristics familiar to the model city proposed are adopted. In addition, a new relationship between worker and employer is critical if trust is to become an everyday fact of life.

The *business sector* must adopt the new attitude of reconstituting the economic contract in which workers are expected to participate in the prosperity that results from a successful businesses. The resorting to using supply and demand as the ultimate framework upon which to pay workers must be replaced with a new kind of employment contract. Within a new democratic perspective, businesses in the planned community must be reorganized to return to the American tradition that one is to be rewarded for adding value to one's work through continual salary rather than through part-time alliances. This is a critical element to the revival of the spirit of camaraderie so necessary to raise the spirits of those in poverty.

With the likelihood that routine and repetitive tasks in today's offices and stores are to be performed by technology, a new perspective is now required for employing heads of households of families in poverty. The skills now required in future organizations are basically people skills such as decision making, team building, and communicating. The good thing about today's workplace is that workers no longer are expected to do it alone but instead to work in groups. However, the bad thing is that higher order level of skills are now required for employment. The model proposed here suggests that to get head of households of families in poverty in a position to be part of this revolutionary workplace, the community will have the responsibility of developing these skills. Therefore, everyday practical experiences related to solving community problems, to counseling students on a one-to-one level as mentoring programs are implemented, and to committing to a new form of democracy whereby citizens in a community bond in efforts to set a direction for their community become the training ground for learning those workplace skills required in today's jobs.

## Those with no vision eventually perish

Without vision, it is concluded that individuals will likely drift without any hope for change. The model city is all about vision. Getting a job is only part of a vision. A vision is something which people dream about. A dream can be something that is perceived as positive, providing hope and inspiration. Being inspired motivates an individual to extend himself or herself on the belief that something can be achieved that is powerful. What the model city is about is feeling sufficiently powerful to overcome obstacles for the purpose of arriving at a goal which provides pleasure.

Those who are 'visionless' lack inspiration, drive, and accomplishment. Such a person can easily spread despair to others. The challenge to change attitudes of those who lack a vision is immense, as complaining becomes the norm. The model city revolves around the reinventing of community spirit. However, becoming part of a vision that leads to reality requires a great deal of work. It also takes coordination to put together a network that one can rely on as steps are taken to move from one stage of development to the next. Having a vision brings hope that the future can be better than the past. Gaining insight as to what it takes to succeed in bringing a vision into reality requires a maturing process. The challenge of the model city is to engage those individuals struggling with the issues of poverty in a way that brings out the best in them. Being willing to put forth an honest effort to create something totally new in this country requires that all involve share in that same vision. It is concluded here that the future can be bright for families in poverty, but only if they are willing to help themselves. Apathy will not bring about creditable welfare reform. Energy and drive will!

## Are you up to the challenge?

It takes a number of factors to build both a community and a career. They are time, financial resources, motivation, vision, short-term and long-term planning ability, and attitude. Of all these, the focus has been on attitude! The premise of this model is that no reform is possible until individuals are prepared to help themselves. Once they reach that point in their lives, then anything is possible. Recreating a new national mood towards welfare reform is an exceptional task, but one that must occur if change is to occur. Avoiding pessimism is a must. To some, the 21st Century looks crowded, mean-spirited, and glum. Some believe that there will be an increasing split between the haves and have-nots, the old and young, and immigrants and the native-born. The social fabric of his nation may become strained due to ethnic tensions and by decaying cities that are surrounded by segregated suburbs. This 'dystopian vision' is one that hopefully will not come true. Predicting the future is always a hazardous business, but change is inevitable.

The continual erosion of the family is a sign of trouble. Nearly half of all American children will experience the breakup of their parents' marriage before the age of 18. Single parenting is on the rise. Children in less affluent families where day care may be out of reach suffer from a lack of quality time with their parents. Left unattended, these kinds of problems will no doubt worsen. The genius of a county is to have the ability to face its challenges and make creative adjustments both socially and technologically. All it takes is a feeling of confidence which is the basis of the process of hope. Uninhibited laissez-faire is not the answer. In a free enterprise system where short-term profits rules decision-making, proposals that do not promise a quick return on investment do not receive much attention. Reclaiming the marketplace and workplace is what this text is all about, and those who are interested in taking this country to the next level must accept the realization that the era of big government is over. Alternate ways must be examined for solving societal problems, and this model city suggests a new role for government.

Lastly, it is also assumed that households who have more invested in their neighborhood are more likely to commit to its ideals. Eventual home ownership is just one example of a mechanism that can change the outlook of a family. Therefore, the challenge here is for each reader (who is committed to enhancing the welfare of those families with special economic needs) to design a community within the confines of the principles set forth in the new democratic framework previously delineated. Each community must have a 'heart and soul' reflected in a core personality whether it be the *educational sector, the health and physical fitness sector, the public sector, or the retailing sector.* Personalizing the planned community by stipulating its size, the criteria of admission, and the handling of grievances and legal matters between residents is critical. The issue of crime must be addressed, and what to do with residents who refuse to adhere to the principles of the community. The objective of this book was not to stipulate step-by-step procedure for putting such a community together. The purpose however was to introduce a new frame of reference when discussing welfare reform and to suggest a reallocating of exiting resources in the search of a new beginning for families who are now facing insurmountable barriers to joining in the telecommunication's revolution.

Do you accept the challenge? What each of us can create is a community of opportunity, a community with a new attitude, and a community of hope. Yes, such a community calls upon our ingenuity and imagination. I would be interested in the community you propose as being feasible, using the parameters indicated in this book. Please send your comments by email to jlm@strauss.udel.edu.

# Bibliography

Akerlof, George and Yellen, Janet (1996), 'Behind Surging U.S. Illegitimacy', *Business Week, 14    October 1996, p. 30 (in Gene Koritz commentary)*

Anne E. Case Foundation. (1994), 'A Working Parent Doesn't Keep Children From Living in Poverty,' (in *American    Demographics* by Diane Crispell).

Aspen Institute. (1997), *Work, Health, and Productivity*, Oxford University Press.

Bane, Mary Jo and Ellwood, David. (1995), *Welfare Realities:    From Rhetoric to Reform*, Harvard University Press, Cambridge.

Barry, David. (1996), 'Looking Back at the Interactive Salad Bowl', Newsweek, November 13, 1996, pp. 53-54.

Barry, Vincent, and Shaw, William. (1995), *Moral Issues in Business*, Wadsworth Publishing: CA.

Becker, Gary. (1996), *Economic Way of Looking At Behavior*, Hoover Institution, CA.

Becker,Gary. (1996), 'Public Schools Need a Little Peer Pressures,' Business Week, November 18, 1996, p. 30.

Becker, Gary. (1996), 'How to End Welfare', *Business Week*, in Economic Viewpoint, June 3, 1996, p. 22

Beer, Samual and Barringer,Richard. ( 1996), *The State and The    Poor*, Winthrop Publishers: Cambridge.

Bernstein. (1996), 'A Minimum Wage Argument You Haven't Heard Before', Economic Policy Institute.

Bianchi, Suzanne and Spain, Daphe *1996 Women, Work, and Family in America*, Russell Sage Foundation: NY.

Blankenhorn, David. (1995) *Fatherless American:  Confronting Our Most Urgent Social Problem*, Basic Books: NY

Boaz, David. (1991), *Liberating Schools: Education in the Inner City*, Cato Institute Report.

Bozell Worldwide. (1996), 'Quality Quotient Pool: A Rude Awakening in Shaping up America', *U.S. News and World Report,* April 1996.

Brookings Institution. (1992), *North American Free Trade,* (report developed by Lustig, Bosworth, and Lawrence)

Burno, Frank. (1948) *Trends in Social Work,* Columbia University Press: New York.

*Business Week. (December 9, 1996),* 'Workforce Patterns of Today's Families',(Special Insert Section)

*Business Week* .(November 11, 1996), 'Low-wage lessons,' (Cover Story), pp. 108-116.

Calmes, Jackie. ( 1996), 'Education Marks a Widening Income Divide', *Wall Street Journal,* June 28, 1996, p. R2.1

Carper, Tom. (1995), 'A Better Chance for Welfare Reform Proposal', *State of the Union Address,* State of Delaware, January 1995.

Center for Budget and Policy Priorities (Report). (1996), *Look At Welfare Reform,* Washington, DC.

Chavez, Denise. (1992), *Shattering the Myth,* Arte Publico Press: Houston, TX.

Chavez, Linda & Miller, John. (1996), 'The Immigration', in R*eader's Digest:* Pleasantville, May 1996, pp. 69-74.

Children's Defense League. (1997), *State of America's Children* (study reported by Marion W. Edelman, president) in *Wilmington News Journal,* March 12, 1997, p. A10.

Children's Defense League. (1994), *Helping Families Work,* Ohio.

Clinton, Hillary. (1996), *It takes a Villag*e *and Other Lessons Children Teach Us,* Simon & Schuster: NY.

Coontz, Stephanie. (1992), *The Way We Never Were: American Families and the Nostalgia Trap,* Basic Books: NY.

Delaware Department of Health and Social Services. (1995), Comments by Secretary Carmen Nazaro during Why-TV News Interview.

Drucker, Peter. (1989), 'Universities Won't Survive', *Forbes,* March 1997, p. 10.

Dupay, Max and Schweitzer, Marc. (1994), 'Are Service-Sector Jobs Inferior?' *Economic Commentary,* Federal Reserve Bank of Cleveland.

*Economic Report of the President.* (1994), Washington, DC, February 1994.

Economic Policy Institute. (1996). *Business Week,* p. 106.

Ehrlich, Everett. (1996), 'Missing in Action', (comment in *Wall Street Journal* ) p.A1 + A-6, May 12, 1996.

Ellwood, D. T. (1988), *Poor Support: Poverty in the American Family,* Basic Books: NY.

Estrich, Susan. (1987), *Real Rape,* Harvard University Press: Cambridge, MA.

Evinger, R. W. (1991), *Directory of Military Bases in the U.S.,* Oryx Press: AZ.

Federal Bank of Cleveland. (1995), *Growth and Poverty Revisited..*

Finley, Rich. (1996), *A New Direction for U.S. welfare,* http://www/mdle.com/welfare.html, pp. 1-12.

Fineman, Howard. (1995), 'Race and Rage', *Newsweek,* April 3, 1995, pp. 23-25.

Flikkema, Luanne. (1996), *News Journal,* December 2, 1996, p. D13.

Freeman, Roger. (1991), *The Wayward State,* Hoover Institution, CA.

Furstenberg, Frank. *(1995),* 'Divorce Doesn't Cripple Kids', *Philadelphia Inquirer,* 16 April 1993.

Gates, Bill. (1995), *The Road Ahead,* Viking Press: NY.

Gilder, George. (1996), *Wealth and Poverty,* Basic Books: NY.

Greider, William. (1996), *One World, Ready or Not,* Simon & Schuster: NY.

Gurr, Ted. (1961), *American Welfare,* NY University Press.

Home Box Office. (1995), *Gang Wars: Bangin in Little Rock,* aired January 22, 1995, 10 p.m.

Healy, Jane. (1996) *Endangered Minds: Why Our Children Don't Think,* Simon & Schuster: NY.

Hernandez, Donald. (1994), *American's Children: Resources From Family, Government, and the Economy,* (reported in *New York Times*) 13 October 1994.

Hira, T. K. (1996). 'Life for Children and Families in 1990s', *Journal of Family and Consumer Sciences,* Fall 1996, pp. 56-59.

Hirsh. (1995), 'The Schools We Need', Doubleday: NY.

Hoffman, Saul. (1996), *Trends in Welfare Reform,* (Special Report), University of Delaware, pp. 440-449.

Hofstetter, Fred (1997), *Multi-Media Literacy,* McGraw-Hill: NY.

Kane, T. J. (1987), 'Giving Back Control: Long-term Poverty and Motivation,' *Social Service Review,* Vol. 612, pp. 405-419.

Karaim, Reed. (1996), 'Beyond Welfare What Works?', *USA Weekend,* December 6-8, 1996, pp. 4-6.

Karsada, John D. (1985), 'Urban Change and Minority Opportunities', in *The New Urban Reality,* Brookings Institution: Washington, DC.

Kasarda, John D. (1988), 'Jobs, Migration, and Emerging Urban Mismatches', in *Urban Change and Poverty,* National Academy Press: Washington, D.C

Katz, Michael, (1983). *Poverty and Policy in American History,* Academic Press: NY.

Katz , Michael. (1993), 'The Urban Underclass as a Metaphor of Social Transformation', In the *Underclass Debate,* (Ed). Michael B. Katz, pp. 3-26, Princeton University Press: NJ.

Katz, Michael. (1995), *Improving poor people*, Princeton University Press: Princeton, NJ.

Katz, Michael. (1996), *In the Shadow of the Poorhouse*, Basic Books: NY.

Katz, Lawrence, (1996), *Differences and Changes in Wage Structure*, University of Chicago Press: Chicago.

Kaus, Mickey, (1992), *The End of Equality*, Basic Books: NY.

Kelso, Willam A. (1994), *Poverty and the Underclass*, New York University Press: NY.

Krugman, Paul. *(1994), Peddling Prosperity*, W. W. Norton: NY.

Krugman, Paul. (1996), *Pop Internationalism*, M.I.T Press: Cambridge.

Krugman, Paul. (1997), 'New Math, Same Story', *New York Times*, January 5, 1997, pp. 32-33.

Kuttner, Robert. (1997), *Everything for Sale: the Virtues and Limits of Markets*, A Twentieth Century Fund Book/ Alfred A. Knoph: NY.

Langer, Ellen J. (1983), *The Psychology of Control*, Sage Publications: Beverly Hills, CA.

Lannon, Larry. (1996), 'Welfare Reform and You: the Role of Telecommunications in Welfare Reform', Vol. 231, No. 7, *Telehpony*, p. 56.

Leone, Richard. (1997), 'Job Training Proposal is Unveiled', Task Force on Retraining the American Work Force (headed by former New Jersey Gov. James Florio), *Wilmington News Journal*, 18 June, 1996, p. B8.

Levy, Frank. (1996), *Dollars and Means*, Competitiveness Policy Council.

Levy, Frank and Murnane Richard. (1996), 'What General Motors Can Teach U.S. Schools About the Proper Role of Markets in educational reform,' *Phi Delta Kappan Magazine*, October 1996, pp. 109-114.

Lewis O. (1968), 'The Culture of Poverty', in On Understanding Poverty, Basic Books: NY, p. 188.

Magnusson, Paul. (1996), 'Why Privatizing Welfare Could Actually Work', *Business Week*, 21 October 1996, p. 94.

Marliow, Julie, Godwin, Deborah, and Maddux, Esther. (1996), 'Barriers to Effective Financial Management Among Welfare Recipients', *Advancing the Consumer Interest*, Vol. 8. No. 2, Fall 1996, pp. 9-13.

Murray, Charles. (1984) *Losing Ground: American Social Policy 1950-1980*, Basic Books: NY.

National Assessment of Educational Progress. (1996), (Study reported in *New York Times*), December 19, 1996, p. 12.

Neckerman, Katherine and Wilson, William. (1986), 'Poverty and Family Structure: The Widening Gap Between Evidence and Public

Policy Issues,' in *Fighting Poverty: What Works and What Doesn't*, Harvard University Press: Cambridge, MA.

*Newsweek.* (1996), 'Washington Washes Its Hands', August 12, 1996, pp. 42-49.

*Newsweek.* (1996), 'Picking a Fight About the Future', December 9, 1996, pp. 30-31.

O'Hare, D.R. (1994). 'GATT Accord Good For All,' *Business Insurance*, Vol. 28, No. 36, p. 29

Pearson, John. (1996), 'Give Me Your Highly Skilled, Yearning to Succeed', *Business Week,* 19 August 1996, p. 41.

Petigrew, T. F. (1980), 'Social Psychology's Potential Contributions to an Understanding of Poverty', . In Covello, Vincent T. (Ed.) *Poverty and Public Policy*, Schenkman Publishing: Cambridge, pp. 189-233.

Pipher, Mary. (1996), *The Shelter of Each Other: Rebuilding Our Families,* Puntnam's Sons: NY.

Poe-Yamagata, Euileen. (1996), 'New Figures for U.S. Justice Dept', *Wilmington News Journal,* 4 Dec. 1996, p. A3.

Rank, Mark Robert. (1994), *Living on the Edge--the Realities of Welfare in America*, Columbia University Press: NY.

Raspberry, William. (1996), 'Build a Better Parent and a Nation Takes Notice', *Wilmington News Journal,* 1 April 1997, p.A-11.

Raspberry,William. (1996), 'Non-Profit Jobs Could Be the Key', *News Journal,* August 26, 1996, pg. A-11.

Reyes, Belinda. (1997), *Mexican Migration Project, Public Policy Institute of California*: San Francisco, 98 pp.

Rich, Spencer. (1995), 'Welfare Mothers Abused', *Washington Post, August 30, 1995*, p. 28.

Rifkin, Jeremy. (1995), *The End of Work, G.P.* Putnman's Sons: NY.

Roiphe, Anne. (1996), *Fruitful: On Motherhood and Feminism,* Houghton Mifflin: Boston.

Roper Center for Public Opinion. ( 1997), *What Americans Think About Their Standard of Living,* Poll Commissioned by Reader's Digest, December, 1996.

Salvoza, M. Fanco. (1996), *Father Figures,* National Parenthood Institute.

Samuelson , Robert J. (1996) 'Great Expectations", *Newsweek, 8 Jan 1996, Vol. 127, No. 2*, pp. 24-33.

Santorum, Rick. (1996), Comments Made During News Interview on KYW, October 15, 1996.

Simon, Julian. (1996), *The Ultimate Resource 2,* Cato Institute Report, Princeton University Press: NJ.

Stern, Mark. (1992), *Calculating Visions,* Rutgers University Press: New Brunswick, NJ.

Stern, Mark. (1987), *Society and Family Strategy,* New York State University Press: Albany, NY.

Strauss, William and Howe, Neil. (1996), *The Fourth Turning,* Broadway Books: NY.

Thompson, Dennis. (1996), 'Traditional Family is Declining', *Wilmington News Journal,* 27 November 1996, p. A-1+A-4.

Thurow, Lester. (1996), *The Future of Capitalism,* William Morrow & Company: NY.

Urbanska, Wanda. (1996), *Circle of Friends,* Doubleday: NY.

U.S. Bureau of the Census. (1994), *Current Populations Reports,* U.S. Government Printing Office: Washington, DC.

U.S. Health Care Financing Administration. (1994), *Health Care Financing Review Quarterly (reported in special tables).*

United States Senate. (1996), *Major Base Closure Summary Report,* Washington, DC.

Wilson, William J. (1996), *When Work Disappears: the World of the New Urban Poor,* Knopf: NY.

Yagaoda , Ben and Westheimer, Ruth. (1996), *The Value of Family: A Blueprint for the 21st Century,* Warner Books: NY.